MISCONCEPTIONS:
UNMARRIED MOTHERHOOD AND THE ONTARIO *CHILDREN OF UNMARRIED PARENTS ACT*, 1921 TO 1969

Despite the passing in 1921 of legislation intended to ease the consequences of illegitimacy for children (the *Children of Unmarried Parents Act*, the *Legitimation Act*, and the *Adoption Act*), reformers in Ontario made little effort to improve the status of unwed mothers throughout much of the last century. Moreover, those reforms that were enacted served as models for other provinces and even for some American states, institutionalizing, in essence, the prejudices inherent in the legislation. Until now, historians have not sufficiently studied these measures that further stigmatized and marginalized unwed mothers. In *Misconceptions*, Lori Chambers seeks to redress this oversight.

Through close analysis and critique, Chambers shows that the solutions to unwed pregnancy promoted in the reforms of 1921 were themselves based upon misconceptions. She explores the experiences of unwed mothers who were subject to the legislation of the time, thus shedding light on the hardships and discrimination they faced. *Misconceptions* argues that child welfare measures designed to simultaneously 'rescue' children and punish errant women could not, and will not, succeed in alleviating child or maternal poverty.

(The Osgoode Society for Canadian Legal History)

LORI CHAMBERS is associate professor in the Department of Women's Studies at Lakehead University.

MISCONCEPTIONS

Unmarried Motherhood and the Ontario *Children of Unmarried Parents Act,* 1921 to 1969

LORI CHAMBERS

Published for The Osgoode Society for Canadian Legal History by
University of Toronto Press
Toronto Buffalo London

© Osgoode Society for Canadian Legal History 2007
Toronto Buffalo London

Printed in Canada

ISBN 978-0-8020-4463-1 (cloth)
ISBN 978-0-8020-8246-6 (paper)

Printed on acid-free paper

Library and Archives Canada Cataloguing in Publication

Chambers, Anne Lorene, 1965–
Misconceptions : unmarried motherhood and the Children of
Unmarried Parents Act in Ontario, 1921 to 1969 / Lori Chambers.

Includes bibliographical references and index.
ISBN 978-0-8020-4463-1 (bound). – ISBN 978-0-8020-8246-6 (pbk.)

1. Unmarried mothers – Legal status, laws, etc. – Ontario.   2. Ontario.
Children of Unmarried Parents Act.   3. Unmarried mothers – Ontario –
Social conditions – 20th century.   4. Parents and child (Law) – Ontario.
I. Osgoode Society for Canadian Legal History.   II. Title.

KEO227.C53 2007   346.71301'7   C2007-902099-2   KF542.C53 2007

This book has been published with the help of a grant from the Canadian
Federation for the Humanities and Social Sciences, through the Aid to
Scholarly Publications Programme, using funds provided by the Social
Sciences and Humanities Research Council of Canada.

University of Toronto Press acknowledges the financial assistance to
its publishing program of the Canada Council for the Arts and the
Ontario Arts Council.

University of Toronto Press acknowledges the financial support for its
publishing activities of the Government of Canada through the Book
Publishing Industry Development Program (BPIDP).

Contents

Foreword

The Osgoode Society
for Canadian Legal History

This book is a study of the operation of the *Children of Unmarried Parents Act*, in the courts and, principally, through the agency responsible for administering the *Act*, the Children's Aid Society. It explores the experiences of unwed mothers regulated under the *Act* by examining a large collection of case files, and in the process tells us a great deal about the operation of law at the level of everyday life. Very much a socio-legal history, Lori Chambers' book also contributes greatly to our knowledge of the history of motherhood and the family, sexuality, and moral regulation. Chambers argues that despite the altruistic objectives emphasized publicly by reformers, the *Act* failed to eliminate the poverty and stigmatization faced by illegitimate children. She also suggests that that failure is not surprising because of the contradictions inherent in a legislative scheme that gave the CAS the mandate both to secure payment from fathers and to provide babies for adoption.

The purpose of The Osgoode Society for Canadian Legal History is to encourage research and writing in the history of Canadian law. The Society, which was incorporated in 1979 and is registered as a charity, was founded at the initiative of the Honourable R. Roy McMurtry, formerly attorney general for Ontario and chief justice of the province, and officials of The Law Society of Upper Canada. The Society seeks to stimulate the study of legal history in Canada by supporting researchers, collecting oral histories, and publishing volumes that contribute to legal-historical scholarship. It has published seventy books on the courts, the judiciary, and the legal profession, as well as on the history of crime and punishment, women and law, law and economy, the legal treatment of ethnic minorities, and famous cases and significant trials in all areas of the law.

Current directors of The Osgoode Society for Canadian Legal History are Robert Armstrong, Kenneth Binks, Patrick Brode, Michael Bryant, Brian Bucknall, David Chernos, Kirby Chown, J. Douglas Ewart, Martin Friedland, John Honsberger, Horace Krever, Gavin MacKenzie, Virginia MacLean, Roy McMurtry, Brendan O'Brien, Jim Phillips, Paul Reinhardt, Joel Richler, William Ross, Robert Sharpe, James Spence, Mary Stokes, Richard Tinsley, and Michael Tulloch.

The annual report and information about membership may be obtained by writing The Osgoode Society for Canadian Legal History, Osgoode Hall, 130 Queen Street West, Toronto, Ontario, M5H 2N6. Telephone: 416-947-3321. Email: mmacfarl@lsuc.on.ca. Website: Osgoodesociety.ca

R. Roy McMurtry
President

Jim Phillips
Editor-in-Chief

Acknowledgments

This book has been several years in the making. Over this (extended) period of time, I have benefited enormously from the support of archivists, funding agencies, the publisher, colleagues and friends, and, of course, my family.

First, my thanks to Jack Choules, who brought the *Children of Unmarried Parents Act* files to my attention, and to the rest of the staff at the Archives of Ontario for their assistance over the years in which this research was completed.

Financial support from this project was received from the Social Science and Humanities Research Council, Lakehead University Senate Research Committee, and the Osgoode Society for Canadian Legal History. To all of these institutions, and to the individuals who reviewed grants and applications, I give my thanks. Reviewers at the Osgoode Society, the University of Toronto Press, and the Aid to Scholarly Publications Programme provided commentary and criticism that helped me to clarify and expand my arguments. The time and effort of these anonymous reviewers is greatly appreciated.

I would also like to specifically thank the Honourable Paul Reinhardt, who provided feedback, without anonymity, that helped greatly in the development of the arguments that follow. Many thanks to Beth McAuley for her excellent editorial work, and to the staff at the University of Toronto Press and the Osgoode Society for Canadian

Legal History, in particular Marilyn MacFarlane, Jim Phillips, Richard Ratzlaff, and Len Husband. Your patience was most appreciated.

Numerous colleagues have been generous with their time and intellectual energy, have challenged and deepened my analysis, and, in the process, have made the task of writing (and rewriting) more enjoyable. Special appreciation must be expressed to my department at Lakehead. I am lucky indeed to work in an environment that is unfailingly supportive. Peggy Tripp, Helen Smith, and Pam Wakewich, thank you. Lakehead colleagues from outside Women's Studies have also encouraged this project, and discussed, on numerous occasions, the ideas that find final form in this manuscript. Particular recognition is due to Rachel Ariss, Nancy Hennen, Bruce Strang, Teresa Socha, and Tom Potter. Over the years, a number of undergraduate and graduate students have also contributed to this research. It is a source of intense satisfaction to see these students move on and succeed in careers related to Women's Studies. I thank, in particular, Dawne-Marie Bernardi, Carrie Gibbons, Angie Gollat, Mandy Hadenko, Terri Kujala, and Stephanie Ross. I have presented portions of this manuscript to a variety of academic audiences, and I thank participants for their feedback. John Weaver, who has followed my career since I was an undergraduate at McMaster in the 1980s, has provided ongoing intellectual support. Ed Montigny, friend and colleague, has debated these ideas *ad nauseum*, has encouraged me through times of frustration, and unfailingly makes me see the funny side of life. Jim Phillips, former thesis supervisor, mentor, and friend, has not only provided intellectual support and constructive criticism, but also has repeatedly made me welcome in Toronto so that I can complete my research. Thank you.

Finally, my family provides untold, and often uncelebrated, support. To la famille Bédard – Rita, Roland, Nathalie, Claude, Manon, et Daniel – merci beaucoup pour l'amitié. Bill Chambers, thank you for the sustenance and companionship in Toronto. My parents, Dave and Kay Chambers, have always encouraged my work. Thank you for your faith in me. My sister, Mary Catherine Chambers, is one of my best (and most candid) critics and has certainly brightened my daily life with her recent move to Thunder Bay. My partner, Michel Bédard, must be thoroughly sick of this project but has patiently lived with the ups and downs of the writing process, providing much intellectual and emotional support. Our children, Geoff and Cat, have gone from babes in arms to young adults in the time it has taken me to complete this book. They enrich my life in ways too numerous to list. The evidence unearthed in the process of researching this book reminds me just how lucky I am to enjoy their love and companionship in conditions of comfort. With much love, I dedicate this book to the two mothers in my own life – Rita Bédard and Kay Chambers.

MISCONCEPTIONS: UNMARRIED MOTHERHOOD AND THE ONTARIO *CHILDREN OF UNMARRIED PARENTS ACT*, 1921 TO 1969

Introduction

Illegitimacy is a social construct that historically has sustained the subordination of women. Stigmatized for her 'sinful' behaviour, the unmarried mother often also suffered material deprivation. Although only a minority of women became pregnant out of wedlock, 'their fate was not lost on the wider community of women.'[1] The unwed mother – and her exclusion and poverty – provided an object lesson in sexual ethics. Illegitimate children, like their mothers, were long considered beyond the pale of polite society. As Charlotte Whitton, a key figure in Canadian child welfare policy, lamented in a retrospective discussion of paternity law in 1943, 'through the centuries, society has made the child the scapegoat and visited upon it (a) life long brand.'[2] In 1921, legislation was passed in Ontario that was ostensibly intended to mitigate the worst social and economic consequences of illegitimacy for children; however, reformers did not seek to improve the status of the unwed mother. She continued to be viewed as culpable in the creation of her own misfortune. The legislation, therefore, had limited effect in reducing child poverty.

Three acts comprised this reform package: the *Legitimation Act* allowed for the retrospective legitimation of children whose biological parents married after their birth;[3] the *Adoption Act* made adoption inexpensive and accessible;[4] and *An Act for the Protection of the Children of Unmarried Parents*, more commonly known as the *Children of Unmarried Parents Act* provided a mechanism by which unwed mothers could obtain financial support from the putative fathers of their children.[5] The reforms in Ontario served as a model for legislation in other provinces and in some American states. Surprisingly, however, historians have not studied these measures.[6] Unwed mothers have also, perhaps unwittingly, been marginalized as historical subjects.[7] Most histories of motherhood examine the experiences of married mothers, implicitly reinforcing the normalization of the heterosexual, two-parent family and reinscribing notions of the 'good' mother.[8] Even studies of single mothers have focused primarily on more 'respectable' widows and deserted wives.[9] This book has two central objectives: first, to analyse and critique the contradictions inherent in the reforms of 1921; and second, to explore the experiences of unwed mothers regulated under the legislation and thus allow these heretofore ignored subjects to emerge from historical obscurity.

The Case Files

The law reports of the province provide little detail about the effects of the 1921 legislation. Cases were reported when they were perceived to set new precedents; most reporting, moreover, was of cases heard in the superior courts of the province. Cases heard at the level of the magistrate or family court, the level of court at which these new acts were administered, were not reported, and decisions are extant in the reports only for cases that reached appeal. Only twenty cases directly involving the *Children of Unmarried Parents Act* appear in the *Ontario Reports* and the *Ontario Journal* for the entire period of 1921 to 1969. Access to court proceedings for child support was mediated by social workers at the Children's Aid Society (CAS), and the primary source materials for this book are 4,023 extant case files created by CAS workers in various locations across the province. Unwed mothers had to report their pregnancies to social workers who kept detailed records of interactions with their clients, made decisions as to whether or not cases would advance to court, and helped mothers formulate plans for themselves and their babies. Unlike law reports, these case files were not intended for public consumption and contain details and commentaries one would not expect to find in traditional legal sources.

The extant cases represent a cross-section of the province geographically, with records available from Algoma, Bruce, Frontenac, Grey, Hamilton, Huron, Kent, Waterloo, Wentworth, and York counties, but with the preponderance of evidence drawn, not surprisingly, from the city of Toronto. They are not, however, representative with regard to religion; in fact, although the Catholic Children's Aid Society (CCAS) developed across the province in parallel with the Children's Aid Society, extant records are from the officially non-denominational, but unofficially Protestant, CAS. It is unclear why particular counties kept extensive records of *Children of Unmarried Parents Act* proceedings or deigned to maintain their files for posterity, when others did not, just as it is unclear why the CCAS records have disappeared. Some files survived by chance alone, languishing in the basements of county courthouses until they were transferred to the Archives of Ontario where they remain unprocessed and unsorted. Although the sample of 4,023 cases is large and geographically and chronologically diverse, it does have obvious limitations. Most importantly, the cases represent a small proportion of the women and children processed under the legislation and an even smaller proportion of women pregnant out of wedlock between 1921 and 1969.

The files used in this study consist of standardized questionnaires given to unwed mothers, transcripts of court proceedings, CAS notes from interviews with mothers and with putative fathers, letters from mothers and children to the CAS, and miscellaneous evidence amassed by mothers to corroborate their claims of paternity. In the questionnaire, unwed mothers were not only asked about their backgrounds, occupations, and education but were also interrogated about smoking, drinking, attendance at cinemas and dance halls, and, of course, their sexual histories. These case files are a rich, but problematic, source for historical inquiry. The unwed mothers' cases were interpreted, mediated, filtered, constructed, and reconstructed through the eyes of social workers and magistrates across the province. Even when women's voices were directly recorded, in letters and in sworn testimony, their language and answers were structured in response to the demands of the legislation, the Children's Aid Society, and the judges. As Joel Braslow asserts with regard to patients and medical transcripts, 'even verbatim' records are not 'pristine "true" accounts,' for the presence of social workers, 'not to mention their often interrogating, adversarial style, colored their patients' responses. Imbalances of power permeate these records in which authorial and real power over bodies and freedom' lay with social workers and the courts, and not with the women who sought their help.[10] But this problem is also a benefit, for the files are an important source for understanding the discourse surrounding illegitimacy and the ways in which social workers translated this discourse into practice. Margaret Little argues in her study of the Ontario *Mothers' Allowance Act* that case files 'enable us to examine how this new relationship between social worker and client was established.'[11]

It is much more difficult to determine how individual women understood and responded to their contact with the CAS and the court. The top-down nature of the sources, however, does not prevent them from being read 'against the grain.'[12] According to Joan Sangster, court transcripts and case files can be interrogated 'critically and skeptically.'[13] The case file, while written and mediated by the social worker, nonetheless represents, as Wendy Mitchinson and Franca Iacovetta assert, 'a dialectic encounter between experts backed by state, medical or religious power and clients possessing far fewer resources.'[14] Unwed mothers, in order to receive the financial support they sought through the CAS, no doubt attempted to appease the authority figures to whom they had to present their stories of pregnancy and their plans for the future. Negotiating one's future in the terms set by regulatory bodies, however, did not necessarily reflect an acceptance of such terms.[15] Regina Kunzel argues that unmarried pregnant women in the United States 'were not passive recipients of others' constructions but struggled to author their own meanings of out-of-wedlock pregnancy.'[16] Case files not only reflect the bias of those with the power to regulate and punish, but also provide a unique window, if one with distorted glass, on the mundane details of the lives of those normally obscured from historical view. Karen Dubinsky points out that while it is easy to dismiss case files as reflecting the values and priorities of the regulator, they also hold great potential for uncovering the private lives of those who have left few other records for posterity.[17]

Historical Context

The reforms detailed throughout this book had their origins in the multiple, overlapping, and contradictory social movements of the early twentieth century. Industrialization, urbanization, and immigration were perceived to threaten the primarily rural and Anglo-Saxon nature of (English) Canadian society.[18] The urban environment was popularly believed to be particularly dangerous for young women, and fears of unrestrained sexuality fuelled the social purity movement. Declining marital birth rates and Darwinian notions of survival of the fittest raised fears of 'race suicide.' Evolutionary ideas also challenged traditional

Christianity. Doctrines of individual salvation and textual literalism, to varying degrees in different Protestant denominations, became secondary to an emphasis on the social gospel and the regeneration of the kingdom of God on earth. The rise of social science and the introduction of the social survey allowed the mapping of poverty and exposed problems of child mortality and ill health that concerned Christian social reformers but also underscored public fears of 'race suicide.' New attitudes towards children, and a belief in the power of scientific education, ensured that reform efforts would be centred on the young. The Great War, the 'war to end all wars,' provided the moment in which concrete proposals for reform coalesced and achieved widespread social legitimacy and support. The legislation under study emerged in this wider context.

Change, of course, continued after the passage of the acts of 1921. Fears about uninhibited youth and the smoking, short-skirted, bobbed and rouged flappers abounded in the 1920s when the legislation was first tested in the magistrates' courts. In the 1930s, depression and unemployment fuelled concern about the growing need for public support for unwanted or unplanned children. During the Second World War, fears of female sexuality and of women as the loci of venereal infection were widespread and even propagated by government. In the post-war period, government endorsement of a wholesale return to domesticity for the nation's women increased the stigmatization attached both to those who were infertile and those who bore children in 'inappropriate' circumstances. The growth of cities continued unabated; industrial production, threatened in the 1930s, grew dramatically during and after the war; and the welfare state expanded exponentially. Any of these changes, and many others, might have been expected to have had significant influence on the treatment experienced by unwed mothers in the offices of the CAS. Instead, procedures and attitudes reflected in CAS and court documents remained largely unchanged until the late 1960s. In part, this reflected the fact that popular attitudes towards unwed mothers remained punitive. In part, it reflected the particular conservatism of social workers and the courts; CAS workers and magistrates often served long terms and reappeared in cases across decades, making the consistency of decisions over time less surprising.

Abruptly, however, in the late 1960s, the case files on which this research is based became both less common and less descriptive. For all years up until 1967, the number of extant cases found at the

Archives was reasonably stable, with an average of 83.8 cases per year and no fewer than 71 or more than 94 (a fact made even more significant by the chance nature of the sample). For 1967, however, only 45 cases are extant – 37 for 1968 and 23 for 1969. This suggests that fewer women were using the legislation and/or that social workers no longer felt justified in demanding extensive personal details about clients. The sudden drop in the number and detail of extant cases in 1969 reflects, in many ways, the end of an era. The decriminalization of birth control that year allowed (at least some) women to prevent unwanted conception.[19] The partial decriminalization of abortion, also in 1969, made it possible (under some circumstances) to terminate unwanted pregnancies without fear of legal punishment and, perhaps more importantly, opened new debates about women's right to reproductive freedom.

The expansion of welfare benefits under the Canada Assistance Plan of 1966 and the *Ontario Family Benefits Act* of 1967 meant that unwed mothers were no longer singled out as undeserving of social assistance and provided a new discourse of welfare as a right, not a privilege. In this context, more women could contemplate keeping children born outside wedlock. For the first time, in 1965 the provincial government assumed the full costs of child welfare measures regulated through the CAS, reducing the financial constraints that had limited the options of social workers and removing the conflict of interest inherent in the agency's concurrent dependency on charity, work in adoption placement, and responsibility for the processing of unwed mothers.[20] A 1969 Supreme Court of Canada decision, *Re Mugford*,[21] sent the message to CAS workers that practices described in this book were coercive and unacceptable. Finally, the liberalization of divorce in 1969 allowed cohabiting couples who wished to do so to formalize their relationships and to rely on the more extensive child support provisions of the *Divorce Act* when relationships broke down. Formal acknowledgement of changing attitudes towards illegitimacy came in the 1970s. Affiliation proceedings were abolished on 31 March 1978,[22] and the designation 'illegitimate' was removed from Ontario law in 1980.[23] Despite this reform, however, the material disadvantage faced by children in single-parent, female-headed households remained endemic.

Organization of the Text

Evidence from the files has been used in two distinct ways. First, I have analysed statistical information about the women's backgrounds, their stories of pregnancy, and their outcomes for their children to provide composite descriptions of the women and the court process and to allow consideration of the concerns that may have influenced women's decisions with regard to the fate of their children. The 4,023 case files reveal strong themes. Statistical descriptions also facilitate the anonymity of subjects. Second, I have used particularly rich case files throughout the text to illustrate, on a more personal level, what it was like to be unmarried, pregnant and in need of the assistance of the state. The identities of the women, their children, families and friends and of the putative fathers and social workers have been disguised to respect the privacy of the living and the dead. Although a specific box number for the archival source is provided to reflect the date and region of each case, the numbering of cases is arbitrary. This was also necessary because the unprocessed boxes do not contain numbered cases; in fact, my first stage of research was the basic sorting and compiling of each case file.

It is also important that I explain the use of language throughout the text. Because the term 'illegitimate' had particular legal meaning, I continue to use this word in describing both children and mothers. This should not be taken as derogatory. The naming is necessary to illustrate the consequences of legal exclusion. Moreover, it is preferable to the other contemporary term often used in these sources, but excised from my discussion: 'bastard.'

Before I embark on an exploration of the case files, I provide the background to the origins of law reform in chapter 1. Evidence about high infant mortality rates, discourses of child welfare, and fears of race suicide combined to create a climate in which reform was possible. In the wake of the Great War and the enormous loss of life it represented, no (white) children were deemed expendable, even those who were illegitimate. The unwed mother, however, was not believed to be worthy of public aid or capable of raising children who would become productive citizens in the 'brave new world' for which 'Canadian soldiers had fought.'[24] What then was to be done with the innocent child of a depraved mother? The *Legitimation Act* was intended to encourage shotgun weddings and the regularization of families living outside the law. The *Adoption Act* aimed to encourage unmarried women to release their children for adoption into legitimate families. Only as a last resort did the *Children of Unmarried Parents Act* provide a mechanism by which an unmarried mother could seek financial support from the putative father of her child; it did so, moreover, in a manner that was deliberately punitive and degrading.

The punitive proceedings mandated under the *Children of Unmarried Parents Act* are explored in detail in chapter 2. As the case files amassed by social workers illustrate, mothers who came before the Children's Aid Society were subjected to invasive questioning about their work, their families, their sexual histories, and their relationships with the fathers of their children. If the story of an unwed mother was believed, CAS workers would attempt to contact the putative father and to convince him either to marry the woman or to enter into a voluntary agreement for the support of his child. If her story was not believed, however, no further action would be taken. Women were routinely questioned, both by the CAS in private and by judges in a public court, in a manner that was degrading and embarrassing; they were assumed to be both promiscuous and liable to lie. Men, despite the vested financial interest they might have had in denying paternity, were not so distrusted. In fact, procedures provided men with ample opportunity to exploit and reinscribe dichotomous ideas about women's sexuality, in particular the notion that a woman was either a Madonna or a Magdalene. Social workers determined whether or not court action would be taken against a putative father. They had the legal right to declare an unwed mother unfit to keep her child and they were simultaneously agents for adoption. The case files reveal that the combined legal and social power of the CAS denied women choice and dignity.

Another important conclusion emerging from the statistical data presented in the second chapter is that two distinct groups of women sought the assistance of the state under the auspices of the *Children of Unmarried Parents Act* and that their stories and experiences must be treated separately.[25] Of the 4,023 women whose case files are extant, 2,031 had cohabited with the fathers of their children and 1,992 were truly single. Although the legislation under study in this book did not distinguish between these two groups of women, over the years of operation of the *Children of Unmarried Parents Act* there is no doubt that cohabiting women and single women received very different treatment in the offices of the CAS. Chapters 3, 4, and 5 explore the experiences of non-cohabiting women, while chapter 6 returns to histories of cohabitation.

In chapter 3, the beliefs, expectations, and stories that social workers and clients brought to the interview process are explored and contrasted. Social work literature and psychiatric discourse decried unwed mothers as delinquent 'girls' of low intelligence, driven by neurotic impulses and poor home lives to seek love and gratification through short, inappropriate relationships with the men who fathered illegitimate children. These beliefs are evident in the judgmental language of the case files. Women themselves, however, suggested alternative meanings and histories of unwed pregnancy. The vast majority of non-cohabiting women claimed to have become pregnant in the context of long-term dating relationships. They realistically acknowledged that they faced considerable pressure to perform sexually for boyfriends. A minority of women asserted that such pressure had culminated in rape, but these stories of violence were often disbelieved and silenced. The stories told by unwed mothers illustrate the contradictions that all women faced under the sexual double standard: powerlessness and, paradoxically, responsibility. The nature of the client/ social worker relationship, however, muted this alternative discourse of sexuality and gender relations.

In chapter 4, I explore the conflict of interest inherent in the fact that the CAS controlled both adoption and access to proceedings for child support. Extant case files illustrate the financial constraints faced by the CAS and the widespread belief in the social work community that adoption would be 'an opportunity, the best life chance for the mother and child in the great majority of cases.'[26] Also evident are the high pressure tactics that were at times used by social workers to convince reluctant young women that adoption was desirable. This chapter explores the characteristics that made young women most vulnerable to pressures regarding adoption: white babies were in demand and poor women who were particularly young, lacked employment or family support, and who were white and recent immigrants were most likely to release their children for adoption. Adoption as facilitated by the CAS served as a form of forced cultural assimilation.

Chapter 5 explores the experiences of women who had not cohabited with the fathers of their children, but who managed none the less to defy the adoption mandate. Far too often, unmarried mothers and their children lived in poverty. The *Children of Unmarried Parents Act* did little to improve this situation. Many women were denied the right to pursue financial support from the fathers of their children because these were deemed immoral and untrustworthy. Even when support was granted, it was based on the man's ability to pay, not the needs of the woman and child, and little effort was put into actually collecting money from recalcitrant men. Moreover, many of the men in these cases could simply not afford to support two households. Mothers worked at dead-end, low-paying jobs, sought help from family and friends with housing and childcare and entered into common-law relationships and marriages to support their children. Sadly, a significant number of mothers lost custody of their children to the state because of their poverty.

In the final chapter I explore now the legislation affected women who bore children during relationships of cohabitation. This chapter begins the process of understanding how ordinary couples constituted and reconstituted family arrangements and engaged, evaded, and contested marriage law, providing important new insights into the history of the family. Women who had cohabited were more likely to be believed both by CAS workers and by judges than were their single counterparts. Nonetheless, the *Children of Unmarried Parents Act* was of limited effectiveness in mitigating the poverty of the children of cohabitation. Even when they were granted child support, families remained outside the law, and fathers who wished to do so could easily evade their obligations. Ironically, they could also be denied access to children with whom they had lived for years but to whom they had no recognized legal connection. Cohabiting men, women, and children were in legal limbo, and by the 1960s social workers recognized that 'except for the legal factor ... [these] may be famil[ies] like any other.'[27] Evidence amassed in cohabitation cases under the *Children of Unmarried Parents Act* helped to fuel public discussion of and support for divorce reform.

This book is not a comprehensive study of illegitimacy as a legal concept or social construct, nor does it pretend to exhaustively portray all the options available to unwed mothers between 1921 and 1969. It is, instead, a focused study of 4,023 women who became pregnant out of wedlock and who sought financial assistance from the fathers of their children via the regulatory structures of the CAS and the state. By exploring the stories of those most vulnerable, this book makes contributions to existing literature on the history of motherhood and the family, the history of sexuality, the history of moral regulation, and the history of poverty, and adds important new knowledge to our understanding of the origins – and limitations – of the modern Ontario welfare state. Since the origins of reform were in many ways national and international, the themes explored in this book may also have resonance in other Canadian and American jurisdictions.

In this work I illustrate that, despite the altruistic objectives emphasized publicly by reformers, the legislative package of 1921 failed to
eliminate the poverty and stigmatization faced by illegitimate children.
This failure, however, is not surprising, given the contradictions inherent in reform. In fact, as a measure intended to punish errant female
sexuality, the legislation was successful. In an era of expanding investment in welfare, the unwed mother occupied an essential ideological
position as outsider, undeserving of state aid. The rhetorical construction of the 'good' mother, central to the modernizing projects of the
interwar period and the post-war welfare state, relied on the counter-
point of the often shadowy and only partially articulated 'bad'/illegiti-
mate mother. This book expands historical critiques of the construction
of the 'good' mother by insisting upon the obvious: legal marriage was
an essential component of acceptable motherhood. Yet the final chapter also illustrates that even as the 'good' mother was constructed
through exclusion of the unwed, fractures and challenges to this discourse emerged. The play on words of the title is intended to reflect
this complexity. Echoing attitudes widely shared in the community,
social workers asserted, as one put it in 1957, that out-of-wedlock pregnancies were 'misconceived,'[28] the result of maladjustment on the part
of the mother. The central assertion of this book, however, is that the
solutions to unwed pregnancy promoted under the *Children of Unmarried Parents Act* were themselves 'misconceived' and based upon 'misconceptions.' Child welfare measures that simultaneously sought to
rescue children and to punish errant women could not, and will not,
succeed in alleviating child (or maternal) poverty. In this, our history
has important lessons for the present.

1

'Such a Program of Legislation': Illegitimacy and Law Reform

Punishment and ostracism – for both mother and child – were central to the legal designation 'illegitimate.' The law traditionally reflected and reinforced the Christian belief that premarital and extramarital sexuality were sinful. In the early decades of the twentieth century, the products of sinful behaviour – children – came to be viewed as innocent and illegitimacy emerged as a subject of concern in the new field of social work. Law reform in Ontario was hastened by the conditions of the Great War. Panic about infant mortality rates, the visible poverty of female-headed households, and a new rhetoric of equality brought censure upon illegitimacy laws. Racism, which was exacerbated by the loss of Anglo-Saxon young men at the front, mass immigration, and a precipitous decline in marital birth rates, fuelled concern about the well-being of the nation's white children. Pity for poor children, however, did not translate into sympathy for the errant women who had produced such babies. In fact, fears of uncontrolled female sexuality led to calls for punishment of the errant and for sterilization of the 'unfit.' As Karen Balcom asserts with regard to illegitimacy in Nova Scotia, 'the "innocent" babe could excite public opinion and become a vehicle for social change in a way that the possibly "destitute" and probably "sinful" unwed mother could not.'[1] How would these contradictory attitudes be reconciled in law reform?

Illegitimacy and the Law Before 1921

The Ontario laws that condemned the unwed mother and her child to outcast status, and often to impoverishment, originated in England. Under the common law the child born to an unmarried mother was a child of nobody. As William Blackstone asserted in 1857, 'the incapacity of a bastard consists principally in this, that he cannot be heir to any one, neither can he have heirs, but of his own body. Being *nullius filius*, he is therefore kin of nobody, and has no ancestor from whom any inheritable blood can be derived.'[2] This reflected patriarchy's denigration of women. Jenny Teichman argues that 'a bastard's mother, being a woman, was in fact that very no-one. In law, lineage, and in matters having to do with property, a woman, until modern times, was a kind of nullity.'[3] Of course, the idea that a child 'is the child of no one and has no kin relations is an obvious absurdity.'[4] The illegitimate child did have kin, including a biological father, but the designation *nullius filius* reflected the patriarchal importance of marriage and of the father as legal head of the household. A child born to a mother who was not formally connected to a man was unlawful.

While married men had exclusive legal rights over their children,[5] in feudal times neither the mother nor the father was responsible for the support of an illegitimate child. As the enclosure movement to seal off common lands and convert them into private property advanced in England, a desire to ensure that individual parents would be responsible for the upkeep of their children became evident. The first English statute regulating the support of illegitimate children was enacted in 1576 and provided for punishment of the mother and the reputed father of the child. Either parent could be charged for the support of the child and committed to jail if they failed to abide by a support order. The act was class specific and, tellingly, was entitled *An Act for Setting the Poor on Work*.[6]

The next legislative enactment, passed in 1609, was more severe. The mother of any illegitimate child who became a charge on the parish could now be imprisoned for a full year. Repeat offenders could be incarcerated on an indefinite basis or until the woman could provide sureties for her good behaviour. In 1662, it was enacted that the goods and income of the mother and the putative father could be seized for the support of the child. A statute of 1733 provided that a single pregnant woman could charge any man with being the father of her child. A warrant for the man could be issued and the putative father was to be imprisoned unless he indemnified the parish or entered into recognizance with sufficient surety.[7] In 1809 this statutory scheme was expanded. The putative father would now be liable for the expenses of the birth and for the costs of his own arrest and affiliation proceedings. Acknowledging the limited economic capacity of most mothers, this act, for the first time, placed primary responsibility for financial support of the child with the father instead of apportioning costs between the mother and the father.[8]

This responsibility of the father, however, was eliminated by the English *Poor Law Amendment Act* of 1834. The Poor Law Report of 1834 reflected disapproval of the regulations of 1809. Martha Bailey argues that '[the previous regime] was [believed to be] procedurally unfair to the putative father. Of far more concern, however, were the women who were [thought to be] greedily feeding at the public trough.'[9] Under the *Poor Law Amendment Act* of 1834, an illegitimate child was to be maintained solely by his or her mother. If the mother's parish became responsible for the child's support, the parish could sue the father for reimbursement. The mother's evidence as to paternity had to be corroborated by a third party; this requirement was based explicitly on the belief that women lied in order to trap wealthy men. The statute provided that 'no part of the monies paid by such putative father in pursuance of such order shall at any time be paid to the mother of such bastard child, nor in any way applied to the maintenance and support of such mother.'[10] The poor laws reflected a Malthusian fear of the unruly reproductive woman as a threat to the nation.[11]

The laws of England, while formative in the legal thinking of administrators in the colonies, were adapted to the perceived needs of local communities. Upper Canada, while sharing punitive attitudes towards illegitimacy that were reinforced by the dominant Christian religious order(s), did not receive and apply England's poor laws because it was believed that poor relief was unnecessary in this land of (supposed) abundance. This left the colony without a system of public relief for paupers and without affiliation proceedings.[12] At law, this meant that neither the mother nor the putative father of an out-of-wedlock child could be held liable for his or her support. Nor, in the absence of poor laws and poorhouses, did the local community have any responsibility to care for an illegitimate child.[13] Under civil seduction procedures, employers could sue the putative father for compensation if they lost the work of an employee due to pregnancy, but the specific requirements of the proceedings limited their usefulness.[14] Many mothers had *de facto* custody of and responsibility for their out-of-wedlock children. When they could not afford to keep such children, they gave them up to the private orphanages that operated from early in the history of the colony, some of which were little more than baby farms where children were housed under appalling conditions and where they too often died.[15] While the infant was a liability, the child who survived beyond infancy became a valuable asset to the family and community.[16] Under apprenticeship legislation, children born out of wedlock, once old enough to be capable of useful labor, could be bound out to masters. There is little doubt that the failure to impose liability for the support of illegitimate children on fathers increased the child labour pool.

Upper Canadian legislators made fathers potentially responsible for the support of their illegitimate children in 1837, but this act reflected the distrust of women evident in the English *Poor Law Amendment Act* of 1834. Under the *Seduction Act*,[17] anyone who furnished necessaries for an illegitimate child could sue the putative father of the child for the costs of such support. The mother's evidence of paternity had to be corroborated by a third party. In cases in which women were successful in affidavits of affiliation, the liability imposed on the father lasted until the child reached his or her age of majority.[18] Perhaps because of the adversarial nature of the proceedings, or the requirement that the woman's testimony be corroborated by a third party despite the new liability of the putative father, unwed mothers and their offspring continued to find refuge in charitable institutions. The harsh laws regarding illegitimacy remained unchanged – and largely unchallenged – until the twentieth century.

Child Welfare, 'Race Suicide,' and the Impact of the Great War

The child welfare package of 1921 reflected the coalescence of a series of reform efforts that were given public legitimacy by the Great War and the resultant rise to political prominence of the social gospel and social purity movements aimed at national regeneration.[19] Concerns that had simmered before the war erupted in a context in which frightening numbers of men were rejected for wartime service because of preventable health problems.[20] Simultaneously, high infant mortality rates raised the spectre that the losses of war would devastate the nation; particularly in a sparsely populated country, 'infant soldiers' needed to be healthy and numerous.[21] Fears regarding the loss of life at the front exacerbated eugenic concerns about race suicide and national security, and the Spanish flu pandemic of 1918 further reinforced these fears.[22] Punitive treatment of illegitimate children also became less acceptable to the public in the context of the rhetoric of the war 'to end all wars.'

Child-saving initially emerged in the nineteenth century as a response to the urban, industrial environment with focus on the neglected and orphaned children who were visible on city streets. The expansion of asylums and orphanages, the creation of the Children's Aid Society, and the establishment of new systems of juvenile justice date from this period.[23] By the twentieth century, however, reformers were more broadly concerned with child health and development. Before the Great War, reformers concerned about the infant mortality rate had been working to ensure a supply of pure milk to babies and to extend public health care through the provision of community nurses and clinics. As early as 1910, Dr Helen MacMurchy prepared reports on infant mortality and child welfare for the Ontario provincial government in which she documented that 6,932 of 52,629 infants born in 1909 had died within the first year after birth.[24] As Alan Brown, a pioneer in Canadian pediatrics and a physician at the Toronto Hospital for Sick Children asserted, 'infant mortality is to-day one of the great national, social and economic problems. The future of every nation depends on its children, their physical, intellectual and moral strength.'[25] It was widely understood by the time of the Great War that poverty was an important causal factor in infant mortality and that babies born out of wedlock were disproportionately likely to live in impoverished conditions, to be sickly, or to die.[26] Improving the prospects of illegitimate infants became part of a more general effort to make advancements in public health and thereby to preserve the strength and vitality of the nation. The altruistic rhetoric of child-saving, moreover, linked children to future regeneration and to notions of the social gospel and Christian-based social reform – movements that were politically powerful during the Great War and in its immediate aftermath.[27]

This rhetoric of child welfare and the Christian origins of much reform, however, did not absolve poor mothers of blame and masked considerable class, ethnic and racial prejudice.[28] Despite an ostensible emphasis on eradicating child poverty, from the beginning the discourse of reform criticized, judged, and categorized mothers. Since not all impoverished children succumbed to disease, some mothers appeared to cope better than others with inadequate housing and sanitation. The editor of *Social Welfare* opined in 1918 that ignorance, not poverty, killed babies.

> Lack of the proper knowledge accounts for possibly the largest number of infant deaths – lack of hygienic and eugenic knowledge; ignorance of the penalties of immorality; of the trouble enacted by defiance of sanitation and toleration of filth; of the fatal results of carelessness and malnutrition; and of the realization of the social and economic value of the child's life.[29]

While asserting that the state must intervene (and invest money) to reduce infant mortality rates, the editor of the *Canadian Public Health Journal* simultaneously argued in 1915 that 'intelligent motherhood alone can give to the infant that which neither wealth nor state nor yet science can offer.'[30]

Infant mortality rates, and fears related to the loss of life at the front, provided a justification for investment in the nation's children. Moreover, wartime was conducive to the expansion of financial support to poor families as the mother whose husband was fighting overseas could not be blamed for the fatherless state of her household.[31] A wartime study of 2,000 institutionalized children in Toronto revealed that most had a living parent and few were 'true orphans.'[32] While apprenticeships had been an acceptable solution to child poverty in the nineteenth century, the modern emphasis on mandatory schooling discredited such approaches to child welfare,[33] and institutional care was increasingly believed to be antithetical to the promotion of family life.[34] Peter Bryce, secretary of Ontario's Board of Health from 1882 to 1904 and prominent member of the Canadian Purity Education Association, argued that

> it has become evident that the normal family life is the only foundation for the State, and that the mother is the one best guardian of the child. But, contrary to this, we have allowed the separation of the mother and child by institutionalization because the mother cannot fulfill the dual obligations of guardian and breadwinner.[35]

Mothers, it was asserted, should be at home with their children.[36] Not only was institutional care undesirable for the child but also it was expensive for the state.[37] It was, as the superintendent of Ontario's prisons and charities put it, 'a most extravagant way of dealing with the children.'[38] In this context, solutions were adopted that would allow the mother to care for her children at home and without requiring young children themselves to be employed.

Initially, aid to lone mothers, in the form of war pensions, was provided by the charitable organization, the Canadian Patriotic Fund (CPF). The CPF was a chartered private agency created by the federal government during the same special session in which the *War Measures Act* was invoked.[39] The CPF asserted that 'the soldier's wife should be entitled to enough money to live decently without having to go out to work as someone's maid.'[40] It was not anticipated that the government would have to provide relief to the dependents of soldiers from public funds; the extent of poverty, however, was grossly underestimated. By 1916 the CPF had recognized that charitable donations were insufficient to meet need and the government began funding pensions to veterans' dependents and supplementing the pay of soldiers overseas; however, the pensions rewarded soldiers for their sacrifices for the nation, not women for their child rearing.[41] Pensions were paid to mothers only because no other option was available while fathers were at the front.[42] Given that pensions were only available for soldiers and that overwhelmingly volunteers for overseas service were of Anglo-Saxon background, such support can be viewed as a response to fears of race suicide, which were heightened by the loss of so many of these young men.[43]

The payment of pensions raised awareness of the illegitimacy issue. As Desmond Morton observes, the 'harried officials' who launched the Order in Council for separation allowances had 'little idea of the complexity of family relations in Canadian society.'[44] Investigation of women's marital status flowed inevitably from the definition of allowances as the husband's right; hundreds of wives who applied for support were not legally married. For example, 184 irregular families were served in Montreal alone.[45] One advocate of the pensions in the House of Commons argued that he regretted the 'complexity of modern social life,' but to deny support would 'simply drive on the streets a woman who had been constantly and regularly living with a man as his wife.'[46] The recognition of cohabitation 'on a bona fide permanent domestic basis for at least two years prior to his enlistment' as equivalent to marriage was endorsed by military authorities and rendered official by the passing of the controversial Order in Council in 1916.[47]

Concerns about infant mortality rates, the poverty of soldiers' families, and the loss of life at the front dovetailed with eugenic fears of race suicide. In a context of increasingly diverse immigration, Anglo-Saxon babies appeared to reformers to be comparatively deserving of state aid. Despite the best efforts of doctors, lawyers, legislators, and other concerned parties, the birth rate among well-to-do married white women was in decline.[48] If women could not be forced to produce adequate numbers of 'desirable' babies, at least those white babies born to poor and single mothers could be given increased odds of survival (and therefore increase the possibility that Canada would remain, fundamentally, a white man's country). Eugenic ideals were given public legitimacy by both the veto rates of the medical examiner and the loss of life at the front.[49]

Implicit in the eugenic world view was the belief that motherhood was not only a woman's highest calling but also a privilege that might be denied or revoked. Racism was evident in assessments of women's potential as mothers; women from the 'backward' – Eastern and Southern European – nations predominant in early-twentieth-century immigration were widely believed by reformers to be prone to deficiencies in child rearing.[50] The rhetoric of contagion was rampant. Children without adequate guidance were likely not only to be unhealthy and the conduits of disease but also to be immoral and therefore sources of pollution and temptation for other children. Such a waste of life, however, was preventable. J.J. Kelso, founding father of the CAS, opined that children, 'if taken hold of at the right time,'[51] could be saved from leading lives of worthlessness, poverty, and vice, and doing so would prevent them from 'polluting' other children. This provided the incentive for intrusive programs of education for motherhood as well as the removal of children from homes deemed beyond reform.[52] Saving babies, therefore, was a more complicated and complex response to social conditions than rhetoric focusing on altruism would suggest.

Altruistic rhetoric, however, had particular resonance with the public in the immediate aftermath of the Great War, which had been justified as a fight for democracy, freedom, and opportunity. Increasing concern over illegitimate children's legal, social, and economic condition was an international phenomenon.[53] In 1915, the U.S. Children's Bureau commissioned a massive three-part series, *Illegitimacy as a Social Welfare Problem*, which was published in 1920. In 1919 and 1920, the Children's Bureau sponsored international conferences that brought together child welfare activists to discuss 'the legal handicaps facing children born out of wedlock and to formulate broad principles of treatment and legislation.'[54] At a 1921 conference in Chicago on the rights of the child, Ernst Freund, a noted professor of jurisprudence, argued that 'every effort should be made by the law to relieve the child of the stigma that attaches to illegitimate birth.' A significant contingent of Canadian social workers attended.[55] While illegitimacy continued to be condemned, the belief, as prominent Canadian reformer Peter Bryce put it, that 'visiting this condemnation on the head of an infant is illogical and unjust'[56] became more widespread in the aftermath of the Great War. Such rhetoric gave a noble tone to discourse promoting legal change for the benefit of illegitimate children. But fears of immorality, as much as altruistic concern about children, drove debates around illegitimacy.[57] Public discussion of prostitution, 'good-time' girls, and venereal disease encouraged a re-examination of laws that regulated sexuality.

Sexual Deviance and the Unwed Mother

The unwed mother was not perceived as innocent or deserving and punishing her was not considered 'illogical [or] unjust.'[58] Ironically, the Christian roots of child welfare reform reinforced the tendency to condemn the sinful behaviour of the mother, even as the child – the product of sin – was discursively (re)constructed as worthy of social investment.[59] The anxieties regarding sexual morality were a product of much larger social issues, in particular the concern that marriage and the family, central institutions of socialization and social control, were being undermined by urbanization, industrialization, and the mass immigration of non-Anglo-Saxons. Racism, ethnocentrism, and fears of immorality overlapped and reinforced one another.

While both men and women engaged in sexual practices of which reformers disapproved, it was women, the supposed guardians of morality, who were blamed and regulated. As Vida Francis argued with regard to errant women in American cities as early as 1906, 'the cost to the state of even one bad girl in her far-reaching influence for social evil is incalculable.'[60] Evidence that the Canadian Expeditionary Force had the highest rates of venereal disease among the troops in Western Europe led, not to disgust with soldiers, but to condemnation of the women who were constructed as the conduits of disease.[61] Heightened fears about unrestrained sexuality led to calls both for preventive measures to improve public morality through education and for punitive measures against those who transgressed the rules of sexual morality, putting the body, and the body politic, at risk. Poor mothering was perceived to be responsible for disease and immorality, as well as impoverishment, thus adding fuel to the fire for those who advocated removal of children from questionable homes.[62] Dr. R.H. Patterson asked rhetorically in the *Canadian Public Health Journal* in 1920, 'who is really to blame?' when young women become diseased or pregnant; his answer, 'the mother.'[63]

Prostitution served as the negative 'master symbol [or] code word'[64] embodying all forms of undesirable sexual behaviour and the fear that unrestrained sexuality would undermine the (white) race and the (Anglo-Saxon) nation. But how was the prostitute to be found and isolated? The working girl, travelling alone, smoking in public and flouting conventional decorum, was believed to be indistinguishable from the professional sinner. The 'modern' girl embodied this fear of sexuality unleashed, of women's rejection of hearth and home and the resultant 'decline of the race.' Geographically, this threat was the terrain of the prostitute, the red light district, the urban slum, the immigrant ghetto and the entertainments of the big city. All who lived in these regions, or who sojourned there for pleasure, were threatened and threatening.[65] In this context, bearing a child out of wedlock was not the ultimate female transgression, but it did ensure that a woman's 'sinful' nature would be exposed to the community.

This fear of women's sexuality was clearly expressed in post-war amendments to the *Female Refuges Act*, which granted wide powers to magistrates and judges to incarcerate any woman under the age of thirty-five who was deemed 'incorrigible' and to be 'leading an idle and dissolute life.'[66] Joan Sangster argues that after the Great War reformers were deeply concerned with 'working girls' transformation into efficient, healthy and moral mothers' and convictions under the *Female Refuges Act* reflected an ongoing fear that unrestrained female sexuality was a threat to the entire nation.[67] Moreover, distinctions between various forms of so-called sexual misbehaviour were blurred. Into the 1960s the belief that 'promiscuity often leads to prostitution – in fact, that between promiscuity and prostitution there is a difference only of degree' – remained widespread.[68]

The reform impulse was particularly strong in the social work community.[69] Charlotte Whitton, writing in the new Canadian social work journal *Social Welfare*, exemplified the complexities and problems in the response of social workers to unwed pregnancy. While she deplored the term 'illegitimacy,' which shamed the child and precluded 'inheritance from either parent,' she nonetheless remained convinced that most unwed mothers were of 'low mentality' and consequently unable to successfully raise their children for the state.[70] It is noteworthy that this construction of illegitimate pregnancy rendered invisible the women who had received some sympathy from the community and the government during the Great War, those who had produced children in the context of ongoing marriage-like relationships. Fathers were completely absent in this discourse of blame and responsibility.

Law Reform and the Mother–Child Relationship

It was in this context – sympathy for the unfortunate illegitimate child, blame and shame for his or her mother, and the invisibility of the father – that public opinion was roused and child protection legislation was passed in Ontario. Lauded internationally as an advanced and humane approach to child welfare, the Ontario legislation served as a model for reform in other provinces and in several American states. While Premier Drury's tenuous coalition government could not agree on economic reforms,[71] his family-centred legislation garnered wide support.[72] He later described the child welfare reforms enacted under his administration as 'such a program of social legislation as Ontario and indeed all of Canada and North America had never seen, or perhaps thought possible.'[73] Charlotte Whitton, a central author of the legislation, consistently asserted that these child welfare reforms were among her crowning achievements.[74] There can be little doubt that reformers and legislators, bureaucrats and reformers were sincerely concerned with improving the economic and social prospects of children; their vision, however, was simultaneously limited by class, ethnic, and racial prejudice and by a propensity to judge the unwed mother.

These acts reflected the desire to maintain a hegemonic, Anglo-Saxon, middle-class model of family life and sexual restraint. Moral concern about lone mothers and sympathy for their innocent, but disadvantaged, children ensured that programs were intended to discourage single motherhood by providing incentives for stable and legal families through marriage, retroactive legitimation of children, and adoption provisions. Little direct aid was offered to the mother who wished to raise her child alone, unless she was a blameless widow. As James Struthers illustrates, 'the origins of income security in Ontario begin with motherhood,'[75] yet public veneration of (good) mothers and concern for children did not translate into widespread income security for lone mothers. Aid was contingent on adherence to strict moral standards, not on need.

The first of these family reforms, the *Mothers' Allowance Act*, excluded unmarried mothers entirely. While women cohabiting with soldiers had been provided with pensions during the wartime emergency, such aid was considered unnecessary, and ill advised, once the exigencies of war had passed. In fact, during public hearings on the possible introduction of mothers' allowance legislation, conducted across the province in 1919, considerable fear was expressed that to allow support for unmarried women would provide a license for immorality and improvident breeding.[76] Representatives of the National Council of Women of Canada asserted that 'the mother with one child should seek support from the father, while unwed mothers with more than one child should be institutionalized.'[77]

Ironically, women with multiple illegitimate children were those most likely to have been living in marriage-like relationships, yet their circumstances, which had aroused some sympathy during the Great War, were now ignored. Children's Aid Society (CAS) workers 'recommended the allowance for needy widows and deserted mothers, but flatly denied unwed mothers. Unwed mothers were considered unfit and the CAS recommended that their children be immediately removed from these homes and placed with foster parents.'[78] 'It was in the better interest of the (illegitimate) child,' asserted one witness at the hearings, 'if it were adopted into some other family.'[79] Labour leaders who testified at the hearings were more sympathetic and argued that 'the child has no choice as to whether it is born into the home of the unmarried or the married mother.'[80] Racism, however, knew no class boundaries. Labour leaders, expressing their (unsubstantiated) fear that 'dangerous foreigners' were a threat to employment, argued for citizenship limitations on the allowance, that 'otherwise there might be a possibility of loading the country up with deserted children from other nationalities.'[81]

The act as passed reflected middle-class definitions of the normal family as well as the racism evidenced both by labour leaders and the elite. To receive the mothers' allowance a woman had to be widowed, had to have been deserted for seven years, or had to have an incapacitated husband. She had to be a British citizen and to have lived in Canada for three years, in Ontario for two. She also had to have two or more children. Birth, death, and marriage certificates were demanded as proof of eligibility, a requirement that effectively precluded First

Nations mothers from collecting the allowance. Thus, for moral, racial, and pecuniary reasons, large numbers of lone mothers were excluded from coverage under this legislation.[82] The act also stipulated that recipients must be 'fit and proper persons.'

Enormous discretionary power was awarded to the *Ontario Mother's Allowance Act* administration. Margaret Little points out that the 'fit and proper' were those who embodied the qualities of worthy (Anglo-Saxon) widowhood: sexual respectability, motherliness, good house-keeping, and habits of home economics.[83] Ontario officials argued that the allowances were justified 'in the interests of the child – the future citizen of the country; the mother being only secondary from the standpoint of the state.'[84] The mother was an employee of the government and could therefore be required to comply with government standards. Once children reached the age of majority, aid would end, whatever the employment prospects and economic circumstances of the mother. The employee could also be fired. As the 1921 Annual Report of the Ontario Mothers' Allowance Commission phrased it, the mother 'is regarded as an applicant for employment as a guardian for future citizens of the state, and if she does not measure up to the State's standards for such guardians other arrangements must be sought.'[85] But what kind of 'other arrangements' would these be? And on whom would they be imposed?

The aid that was offered, even to the 'virtuous and deserving' few, was inadequate. In order to save the provincial treasury money, mothers' allowance payments, were based on a maximum per family that amounted to much less than that which had been given to soldiers' wives during the war under the Canadian Patriotic Fund.[86] These provisions undermined the stated purpose of the allowance; mothers could not avoid paid work outside the home. In justifying this approach, the 1924 annual report of the Mothers' Allowance Commission made a virtue out of parsimony. It was argued that

> while the allowance does not cover the full maintenance of the family it is just enough to give encouragement to the mother. With careful management on her part and by doing a little work to supplement the allowance, she is able to keep herself and her family comfortable in every respect. Were the allowance made to cover full maintenance it would create wastefulness and probably laziness.[87]

This imperative to work for wages gave mothers mixed messages about proper behaviour and created standards that were impossible for any single parent to meet – economic self-sufficiency and simultaneous in-home care for children. This discourse also encouraged the moral scrutiny of all mothers.[88]

The tension between concern for the welfare of children and disapproval of errant mothers is evident in the three pieces of legislation passed in 1921: the *Legitimation Act*, the *Adoption Act*, and the *Children of Unmarried Parents Act*. The intention of these acts was to provide various forms of support for children whom legislators knew had been excluded under the *Mothers' Allowance Act*. The acts illustrate that concern regarding the health, welfare, and opportunities of poor, illegitimate children provided an incentive to protect such children from both poverty and immorality. This necessitated their removal from the baneful influence of degenerate women, not the provision of material aid to 'illegitimate' mothers who were single by choice.

These three acts delegated enormous discretionary power to local Children's Aid Societies. The CAS was a unique institution. It assumed responsibility for a wide range of child welfare legislation and was empowered to claim custody of children as well as to enforce the acts. The CAS operated as a private agency run by its own boards at the local level. Although enforcing state policies, the CAS experienced only minimal government regulation and financial support, rendering each institution dependent upon charity and ensuring that little cash was available to support single mothers (or to cover the costs of other child welfare programs facilitated by the CAS).[89] The CAS was staffed by middle-class, Anglo-Saxon child welfare workers, many of whom were women who had obtained training in the emergent professional discipline of social work and who shared the biases and preconceived notions of their contemporaries.[90] Moreover, even the most open-minded of social workers were constrained by the requirements of the legislation under which decisions were made.

The first act in this child welfare package, the *Legitimation Act*, allowed for the subsequent legitimation of children, born outside of lawful wedlock, whose biological parents later married.[91] This measure was intended not only to improve the legal and social status of illegitimate children but also to provide an incentive for cohabiting couples to formalize their relationships and for couples caught pregnant to have shotgun weddings; the state rewarded conformity rather than explicitly punishing non-marital cohabitation. It would be easy, from a modern perspective, to assume that this legislation faced little opposition, yet in the early decades of the twentieth century more punitive measures had considerable support. For example, the Presbyterian Church called for adultery and lewd cohabitation to be made punishable offences under the Criminal Code. The Federal Department of Justice gave some consideration to such legislation, although it was ultimately deemed unwise, largely because it would have been completely unenforceable.[92]

The *Legitimation Act* was controversial. Retroactive legitimation represented a considerable departure from the common law. Retroactive legitimation of children had been rejected 'because of the very great uncertainty there will generally be in the proof that the issue was really begotten by the same man.'[93] In order to promote family stability and to reduce state responsibility for the maintenance of children, the state would now accept the father's word regarding paternity.[94] Such a policy may have had particular resonance for the public in the immediate aftermath of war. A woman who became pregnant when her boyfriend was about to depart overseas, or was home on furlough, could not solve her problem through a shotgun marriage. This legislation allowed couples who married as soon as possible after the war to eliminate the stigma to which their children otherwise would have been subjected and to ensure that they were not precluded from inheritance. In peacetime, however, it was unrealistic to hope that many couples would make use of such legislation. Couples who were able – and wanted – to marry were likely to do so as early in the pregnancy as possible and thereby avoid recourse to the state. Most couples who cohabited outside legal marriage did so because one or both partners were separated from legal spouses but unable to afford divorce. It is also worth emphasizing that it was the uncorroborated word of the father, not of the mother, that was accepted under this legislation, thus reinforcing patriarchal definitions of the family.

The second act in the package, the *Adoption Act*, provided a mechanism for the permanent adoption of children either by strangers or by kin.[95] Ontario based its legislation explicitly on that of Massachusetts, the first state in the United States to amend the common law by providing means for formalizing adoptions and giving familial status to the non-biological child.[96] In Ontario, until 1921, adoption was possible only through private members' bills in the provincial legislature;[97] the *Adoption Act* created cheap and informal proceedings that could be undertaken at the level of the magistrate's court. As the Social Service Council of Ontario asserted in a 1921 memo to then Attorney General

W.E. Raney, 'one of the objectives of the act is to encourage the adoption of children by ... people who have the means and can provide a suitable home.'[98] Adoption, of course, would thereby serve state interests because adoptive parents, selected carefully as 'people with the means,' assumed legal responsibility for their new children, making these infants and youngsters less likely to become charges upon the public purse. In a context of fears of race suicide, moreover, adoption of white non-Anglo-Saxon infants into Anglo-Saxon homes represented the ultimate form of forced cultural assimilation.[99]

It was also argued that adoption should be supported because it was superior to institutional care. Institutional care, in the wake of epidemics and evidence of continued high death rates, was being phased out by the CAS and emphasis was instead being placed on foster care.[100] Why not give foster parents the opportunity to have permanent and legally binding relationships with the children in their care? These homes be good for children and foster care could lead to adoption which would save the state money. In cases in which marriage was not possible, relinquishment for adoption was believed to be in the best interest of the child. Reformer J.J. Kelso, whose work had been central to the creation of the CAS itself, argued that 'the experience of ages has proved conclusively that no unmarried mother can successfully bring up her child and save it from disgrace and obloquy. [But] the child, if adopted young by respectable, childless people, will grow up creditably, and without any painful reminders of its origins.'[101]

Legislators clearly hoped that unwed mothers would either legitimate their children through marriage or release their babies for adoption. Both retroactive legitimation and adoption represented dramatic departures from the common law, and both met the ambition of legislators and CAS workers to promote two-parent, patriarchal, traditional families and provided an opportunity to 'rescue' children while combating potential 'race suicide.' This policy would come to full fruition in the 'sixties scoop' of First Nations children for adoption by white families.[102] The acts reflected the belief that children whose parents married should not suffer the stigmatization associated with illegitimacy and that children in institutions should instead be placed in loving homes. The acts also embodied the widespread belief that unmarried mothers, for a variety of reasons – immorality, intellectual inferiority, and economic disadvantage being the most widely discussed – were unable to provide stable homes for their children. In effect, while promoting child welfare and greater equality of opportunity for children and challenging the idea that any child could be socially 'illegitimate,' the rhetoric of reform discursively constructed the unwed mother as the locus of sin, as a 'bad' or 'illegitimate' mother. The contradictions inherent in reform are clearly revealed in the third statute passed in this child welfare package – the *Children of Unmarried Parents Act*, formally known as *An Act for the Protection of the Children of Unmarried Parents*. [103]

The *Children of Unmarried Parents Act* provided a mechanism by which unwed mothers could obtain financial support from the putative fathers of their children, but it did so in a manner that was deliberately punitive and degrading. The CAS, the court, and society remained reluctant to provide financial support for unwed mothers lest this encourage immorality and 'improvident breeding.' The most explicitly punitive aspect of the act was that it undermined the common law assumption that the mother was the *de facto* guardian of her illegitimate child. Instead, it provided in section 10 that 'the provincial officer [the government employee appointed to enforce these three acts] may upon his own application be appointed guardian of a child born out of wedlock either alone or jointly with the mother of such child.'[104] Under child welfare legislation, the CAS had the right to remove children from the custody and control of unfit parents and to make such children Crown wards and then to release them for adoption without parental consent to relinquishment.[105] This power was expanded under the *Children of Unmarried Parents Act*. Section 11 established that when 'the mother ... through lack of means is unable, or through misconduct is unfit to have the care of the child, the child may, with the consent of the provincial officer, be dealt with as a "neglected child."' Simply put, an unwed mother could be deemed unfit purely because of her poverty.[106]

The state, not the mother, had the primary right to claim child support from the putative father.[107] The mother, or 'any person who has custody of a child born out of wedlock,' could also apply for support from the putative father of the child, but such applicants had to bear the cost of the proceedings themselves. For poor, single mothers and their families the cost of affiliation hearings was a disincentive to independent application. The CAS, in a manner that paralleled the workings of the administrators of the *Ontario Mother's Allowance Act*, had enormous discretionary power in determining which mothers did and did not have adequate corroboration of their stories of paternity to warrant court proceedings. When cases did proceed to court, the judge could only make an affiliation order 'on sufficient evidence' and women were put on the defensive as it was explicitly enacted that 'no order of affiliation shall be made upon the evidence of the mother of the child unless her evidence is corroborated by some other material evidence.' The term 'putative' father illustrates the distrust of women that underlay this ostensibly child-centred legislation; as one forthright Ontario judge put it in 1942, the court was inherently 'doubtful of her [the mother's] veracity.'[108]

When convinced by the evidence, the judge could declare 'the person named to be the father.'[109] The judge could also order the father to pay 'reasonable expenses for the mother' resulting from the pregnancy and during her recovery and 'a sum of money weekly towards the maintenance of the child.' The sum to be awarded was to be based not on need but on the father's 'ability to provide and (his) prospective means.' This, of course, undermined the purpose of the legislation in providing economic support for the illegitimate child and rendered the mother vulnerable. The putative father could not be required to pay beyond his means, but without such money, the mother might find her child dealt with as a 'neglected child.' The mother might go without food and other necessities in order to feed her child, but this would never be expected of the father, whose needs, under this legislation, explicitly superceded those of his offspring.

This act was intended to privatize the costs of reproduction, to prevent illegitimate children who could not be placed in normative families, as one judge put it, from 'becoming a burden' on society.[110] The order, when granted, imposed obligations of support on the putative father but did not give him any meaningful status with regard to his child.[111] This provided little positive incentive for responsible behaviour on the part of fathers. Neither did the child have any claim, beyond maintenance, against his or her father; the child remained *nullius filius*, without rights of inheritance or membership in the father's family. In a patriarchal world in which carrying the father's name had legal, symbolic, and social importance, the *Children of Unmarried Parents Act* did nothing to reduce the stigma to which the illegitimate child was subjected.[112] No distinction was made under the act between the father who had never lived with his child and the circumstances of the functional, informal, family after dissolution. Given the origins of the legislation in the provision of pensions by the Canadian Patriotic Fund during the Great War, this omission was ironic.

The *Children of Unmarried Parents Act* offered illegitimate children limited and precarious economic relief. It privatized the costs of reproduction and made no provision for state support of illegitimate children, while in the care of their mothers, if putative fathers were not deemed to be biological fathers, if they disappeared, or if they were simply unwilling or unable to pay support. The state had provided mechanisms for legitimating the child or for releasing it for adoption, and women who refused to conform could be blamed for their own 'stubborn refusal to think of their children before (themselves).'[113] While the impact of the new acts would clearly depend upon the discretionary power exercised by the CAS, the legislation had enormous potential to punish women who defied community standards of appropriate sexual expression and family formation. Significantly, the act was not modified in any meaningful way during the almost fifty-year period under study.

These acts reinforced a hierarchical ordering of families, were not-so-subtly coercive, and defined motherhood as appropriate only for women who met specific moral criteria.[114] The legislation encouraged women to release their children for adoption, and parsimonious approaches to welfare ensured that the single mother who kept her child would be obligated to work in a world that denied women fair wages and in which child care was difficult to obtain and expensive. At the same time, mothers were castigated for working outside the home. In supporting this family form and sexual division of labour, these acts reinforced the traditional family and its traditional gender roles. The legislation also set the precedent that the state would clearly distinguish between the deserving and the undeserving poor, even with respect to children.

2

'Doubtful of Her Veracity':
Procedures and Judgment under the
Children of Unmarried Parents Act

The contradictions inherent in the child welfare legislation of 1921 become starkly evident when the case files amassed by social workers are examined. The rhetoric surrounding reform emphasized child welfare and altruism, but the experiences of women in interaction with social workers suggest that judgmental and punitive attitudes towards unwed mothers pervaded the implementation of child welfare reform. Under the procedures mandated by the *Children of Unmarried Parents Act*, women were subjected to humiliating interrogation by CAS workers and were required to provide extensive corroboration of their stories of pregnancy. Putative fathers were also interviewed by CAS workers, but they were not distrusted in the same way as unwed mothers. Although the legislation did not differentiate between the circumstances of non-cohabiting women and former cohabitants, social workers did. Women who could provide evidence of cohabitation with the fathers of their children were rarely disbelieved. Women who had not cohabited with the fathers of their children, however, faced enormous procedural barriers in proving paternity. While determining women's access to child support, CAS workers were simultaneously responsible for helping women to plan for the future of their children, and non-cohabiting women were pressured to marry former lovers and to release children for adoption.

When cases did proceed to court, further humiliation for the mother ensued and, even when the CAS supported a woman's application, victory in court was not guaranteed. Few mothers had money with which to hire private lawyers to challenge the decisions of social workers or to appeal decisions from the magistrate's court. These problems with the legislation, however, are not apparent in the law reports.

The Law Reports and the Invisibility of Unmarried Mothers

The law reports are largely silent about the *Children of Unmarried Parents Act*.[1] Given the educational purpose of the law reports for practising lawyers, the paucity of cases would have raised considerable difficulties for lawyers trying to prepare themselves for court proceedings on behalf of single mothers. Of equal importance, this ensures that the historical evidence that today might be gleaned from the law reports is limited (and potentially misleading). Of the twenty higher court cases that appear in the law reports, three were purely about technicalities in the interpretation of the legislation and provide little insight into the impact of legislation on women, putative fathers, or children.[2] Of the other seventeen cases, fifteen were those in which putative fathers either sought leave to appeal the decisions of the lower court, or appealed an award of child support. In only two cases did appeals come from mothers. None of the reported cases involve cohabitation.

Ten of the fifteen cases in which putative fathers challenged the decisions of a lower court were unsuccessful. Two cases were leave to appeal decisions and both were denied. In one case the putative father had failed to contradict the evidence provided by the mother and refused to enter the witness box,[3] and in the other he had corroborated her story to a third party.[4] Of the thirteen cases in which putative fathers challenged decisions of the lower court, eight were denied. In one case the appeal occurred after the death of a mother in childbirth; the woman's father sought compensation for the costs of her illness and subsequent burial.[5] Two other cases involved very limited costs to the putative fathers as one child had been adopted[6] and another had been stillborn.[7] In the other five cases in which the appeal by the putative father was denied, evidence of paternity was overwhelming. Two fathers had signed detailed voluntary agreements for support in which they admitted paternity.[8] The third father had written extensive love letters confirming the nature of his relationship with the mother of the child and these letters had been entered into evidence at trial.[9] The fourth father had admitted paternity to several third parties (who gave evidence at trial) and the young woman, who worked for him as a domestic servant, asserted that the putative father 'compelled her to have intercourse with him.'[10] In the final case, the court stated that the decision of a lower court should not be overturned where 'the learned trial judge is satisfied that there is corroborative evidence.'[11]

In five of fifteen cases in which putative fathers appealed the rulings of the lower court, orders for support were vacated. One award was overturned on the technicality that the mother was legally married at the time of conception and had failed to provide evidence of non-access by her husband,[12] but the remaining four provide important hints regarding the difficulty that women faced in providing legally acceptable corroboration of their stories of pregnancy. One appeal was granted on the basis that the mother's claims of keeping company with the putative father, and the resemblance of the baby to him, did not constitute proof of paternity.[13] In another case evidence of the mother's alleged promiscuity was fatal to her claim for maintenance. She admitted that she had had sexual relations with two men. It did not matter that one of these relationships had ended long before the period relevant to conception. The judge argued that he could 'not escape the conclusion that the evidence falls short of amounting to proof sufficient to support a judicial determination.'[14] Another appeal was allowed on the assertion by the judge that any 'doubt – reasonably entertained – should, as in any penal proceeding, have inured to the benefit of the accused.'[15] This was despite the fact that officially the proceedings were civil, not criminal, and that the standard of proof should have been the balance of probabilities, not the criminal requirement of proof beyond a reasonable doubt.[16] In an ironic admission, while granting the appeal of another putative father, the court asserted in 1921 that 'the new Act in many of its terms [was] more onerous' than the regime that had preceded it.[17]

Of the twenty cases to appear in the law reports, only two were cases in which mothers challenged the dismissal of their claims by a lower court. The paucity of such cases, in itself, is suggestive; few mothers, it appears, had the resources necessary for appeal. One of these cases was dismissed, and in the other the mother was vindicated and an order for child support established. In the case of the dismissal of the mother's appeal, the report provides no detail regarding the reasoning behind the judge's determination that the mother's claim was fraudulent.[18] In the case in which the mother's appeal was granted, her evidence was accepted as sufficient to prove that 'she did not keep company with any other man during the year or more she and the defendant were continually going about together.' Perhaps more importantly, 'the defendant's staying out of the witness box and omitting to give any explanation of a series of circumstances so suspicious as to call for explanation' was fatal to his desire to see the claim dismissed.[19]

While the ratios of success in the reported cases might be interpreted to prove that the playing field was level between men and women in affiliation proceedings, both the number of cases initiated by men (fifteen) versus those initiated by women (two) and the reasons given in the decisions belie such findings. Few women challenged lower court decisions. Men who denied paternity were largely believed; it was when men refused to speak in their own defence that their claims were dismissed. Perhaps more importantly, the brief and legalistic disposition of cases in the law reports renders invisible the lengthy negotiations and struggles that preceded the arrival of cases in court. To fully understand the Kafkaesque procedures to which women were subjected, the case files produced by social workers must be explored.

Intake Proceedings at the Children's Aid Society

The unwed mother was required to report her pregnancy to the local Children's Aid Society, and it was 'the duty of the provincial officer, by inquiry through Children's Aid Societies, to obtain all information possible with respect to every child born out of wedlock.'[20] While reported cases provide no detail about the role of the CAS in *Children of Unmarried Parents Act* cases, the files produced during the process of the interrogation of the client at intake (which include full court transcripts in cases which advanced to litigation) are rich in detail. Impoverished, often disappointed by the conduct of men they had loved, fearful for their futures, and potentially intimidated by the power of CAS workers, young women arrived at the CAS offices seeking assistance in obtaining financial support for their children. Before any help would be forthcoming, however, the unwed mother had to convince the CAS worker that she was worthy and that her proof of paternity was overwhelming.[21]

Ironically, by reporting her pregnancy to the CAS, a woman subjected herself to potential punishment. Under the *Female Refuges Act*, first passed in 1897, updated in 1919 and not repealed until 1958, any woman under the age of thirty-five could be incarcerated on a complaint regarding her immorality and incorrigibility. No appeal was possible until 1942.[22] As evidence amassed by Joan Sangster amply demonstrates, unwed pregnancy often precipitated incarceration;[23] the CAS had the power to make complaints regarding clients and women were made aware of this fact in the course of their interrogations by CAS workers. It is clear from the case files that at least twenty-three women were reported by the CAS under the *Female Refuges Act*, although the case files do not record what happened to them. CAS workers also had the power to decide whether or not the mother was entitled to her child's 'custody and guardianship.'[24] The process of interrogation to which women were subjected replicated what Foucault and others have described as 'the ritual of the confessional.'[25] It was in an atmosphere of extremely unequal power relations that young women were subjected to intense questioning and forced – with the aid of social workers but without the opportunity to consult lawyers – to complete standardized questionnaires.

Basic demographic information – detailing age, employment status, place of residence, and sometimes religious affiliation – was collected. Although the majority of women in these cases appear to have been English-speaking and Anglo-Saxon, 'the designation "white," "British," or "English" was absent'[26] from the case files. In such cases, background was not considered a causal factor in women's immorality. In a manner that parallels the evidence unearthed by Joan Sangster with regard to criminal case files, however, 'if non-Anglos were involved, ethnicity was more likely to be mentioned, with the underlying implication that this might explain the presence of immorality.'[27] This was particularly true with regard to non-white women. With disturbing regularity, insulting asides appeared in the descriptions of the fourteen women who were Black[28] and the nine who were Aboriginal.[29] In all but one of these cases, gratuitous remarks about women's supposedly slovenly habits, drunkenness, and 'low moral character' appeared in the files, often with a note that the family in question was already under surveillance by the CAS. It is also significant that of the twenty-three cases in which women were reported to the authorities under the *Female Refuges Act*, eleven were either Aboriginal or Black. The contrast with white women is stark. While eleven of twenty-three Black and Aboriginal women endured prosecution under the *Female Refuges Act*, only twelve of 4,000 white women were charged under this mechanism.

Women had to describe in detail the circumstances under which they had become pregnant, naming the putative fathers of their children and outlining any previous sexual history.[30] But the details that they shared could be and were used against them. Women who admitted previous sexual relationships, or having met boyfriends in circumstances of which social workers disapproved, reduced the chances that their stories of pregnancy would be believed. The questionnaire also solicited information about smoking, drinking, and attendance at dance halls and moving picture houses.[31] As one social worker argued in the 1950s, this inquisition could prove to be a time-consuming endeavour: 'It is the concern of the caseworker to ascertain how much evidence the mother can produce in support of her claim. The compilation of a detailed history of the relationship may demand much time and patience.'[32]

There is no doubt that these proceedings and interviews were unpleasant for unwed mothers. Of more importance in this chapter, however, is the discretionary power that CAS workers had to determine women's access to court proceedings and thereby to limit their options with regard to the futures of their children. As Linda Gordon asserts in her path-breaking study of the interaction between battered women and the 'helping' bureaucracies, in articulating one's story to state agencies 'one rarely gets what one wants but rather another interpretation of one's needs.'[33] If a woman's story was believed, the putative father would be sought for questioning. If, however, CAS workers determined that the woman was untruthful, that she was promiscuous and therefore could not prove paternity, if she was unable to provide contact information for the putative father of her child, or if she was believed to be unworthy and incapable of being a proper mother, no further action would be taken on the case. In most cases, no specific reason for the decision was recorded in the file when a woman's claim was dismissed at intake. Complex factors, including race, ethnicity, the woman's manner of presentation, the evidence she might have brought with her to the CAS office, and admissions regarding sexual activity at times not related to pregnancy would all have had some influence on the attitude of CAS workers and the decisions they made about taking cases to court. Such discretionary power was amorphous and difficult to challenge.

In 526 of 4,023 cases, no further action was taken after the interview with the mother. Such aggregate numbers, however, hide the disproportionate disadvantage faced by young women who had not cohabited with the fathers of their children. Only eighteen women of 2,031 who had cohabited with the fathers of their children were disbelieved at this stage of the proceedings. By contrast, of the 1,992 women who had not cohabited with the fathers of their children, 508 saw their cases dismissed informally by the CAS at intake. Importantly, this failure to believe women did not decline significantly over time. In the 1920s, 98 of 386 non-cohabiting women (25.3 per cent) were dismissed at intake; in the 1930s, 105 of 418 (25.1 per cent); in the 1940s, 106 of 406 (26.1 per cent); in the 1950s, 119 of 467 (25.5 per cent); and even in the 1960s, 80 of 323 non-cohabiting women (24.8 per cent) were summarily dismissed at this early stage of proceedings. Condemnation of the unwed mother, and the propensity to disbelieve her, remained pervasive into the 1960s.

Corroborating the Woman's Story

If the social worker believed the woman's story, the next step in the process was to determine whether or not the woman had sufficient evidence to corroborate her claim. Convincing the social worker was not enough, as under the act it was explicitly provided that 'no order of affiliation shall be made upon the evidence of the mother of the child unless her evidence is corroborated by some other material evidence.'[34] First and foremost, the CAS sought such corroboration through an admission of paternity from the putative father. Finding the father was the essential first step in obtaining an admission of paternity. In 443 of 4,023 cases, men disappeared. As CAS workers noted in one case, 'it looks as though our bird has flown the coop ... we have been informed that he quit his job and nobody knows where he is.'[35] Again, however, aggregate numbers erase the particular disadvantage faced by young women who had not cohabited with the fathers of their children. While only 42 of 2,031 cohabiting fathers (2.1 per cent) disappeared at this stage of proceedings, 401 of 1,992 non-cohabiting fathers (20.1 per cent) could not be located for interviews with the CAS, 401 of 1,484 if we consider that 508 women had already been summarily dismissed because they were not believed by social workers.

Although paternity proceedings had originally had a quasi-criminal element to them, with magistrates under the Elizabethan poor laws having the right to arrest the defendant until a preliminary hearing had been conducted, the CAS did not have such power.[36] If a judge felt that a man was at risk of disappearing, he could be 'detained as a material witness';[37] in practice, however, men who wanted to disap-

pear did so long before cases proceeded to court and before such procedures could be invoked. One sarcastic putative father taunted his
former girlfriend in a letter that he wrote to her after he had fled the
jurisdiction of the court: 'Since I am now residing in Vancouver, it will
be impossible for me to appear on May 3. I would appreciate a more
convenient time and place.'[38]

When they could find putative fathers, CAS workers tried to convince them to enter into voluntary agreements for the support of children. In 1,533 of 4,023 cases, men entered into such voluntary
agreements and admitted their paternity. [39] It is important to emphasize, however, that again aggregate numbers do not reflect the differential outcome in two types of cases. Of the 1,533 men who freely
entered into voluntary agreements, 1,242 had cohabited with their girlfriends and had lived with their children for extended periods of time.
By contrast, only 291 of 1,083 non-cohabiting men who were interviewed (not 1,992 because of the attrition due to dismissal of mothers
and disappearance of fathers) admitted paternity. Ultimately, most
cohabitation cases that came before the court involved the enforcement
of a voluntary agreement or an adjudication of the quantum of the
award. These cases are so different from those not involving cohabitation that the remainder of this chapter will focus exclusively on non-
cohabiting women; stories of cohabitation will be the subject of a later
chapter.

Of the 1,083 men who had not cohabited with women prior to pregnancy and who were interviewed by CAS workers, 409 denied paternity and sought to impugn the reputations of former girlfriends.[40] Of
course, both men and women might well have lied to CAS workers,
but women were much more often suspected of being untruthful than
were men. The distrust of women that underlay legislation, and the
informality of the interviews of the CAS with putative fathers,
rewarded the most recalcitrant, irresponsible, and dishonest of men.
Men were not under oath when they spoke to CAS workers. While
these workers often pre-judged the unwed mother as 'untrustworthy,'[41] the putative father was not so judged. Despite the fact that men
had a financial interest in disproving paternity, their veracity was
rarely questioned. Engaging in sex without marriage was not believed
to reflect on the man's wider morality, but the woman who had sex
outside of marriage was constructed as both promiscuous and dishonest. As Renee Monson argues with regard to contemporary paternity
cases in the United States,

the majority of questions asked of women revolved around their sexual practices and partners; the questions asked of men focused more on their employment, income and expenses. Even when men were asked questions about sexual behavior, it was the woman's veracity and sexual practices that were almost always at issue.[42]

Men were not subjected to the standard questionnaire and even those who were described as 'unreliable'[43] or who had 'never been known to be steadily employed'[44] were not thereby judged as likely to be dishonest. Informal discussions with the CAS, while putting women on the defensive in having to explain their 'promiscuity,' provided men with ample opportunity to humiliate their girlfriends and to impugn their reputations. This is not to say that interviews might not also have been unpleasant and intimidating for putative fathers; however, the father, unlike the mother, was considered to be innocent until proven guilty.

To combat a denial of paternity a mother could bring her friends, family and work associates into the CAS office to provide evidence of intimacy between the parties or public admissions by the father of his role in the pregnancy. Evidence that would be considered by the CAS was explicitly listed by one social worker when interviewing a recalcitrant (and very obviously·dishonest) putative father:

> How are you going to establish you are not the father. We have the evidence now first from the mother of the child who says you are the father. You had relations with her from time to time. There is corroboration from her mother, discussions you had with her, promises to marry, the arrangements for the marriage, setting the dates, the fact you bought her that ring after the child was born, you paid her money after the child was born. These things would indicate you are likely to be the father of the child.[45]

Ironically, however, the father in this case remained evasive and refused to admit paternity; although he was harangued and repeatedly questioned, the CAS chose not to pursue the case in court.

The mother had to provide evidence of ongoing intimacy with the putative father and of her good character, in particular with regard to her chastity outside of the relationship in question. But proving chastity was a challenge for a woman who was pregnant outside of lawful marriage. And how did one provide material evidence and corroboration of a quintessentially private activity? Moreover, as the previous

Figure 2.1: Dismissal of cases at intake and after interviews with putative fathers (%)

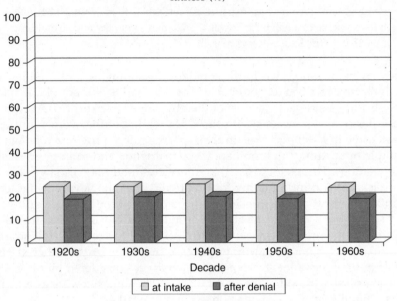

case illustrates, such evidence was often not enough when men denied paternity or simply refused to answer questions. As was observed by one expert who challenged the discretionary power of the CAS and the administration of paternity law, 'one of the unmarried mother's knottiest problems was to provide legally acceptable evidence that the man she names is actually the father of her child.'[46] The propensity to disbelieve mothers, and to dismiss cases after informal interviews with putative fathers, did not change significantly over time. In the 1920s, 77 of 386 non-cohabiting women (19.9 per cent) saw their cases dismissed after the CAS had interviewed the putative father; in the 1930s, 87 of 105 (20.8 per cent); in the 1940s, 87 of 406 (21.4 per cent); in the 1950s, 94 of 467 (20.1 per cent); and even in the 1960s, of 323 noncohabiting women, 64 (19.8 per cent) were disbelieved after the interview with the putative father (see fig. 2.1).

If the CAS denied woman access to court proceedings, her only alternative was to pursue support in court at her own expense. Financial concerns at the CAS, in part, underscored this policy. W.H. Bury, the provincial officer in charge of the Department of Public Welfare,

Children's Division, put government policy on this issue bluntly in 1953:

> An application for an affiliation order is usually made by the Provincial Officer [Section 8 (g) C.U.P.A.] acting through the Superintendent of a Children's Aid Society, who is the representative of the Provincial Officer. As the Provincial Officer is liable in the first instance for the costs of the action, including court and solicitor's fees, the P.O. will authorize an application for an order only where a mother's claims can be fully corroborated.[47]

The CAS received very limited state funds, reinforcing the propensity to disbelieve women and to dismiss their cases.[48] Of course, mothers also faced financial limitations, and for the most part, the refusal of the CAS to pursue a case ended the story of the woman's attempts to seek justice and support for her child. Ultimately, of the 1,992 extant case files involving non-cohabiting women, 917 were dismissed at intake or after the interview with the putative father, but only in thirty-one cases did such women, or their parents, hire lawyers and fund their own petitions to the court.

This does not mean, however, that women were unaware of the unequal terms under which they negotiated with putative fathers and the CAS. But they had little power to protest. If they were critical of social workers, all services to them could be withdrawn. As one CAS worker put it in a letter to a young woman, 'no further services would be available' for the simple reason that the woman had 'been very critical of our handling of this case.'[49] A minimum of thirty-seven non-cohabiting women were sent letters threatening that if they were not more cooperative, services to them would cease; it is impossible to know how many times such verbal threats were made. As the Social Planning Council of Toronto admitted in 1960, 'legal counsel to unmarried mothers is very limited and the laws protecting children give Children's Aid Societies extraordinary power and authority.'[50] This should not be surprising to historians of women. Mariana Valverde argues that the differential treatment of male and female juvenile 'delinquents' during this period meant that 'many of the girls were victims of processes on the margins of the legal system. It would seem that girls were more subject to the opinions of social workers, parents and other authorities than to the letter of the law.'[51]

Ironically, social workers claimed that processes outside the law were more humane than court proceedings, stating that it 'would be advantageous from every point of view if all courts would engage the services of trained social workers.'[52] Dorothy Chunn points out, however, that so-called 'scientific and exhaustive investigation of all circumstances surrounding family cases before they came to court'[53] did not deliver a 'humane, effective alternative'[54] to the court system but instead denied women choice; this argument is clearly proven in the cases adjudicated under the act. Not only were the vast majority of women who were pregnant without cohabitation denied the opportunity to seek child support from the fathers of their children, but also, because of the simultaneous legal and social powers of the CAS, they were pressured to marry men against their wishes and/or to release their children for adoption. Refusal to pursue support through court proceedings could itself be used as a pressure tactic to influence the mother's plans for the child.

Determining the Future of the Child

In the opinion of CAS workers, the obvious and most desirable solution in cases of unwed pregnancy was marriage. In the words of one American social worker, 'the cases in which the girl married the father of her baby are, of course, instances of a solution that is as nearly perfect as possible under the complex circumstances.'[55] Given the legal disadvantages and social opprobrium attendant upon illegitimacy, it was not unreasonable for CAS workers to recommend marriage to the mother and the putative father as the best solution for the child, particularly given the passage of the *Legitimation Act*. The hope that many couples would marry, however, was misplaced. Marriage occurred in only 56 of 1,992 cases not involving cohabitation.

More importantly, CAS workers denied women choice. Women who did not want to marry the fathers of their children, who asserted that 'we fought like cats and dogs every time I saw him,'[56] or that 'he never got a steady job or settled down and he would not be a good prospect as a husband,'[57] were perceived to be irresponsible and undeserving of financial support. As was asserted in one case by a social worker, 'I have pointed out to the woman that her marriage now with H would legitimize the child and relieve him for the rest of his life of a handicapping stigma. She, however, persists in her refusal to marry H and insists on keeping the child.'[58] Despite the fact that the man in this case was domineering and abusive,[59] the CAS determined that the only correct option for this mother was to accept his offer of marriage. When she refused to do so, they decided that her case would receive no further attention. Although her parents, with whom both she and the baby were living, hired a lawyer and funded a petition to the court, the judge concurred with the CAS, asserting that 'he is quite willing to marry the woman or to take the child and maintain it at his own expense. She quite stubbornly refuses either of these proposals ... Under the circumstances I do not think that he should be tied up to a periodic payment.'[60]

That the CAS had the power simultaneously to provide counselling suggesting that the mother should get married and to determine whether or not she would be provided with legal assistance in obtaining support from the father of her child, even when paternity was not under dispute, reveals the conflict of interest embedded in legislation.[61] Moreover, men could exploit the emphasis on marriage for their own advantage. For example, one mother delayed proceedings against her ex-boyfriend for over a year, 'trusting and believing in promises that he falsely and maliciously made to marry me'; ironically, she was then told that the one-year time limit on prosecution had expired and that, whatever her evidence of paternity, the CAS could not help her.[62]

The marriage solution was also racially specific. White men were not expected to marry non-white women with whom they had been involved, even when they were unmarried and admitted paternity of children. The number of such cases recorded in these files is limited (only eleven cases were found in which a white man was involved with a non-white woman) but evidence is nonetheless convincing that racist fears of miscegenation prevailed over the moralistic desire to see couples legally wed. CAS workers, in fact, actively intervened to prevent mixed-race marriages. One white man had admitted paternity to his 'Negro' girlfriend's family and he had initially planned to marry her. Pressure from his family and the CAS led him instead to negotiate a settlement in which he agreed to pay $6 a week in support for the child. When he married a white woman shortly thereafter, he stopped paying; when he was called into court about this, the amount of support was reduced to $3 a week. The agreement was taken as *prima facie* evidence of paternity, despite the fact that the CAS asserted that the case should be reopened entirely. This was an unusual, and undoubtedly racist, response; normally, CAS workers did not actively seek to overturn an admission of paternity. Although ostensibly it was the social worker's job to defend the mother's interests in court, instead the social worker asserted that the putative father 'feels that there is a very definite possibility that other men could also be the father of this child. He indicated that he felt that he was by no means certain that he was the only boy to be intimate with Miss T. The girl's family is not known for its truthfulness or good habits.' Although she did not explicitly refer to Miss T's race when making this assertion, descriptions of her 'Negroid' appearance throughout the evidence suggest that race was a prominent consideration in the disposition of the case.[63]

White women, too, were dissuaded from marriage when their sexual partners were non-white. In all seven cases in these files in which white women were pregnant with mixed-race children, they were discouraged by the CAS from marrying their lovers, despite the fact that their babies were not considered desirable for adoption. As one mother was told, marrying her Chinese lover would simply 'compound one mistake with one that is even greater.'[64] In her devastating autobiographical critique of the *Female Refuges Act*, under which she was incarcerated for out-of-wedlock pregnancy and incorrigibility, Viola Demerson recalls pacing her cell in shock, thinking 'how could it be that a judge, knowing that I'm pregnant, would refuse to allow me to marry the father of my child?'[65] The father of her child was Chinese and such a marriage was to be prevented whenever possible.

In most cases, however, both parties were white, but marriage did not occur and social workers had to help mothers to formulate other plans for their babies. The possibility of adoption, with its limited financial implications for putative fathers and, notably, for the CAS itself, was always suggested to mothers and was part of the informal negotiations carried out by the CAS with unmarried fathers. In fact, social workers seem to have introduced the possibility of adoption into negotiations with putative fathers even when mothers were adamant that they did not want to relinquish their children. Social workers could use the threats that corroboration was absent and that cases would not advance to court to encourage women to consider adoption.

The informality of negotiations with putative fathers indirectly empowered men, via the CAS, to influence the decisions of mothers with regard to the futures of their children, despite the fact that legally the mother of an illegitimate child was the only parent required to sign consent to relinquishment papers.[66] In 203 of the 1,083 cases in which non-cohabiting fathers were interviewed, men admitted paternity informally to the CAS and agreed to pay costs pending adoption, but refused to provide a formal admission of paternity and threatened to force the issue into court if the mother wanted long-term support. The proportion of such cases increased slowly but steadily over time. In the 1920s, 8.9 per cent entered into such arrangements; in the 1930s, 9.3 per cent; in the 1940s, 10.8 per cent; in the 1950s, 10.7 per cent; and in the 1960s, 11.1 per cent. One father asserted to a CAS worker in 1952 that 'he was not going to do anything more than this $200. If the girl did not take that, he would just live outside of the Province of Ontario and she could not collect anything.'[67] Another man threatened his pregnant ex-girlfriend and the CAS. 'If Miss K is prepared to place her child for adoption he would be prepared to enter into an agreement for confinement expenses and maintenance from the date of the child's birth until placement. He stated that if Miss K wished to keep the child that he would be prepared to have the matter brought before the court.' She was unemployed, unable to speak English and, as a recent immigrant, had no local family to help her. It is not surprising that ultimately she accepted her former lover's offer of $120 and gave her child up for adoption.[68]

Another father was explicit that he would provide no support 'for the care of the child in this case while in the care of her mother' and stated that it was his intention, if an order was made against him, 'to leave the province in order that he might not be forced to pay.'[69] CAS workers did not use such admissions against men in court, but seem to have assumed that men would carry through with threats to abscond or to deny paternity and that it was therefore a waste of time and money to pursue support for mothers. Women themselves, however, recognized the power of putative fathers in negotiations; as one mother lamented, 'he is trying to force me to place the baby for adoption so he can evade payment.'[70]

Social workers refused to go to court without an admission of paternity from the father and without extensive corroborative evidence on the part of the mother, and they used their control over court proceedings to influence women's decisions with regard to marriage and adoption. Interviews with putative fathers put women, not men, on the defensive. While CAS workers might threaten putative fathers in the hopes of eliciting an admission of paternity, or at least an agreement for support pending adoption, men held considerable power, as without an admission of paternity, the CAS would not go to court. Only 291 agreements for support emerged from the interview process and in 203 of these cases court proceedings ensued after non-payment. Ironically, however, court cases, ostensibly about enforcement, instead engaged questions of paternity. Fathers who had admitted paternity raised new questions about evidence and women faced yet another layer of interrogation and humiliation.

Court Proceedings

Paternity suits, as one contemporary observer noted, were 'barbaric in terms of consideration for human dignity ... [the mother had to describe] in open court in very explicit terms how, when, and where the male defendant's penis [had] entered her vagina. The entire procedure implicitly indicates that the court regards her as a whore, and that the court listens to her at all only for the sake of the taxpayers.'[71] Judges routinely allowed invasive, highly personal, and condescending questioning to continue unabated, even when such questions were obviously irrelevant to the issue of paternity. The court took 'the point of view that the unwed mother [was] merely a witness for the prosecution.'[72] It is not surprising that he said/she said contests produced transcripts that exhibit a remarkable resemblance to those produced during rape cases.[73] This, moreover, was in a context in which men had previously admitted paternity in the offices of the CAS.

At times, the tone of interrogations can only be classified as pornographic. Putative fathers attempted to convince the court that, as one man put it, although he didn't know of any specific men who had been sexually active with his ex-girlfriend, she had slept with him on their first date and therefore 'it would have been easy for any guy.'[74] The lawyer representing another defendant asserted that 'it is important to show persons with whom she had intercourse because normally once a woman has intercourse with a man, as a matter of normal probative value, she will enjoy intercourse with that man ... and he will be able to call upon her from time to time in the future.'[75] As one young woman asserted, the entire focus of the defendant seemed to be 'trying to class me as a girl of the streets.'[76] But while women contested the erroneous and damaging stereotypes invoked by defendants and their lawyers, judges and magistrates did not. In fact, even under the most extreme and compelling of circumstances, women could be disbelieved and denied support; judges, too often, shared rather than contested hostile attitudes and misconceptions.

In 160 of 203 cases brought to court by the CAS, women were disbelieved and financial support for their children was denied. This high rate of dismissal of women's claims by the court seems surprising, given that more 'difficult' cases were either dismissed at intake or after the interview with the putative father. More importantly, the men had signed agreements for support, so their testimony should have been subjected to close scrutiny. Instead, as one forthright Ontario judge put it in 1942, the court was inherently 'doubtful of her [the mother's] veracity.'[77] Technically, these should have been civil proceedings in which the standard of preponderance of the evidence would have been applied in reaching a verdict. In practice, however, the mother had to prove her case beyond a reasonable doubt. In fact, confirmation that the civil, not the criminal, burden of proof applied in affiliation cases did not come into practice in Ontario until 1976.[78] This led to egregious miscarriages of justice against which poor women had little recourse.

For example, a woman who had borne an illegitimate child in 1952 had charged the father of the child with rape. He had been acquitted, however, when his wife, after initially refusing to do so, provided him with an alibi. Physical evidence provided strong proof that the rape had indeed occurred. The woman claimed that she had been 'previously chaste' and several witnesses came forward to attest to her 'good character.' The CAS supported her claim throughout the proceedings and described the putative father in extremely unflattering terms. In his initial contact with the CAS, the putative father had admitted paternity, yet the judge asserted that he was 'not certain that this woman was entirely truthful.'[79] The woman did not appeal.

Another woman, whose child was born in 1935, claimed to have consented to intercourse only upon a promise of marriage. When she became pregnant, the putative father provided her with medicine intended to produce a miscarriage. She became violently ill, ending up in emergency care. The boyfriend was then charged with administering drugs intended to induce an abortion and was given a suspended sentence. Despite his admission of paternity in the attempted abortion case, and in his initial dealings with the CAS, when called to court in the affiliation hearing he denied responsibility for the pregnancy. The judge dismissed the case with the following denigrating commentary about the unwed mother:

> She admits that she was quite willing for the intercourse. No blood was produced by the intercourse. The witness, W (a friend of the accused)

swears that the girl told him that if he would come out with her she would rob him of his purity. Considering these doubts cast upon the previous chastity of the girl I find myself unable to conclude in any satisfactory way that M was the father of this child. The application is therefore dismissed.[80]

At no point in the proceedings had it been suggested that the mother had had intercourse with anyone other than the putative father at a time material to conception. Her alleged promiscuity was adequate evidence to prove that her 'veracity could not be trusted,' despite the fact that all so-called evidence of promiscuity had been obtained from friends of the putative father. She did not appeal.

Women were repeatedly disbelieved by the courts and they were punished when they were honest about behavior that contradicted the ideal model of femininity. A twenty-seven-year-old mother whose case was supported by the CAS admitted in 1932 that she had not been a virgin when she became involved with the putative father of her child; she had had one other long-term relationship in which she had been sexually active. Despite the initial admission of paternity by the putative father and the fact that family members could corroborate a long-standing relationship between the parties, her application was dismissed by the judge with the following commentary:

This unfortunate young woman has, during the last few years, lived in a loose manner, careless even of appearances. She has admitted also being in the company of other men under suspicious circumstances. She denies, of course, that any other man had intercourse with her over a period of time during which the pregnancy must have been created ... but the charge has not been proven and must be dismissed.[81]

In another case, a judge dismissed an application which had been supported by the CAS in terms that reveal the propensity of the court to disbelieve the word of women: 'Any one of the men named could have provided the vital sperm and would have been permitted to do so at any time ... at 15 the applicant was a potential tramp and now has fully realized that potential.' All evidence regarding the young woman's so-called promiscuity had been provided by friends of the accused, but the woman did not appeal. Not surprisingly, however, the CAS worker described her departure from the court as 'marked by tears.'[82] The same judge, as late as 1966, dismissed a case in which evidence from the woman's roommate provided corroboration that the putative father had 'pretty much lived with them for the last year,' and that no one else had been intimate with the mother. The judge, however, argued that such living arrangements revealed the promiscuity of the mother, that young women 'shouldn't live unchaperoned' and that he therefore 'just cannot believe it. I am sure that he did have intercourse with her, however, I am not satisfied with the quality of the corroborative evidence.'[83] Judges could – and did – display deep hostility towards women.

They also failed to understand the power dynamics that permeated the court. For example, one magistrate ejected an unwed mother as an unfit witness and dismissed her case without ever hearing her evidence: 'Just a minute ... first of all, you don't speak English very well – secondly you seem to be very concerned about this case because I have never seen anyone more emotionally disturbed than you ... I don't understand you and if I don't understand you there is no point in you coming down here today.'[84] No translation services were provided, nor did the judge consider why she might justifiably 'be very concerned about this case.' Although supported by her CAS worker, the young woman did not contest the decision of the court.

Women who funded their own appeals to the court were treated with equal contempt. It must have been heartbreaking for women and families who had invested their limited resources to hire lawyers and go to court to be denied redress. Moreover, in the process, like other women who appeared in court, they were humiliated; lawyers for the defence exploited the double standard, racial stereotypes, and any and all other arguments that might embarrass and discredit pregnant women. For example, one defence lawyer, in questioning a French-Canadian mother about the time at which intercourse had first taken place with the putative father of her child, tried to portray her as wanton and depraved, more sexually experienced than his 'unfortunate' client. He asked probing and embarrassing questions about her alleged previous sexual partners, without even deeming it necessary to argue that intercourse had occurred with any other partners at a time relevant to conception. He implied that her veracity was in question because of her so-called promiscuity and he subjected her to nasty insinuations about other bad habits, such as drinking, going out unescorted, and necking at parties. All of these bad habits, he asserted, were linked to her degraded upbringing and the lack of civilization among French-Canadian families:

Q: Approximately how old were you when you started to have intercourse?

A: I can't remember, but I know that I was older than 16.

Q: Were you 16 and a half, 17?

A: I don't know.

Q: 18?

A: I don't know.

Q: You are not impressing anyone with this kind of evasive answer.

Q: Do you remember the name of the boy?

A: No.

Q: Just picked him up off the street?

A: No.

Q: Someone you knew.

A: Yes.

Q: If you know him, give us his name.

A: He was LM.

Q: Just about thirty seconds ago you told us you couldn't remember the
name.

Interjection by her lawyer: I would like to address the Court if I may.
Your Honor, I know cross-examination should be broad but I submit that
it should also be relevant and intercourse that does not, and cannot, affect
the pregnancy, which is the subject of the matter of this action, is not relevant in my humble submission.

By the Court: There may be an attempt to prove promiscuity.

By her lawyer: If so, a prostitute if there were one, would have a right to
come to this Court and promiscuity, I submit, is not relevant, I just make
the point.

Q: I kind of thought you would say that you were an experienced woman
when you had intercourse with JG (the defendant).

A: Not that much.

Q: How much do you think of as that much?

A: I don't know.

Q: You go to a man's apartment. You take your clothes off and get into
bed with him, is that right, and then you can say that G was only the second man.

A: He was.

Q: Sure he was. You girls tell the same lies every time you come into these court rooms ... Do you smoke?

A: Yes.

Q: Do you drink?

A: A bit, yes.

Q: I suppose beer affects you?

A: I guess it does, if you drink enough.

Q: You drink enough?

A: I didn't drink that much.

Q: Not that much, whatever that means. Does liquor make you passionate?

A: I don't know.

Q: If you don't know, who does? You are an experienced drinker. You drink liquor. You drink beer. Does it make you passionate?

A: I guess it does.

Q: Lots of necking goes on at your parties? Don't shrug your shoulders. We cannot get that on to the record ... [now, with regard to a party unrelated to the time of conception] You had a nice party in Hamilton and came back to the house. You were left alone with PJ [who was not the man named in the paternity suit] in this recreation room dancing and kissing. Be fair.

A: Yes.

Q: Then I suggest that you did what came natural with him.

A: I did not.

Q: Then did he take you home?

A: No, I called for a cab.

Q: I even know your answers before you utter them. I want truthful answers. Whatever other virtues you might have, frankness is not one of them.[85]

The case was dismissed. The mother's sister and brother came to court asserting that the putative father had admitted paternity to them and that he had initially planned to marry the young woman. Another woman, who had been a boarder in the same house as the mother, testified that he had also admitted paternity to her and that, since she was a nurse, he had sought her advice about an abortion. The putative father did not deny intercourse at the material time and admitted to a long-standing sexual relationship with the mother of the child. He was not able to name any other men who might be responsible for paternity. In questioning the young woman, the lawyer for the defence made several derogatory remarks about the 'known sexual habits of her race.' He asserted that she, unlike his client, 'did not have the benefit of a civilized upbringing' and that the 'veracity of these people [the French-Canadians] was often to be doubted.' The fact that the case had not been deemed worthy of court action by the CAS, that it was being prosecuted by the woman's family, and that it was dismissed, all illustrate the persuasive power of both gender and ethnic stereotypes. It is also striking that, although it was noted at several points during the interrogation that questions had to be repeated because the woman's English was poor and she had not understood the proceedings, no translation services were provided for her. Neither had the CAS considered it necessary to provide such services during the informal negotiations that preceded their decision not to prosecute on the woman's behalf.

Cases that advanced to court illustrate a pervasive mistrust of women that did not abate over time. Women pregnant outside the context of cohabitation were extraordinarily vulnerable; of 1,992 women in such circumstances; 508 (25.5 per cent) were dismissed at intake; 401 (20.1 per cent) saw boyfriends (or attackers) disappear; 409 (20.5 per cent) had their cases dismissed once CAS workers had interviewed putative fathers; 56 (2.8 per cent) married their lovers (sometimes under duress); and in 203 (10.2 per cent) cases fathers were willing only to pay costs pending adoption. Only 291 men (14.6 per cent) admitted paternity. In 124 cases (6.2 per cent) proceedings failed to advance to court, but evidence in the case files is inadequate to understand and categorize the reasons why and at what stage of the proceedings cases were not pursued. After the attrition of cases at the CAS, 203 fathers who had previously admitted paternity denied responsibility in court and in 160 of these cases they were successful in overturning agreements for support. The proportion of cases in which men were successful when they denied paternity in court did not decline over time; in the 1920s, 29 of 39 (74 per cent) such applications were successful; in the 1930s, 34 of 42 (80.1 per cent); in the 1940s, 31 of 41 (75.6 per cent); in the 1950s, 39 of 48 (81.2 per cent); and in the 1960s, 27 of 33 (81.8 per cent).

Women faced hostility and distrust of their word in the court, as much as in the offices of the CAS. Yet, because of their poverty, few were able to challenge either the refusal of the CAS to initiate proceedings against putative fathers or the dismissal of their cases by the magistrate or family court judge. Despite the rate of attrition outlined, only

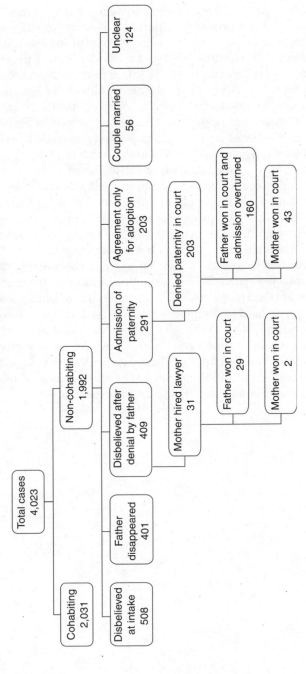

Figure 2.2: Outcomes in non-cohabitation cases

thirty-one non-cohabiting women challenged the powers of the CAS and funded their own applications for declarations of paternity. Of these cases, only two women were successful in obtaining orders of support for their children (see fig. 2.2). Evidence from unreported case files reveals the limitations of the law reports as a source of information about the workings of the *Children of Unmarried Parents Act*.

Although reported cases provide no insight into the informal proceedings mandated under the *Children of Unmarried Parents Act*, the case files produced by the CAS provide incontestable evidence that unwed mothers who had not cohabited with the fathers of their children were humiliated, insulted, and disbelieved by social workers and judges. Subjected to intense questioning by CAS workers, they were far too often denied the right to pursue the fathers of their children in court. When cases did proceed to court, the humiliation of women continued unabated. As contemporaries recognized, 'the courtroom presentation of a bastardy case is at best a sordid spectacle.'[86] But it was a spectacle that humiliated the mother, not the putative father, and which inflicted economic and social punishment on the innocent.[87] Yet, because of poverty, women had few alternatives but to seek aid from the CAS. It is hard to disagree with the assertion of one observer, arguing for reform, that 'the cruelty of the law [was] most intense in its treatment of unwed mothers.'[88] Procedures on the margins of the law were equally cruel and perhaps more difficult to challenge. In illustrating the magnitude and frequency of the mistreatment of unwed mothers, the case files amassed by the CAS are essential.

3

'I Did Not Bring This Child into the World BY MYSELF': Stories of Unwed Pregnancy

Pregnancy 'makes sex visible; it converts private behavior into public behavior,'[1] and unwed pregnancy brought women under the scrutiny and judgment of social workers. This chapter uses case files produced by CAS workers to explore preconceived notions about the etiology of unwed pregnancy that permeated interviews with young women, and to contrast professional misconceptions with the stories told by pregnant women themselves. Case files provide an unusual, if distorted, window into the private lives of young women usually obscured from historical view. This is important because, as Kathy Piess argues, a shortage of primary sources has made 'uncovering the history of working-class sexuality ... a particularly intractable task.'[2]

The stories told by unwed mothers illustrate the contradictions that all women faced under the sexual double standard: powerlessness and, paradoxically, responsibility. The sexual double standard provided men with a ready-made excuse to abandon pregnant girlfriends, implicitly endorsed violence within dating relationships, and prevented women and men from obtaining the means to control the consequences of sexual expression. Working-class women – and their families – recognized these problems. The central irony of these case files is how little social workers learned from the repeated stories of the women they were supposedly helping. Young women's critiques of the sexual double standard were silenced.

Professional Discourse and the Etiology of Unwed Pregnancy

Simplistic ·ideas about out-of-wedlock pregnancy dominated professional and public discourse. Social work and psychiatric literature condemned the unwed mother as young, unintelligent, delinquent, and
maladjusted, while popular media, films, novels, and newspapers told
cautionary tales that emphasized the tragedy that would befall any
young unmarried woman who 'got herself' pregnant. The starting
point of the inquiry at the CAS was the assertion that unwed pregnancy was a moral problem; the client, not the society in which she
struggled, required transformation. As social workers asserted, the
objective of the case file was to collect 'any and all facts as to personal
or family history which indicate the nature of a given client's difficulties and the means to their solution.'[3] This rhetoric erased the social
challenges that young women faced, as well as the role that men
played in creating out-of-wedlock pregnancy. As critics of the modern
welfare state still argue, when 'clients are constructed as deviant and
defective, the response is service provisions that include a therapeutic
dimension that reconfigures social and economic problems as individual pathologies.'[4] Throughout the period 1921 to 1969, young women
experienced judgment and prejudice in the offices of the CAS; over
time, however, the predominant social work paradigm of single pregnancy shifted from a model that linked pregnancy to delinquent
behaviour to one that stressed the young mother's psychological maladjustment.

Charlotte Whitton, a leading child welfare advocate and a central
author of the legislation under study, clearly expressed the paradigm
of unwed pregnancy to which she subscribed and which dominated
social work practice until after the Second World War. She asserted
that most unwed mothers were 'delinquents' of 'low mentality' and
were consequently unable to successfully raise their children for the
state.[5] Under eugenic beliefs of the 1920s and 1930s, influential not
only in Canada but throughout the Western world, it was believed that
'unmarried mothers are mostly young, they come from the economically inferior strata of the population, they are of inferior mentality and
they have previously been delinquent or immoral.'[6]

Young women were believed to embody delinquency in ways that
young men could not. Delinquency was widely understood – but
loosely defined – as behaviour that threatened to undermine the expec-
tation that young women would be sexually innocent and passive; it

was not coincidental that young women arriving at the CAS offices were questioned extensively not only about the pregnancy itself but also about their other 'bad [modern] habits,' such as rouging themselves, smoking, drinking, and attending dance halls and movies.[7] Females had 'a much narrower range of acceptable behavior [than did males], and even minor deviance [could] be seen as a substantial challenge to the authority of the family and the viability of the double standard.'[8] Sexual activity, confirmed by unwed pregnancy, was not a 'minor deviance.' Dale Harris argued in his 1944 study of female delinquency in the United States that 'sex behavior is the greatest source of difficulty ... the typical delinquent girl is a sex delinquent.'[9] For boys, however, sexual misbehaviour was excused and delinquency was directly linked to criminal behaviors.

The codification of sexual misbehaviour as delinquency for young women led to extensive incarceration. Sociological studies of delinquency were based on evidence from incarcerated populations and these studies confounded correlation with causation and thus rendered self-fulfilling the presupposition that delinquency caused and was caused by out-of-wedlock pregnancy.[10] Because all women pregnant out-of-wedlock were assumed to be sexual delinquents and sexual delinquents were believed to be undiscriminating and promiscuous, experts asserted that unwed mothers had had 'short and meaningless relationships'[11] with the fathers of their children. Early theorists posited that delinquency was linked to organic intellectual deficiency.[12] It was also widely believed that immigrant women, and those of non-Anglo-Saxon descent, were more likely to be delinquent and to lack sexual control. 'Geneologies of defectiveness'[13] targeted criminals, recent immigrants, and women for social intervention. The fact that studies of illegitimacy and delinquency were linked and were based on incarcerated populations makes this project particularly important; the women who sought support under the *Children of Unmarried Parents Act* were not incarcerated and their stories offer a corrective to the belief, embodied in social work literature, that only 'problem' young women became pregnant out of wedlock.

The language of judgment of the unwed mother was transformed in the post–Second World War period. In the psychiatric, sociological, and social work literature, women pregnant out of wedlock were no longer described primarily as delinquents or as organically flawed. Instead, under the growing influence of Freudian analysis,[14] social workers described unwed mothers as very young, overly sexual, and psychologically disturbed. Myriad social factors, including home conditions, family, and education were now constructed as causative in the etiology of unwed pregnancy. This change in language, however, did not reflect any softening of the condemnation of out-of-wedlock pregnancy which became, if anything, increasingly shrill by the 1950s under the cultural imperative of idealized domestic and family life. Canadian social worker Betty Isserman succinctly delineated the etiology of pregnancy accepted by most post-war social workers: 'Unmarried mothers are usually emotionally immature, they come from families that have given them little affection and security, often there is neurosis.'[15]

A number of theorists also posited that the etiology of unwed pregnancy included not only family dysfunction but also confusion with regard to sexual identity. Helene Deutsch, a prominent figure in the growing field of the psychology of women, argued that the unwed mother was aggressive and masculine. The unwed mother asserted a 'parthenogenic, puberal fantasy' in the deliberate act of becoming pregnant: 'I have a child born of me alone. I am its mother and father. I do not want or need a man for the begetting of a child.'[16] The core of the unmarried mother's failure lay in her refusal of married heterosexuality: 'Certainly, the girl's wish to have a baby without a husband is neither an adult nor a normal desire.'[17] Two damning post-war epithets – immaturity and abnormality – were unequivocally invoked in this description of the unwed mother. These ideas had considerable longevity; two prominent Harvard-based psychiatrists argued as late as 1965 that 'every unmarried mother is to some degree a psychiatric problem ... the victim of mild, moderate, or severe emotional or mental disturbance.'[18] The unmarried pregnant woman was described as having satisfied her neurosis through premature sexuality, but ironically heterosexual interest, if not intercourse, was, according to psychological experts, essential to normal female development.[19] These views were widely shared in the larger community in which popular psychology had unprecedented power.[20]

The undesirable characteristics that social workers often attributed to non-cohabiting pregnant young women were assumed to reveal much not only about a woman's sexual morality but also about her veracity. The case files provide clear evidence that social workers borrowed interpretive concepts and vocabulary from sociology, psychology, and medicine and used diagnostic labels and 'the language of clinical blaming' as a 'socially acceptable way to speak pejoratively' about unwed mothers and their so-called pathologies.[21] Unlike law reports, the files amassed by social workers were not intended for public consumption. Social workers did not censure their judgments and employed blunt language and colourful shorthand in transcribing interviews with mothers. Pregnant women were repeatedly described in derogatory terms. In total, 1,404 of 1992 (70.5 per cent) non-cohabiting women were described as 'delinquent,' 'immature,' 'neurotic,' 'unstable,' 'promiscuous,' and 'dishonest.'[22] Interestingly, the percentage of women described as 'delinquent' declined steadily after the war, while the use of the terms 'neurotic' and 'unstable' increased, reflecting the changing social work paradigm of the etiology of unwed pregnancy. Women repeatedly challenged these categorizations; they lacked the power, however, to insert these challenges into public discourse or to overcome the prejudice that they faced in the offices of the CAS.

Who Were the Pregnant Women?

While they accepted and reinforced preconceived notions about the etiology of unwed pregnancy, social workers were simultaneously collecting data that (should have) discredited the idea that women pregnant out of wedlock could be readily categorized. Social workers' own detailed information – collected during the process of client intake – proves the erroneousness of popular misconceptions regarding illegitimate pregnancy and unwed mothers. The most glaring refutation of the 'problem girl' stereotype – the assertion that the illegitimately pregnant woman had had a 'short and meaningless relationship'[23] with the father of her child – is the fact that the majority of the women in these case files had borne children in the context of long-term cohabitation. Although social work literature did not discuss the plight of the informal wife, it is clear that women who could prove cohabitation were treated differently than were single pregnant women. For this reason, this chapter focuses exclusively on the evidence of pregnancy provided by the 1,992 young women who were not involved in cohabitation relationships; we will return to cohabitation in a later chapter.

Beliefs regarding non-cohabiting mothers were also erroneous. Contrary to contemporary popular beliefs, the women who sought the help of the Children's Aid Society in Ontario were not overwhelmingly young; few had any history of delinquency; and no evidence suggests that their level of intelligence set them apart from the remainder of the female population.[24] Most came from families that showed no evidence of the 'maladjustment' so often assumed by social workers. They lived with their families of origin because independence was beyond their means. They worked in the low-income female job ghettoes of the modern city. Repeated out-of-wedlock pregnancies were uncommon. These women, in other words, were statistically ordinary. The only consistent factor that united them (apart from pregnancy itself) was poverty. Of course, women who were not impoverished also became pregnant out of wedlock, but they could afford options that helped them to avoid the judgmental gaze of government agencies and social workers.

The age of the women who sought help from the CAS fluctuated by decade, with a mean of 22 in the 1920s and 1930s, 26 in the 1940s, 23 in the 1950s; and 21 in the 1960s.[25] The ages of these women at time of confinement suggest that pregnancies resulted from adult relationships, many of which had probably been headed towards marriage. This hypothesis is strengthened when one considers that the average age of these first pregnancies mirrored closely the average age at first marriage of women in the general population. The average age of women at first marriage in Canada in the 1920s and 1930s was 24.5 and 24.2 respectively; in the 1940s, 24.9; in the 1950s, 23.6; and in the 1960s, 22.6.[26] (See fig. 3.1.) And these were, overwhelmingly, first pregnancies; only nineteen women of 1,992 (0.9 per cent) had a second or subsequent illegitimate pregnancy. These women were not sexual delinquents. Nor did they have histories of other forms of delinquent behaviour; only thirteen of these 1,992 women had previous records of conflict with the law.

Also contrary to popular misconceptions, the majority of the women – like the majority of the general population – appear to have been white or Anglo-Saxon. However, 'the designation "white," "British," or "English" was absent'[27] from the case files. For those who were neither white nor Anglo-Saxon, however, race and ethnicity were constructed as causative of pregnancy.[28] In fourteen cases (0.7 per cent) women were described as 'Negroid.' In nine cases (0.5 per cent) mothers were described as Aboriginal. In 251 cases (12.6 per cent), women of various European backgrounds were explicitly described as non-Anglo-Saxon (but white) or were unable to comfortably converse in English, suggesting a non-Anglo-Saxon, immigrant background (or, in some cases, French-Canadian ancestry). Documenting the precise impact of racial and ethnic prejudice in the disposition of cases is

Figure 3.1: Age of women by decade

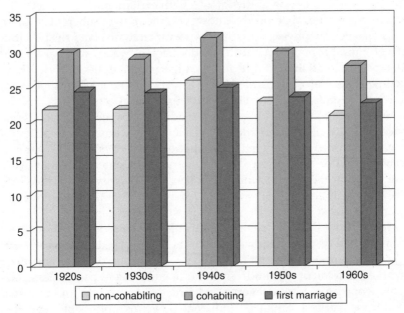

impossible, but derogatory comments in case files suggest that non-white and non-Anglo-Saxon women faced significant hostility and additional challenges in convincing social workers of their morality and veracity.

Overwhelmingly, the women who came to the CAS seeking assistance were 'working girls,' employed in the ghettoized and exploitative sectors of Ontario's growing commercial and industrial economy. In this, also, they were ordinary. From the turn of the century onwards, many young women worked outside the home, particularly in the years before marriage. While the employment of women served the needs of business and industry, as they could be paid significantly lower wages than men, the spectre of independent employed women was unsettling to many. Paid work appeared to conflict with prescribed ideals of feminine behaviour as dependent, domestic, and subordinate. What disturbed reformers in the early decades of the twentieth century was not the exploitative nature of women's work, but the fact that young women were meeting men away from the control of family. Reformers in the early twentieth century explicitly pointed to women's work outside the home as dangerous: 'Many young girls find opportunities at jobs with certain moral hazards.'[29]

From a modern perspective, however, the danger inherent in these jobs was not the physical proximity of women to men and the possibility of 'moral contagion,' but the inadequacy of wages, an overwhelming reality that limited the independence and options of working women. As Veronica Strong-Boag asserts, women were 'first ghettoized by gender' and 'further restricted by the effects of class. For the daughters of many working-class Canadians, jobs meant personal service or blue-collar occupations.'[30] The young women in these cases were employed in the female job ghettoes that offered little material reward and no security; 1,130 of 1,992 women stated that they were employed at the time at which they sought the assistance of the CAS. Of the 634 non-cohabiting women for whom details of employment were recorded on the standard questionnaire (another 496 were employed but did not provide details of their employment), 102 were semi-skilled or unskilled factory workers, 80 worked as domestic servants, 81 worked as secretaries, and 51 as waitresses. The remainder worked in retail or as laundresses and hospital aides, bank tellers, telephone operators, dressmakers and hairdressers, janitors, and informal childcare workers. Financial independence was impossible, and this problem had not been overcome by the 1960s. The only significant change noted over time was that the percentage of women employed as domestic servants declined precipitously after the outbreak of the Second World War. This does not mean, however, that women working in the more modern job sectors were earning a living wage.

Perhaps because they earned so little, the women in these cases lived, overwhelmingly, with their parents; 1,384 (69.5 per cent) of the 1,992 women who were not cohabiting with the fathers of their children resided with their families of origin at the time of conception. These families were statistically ordinary. Only thirteen families had records of previous interaction with the CAS; of these, three families were described as 'Negro' and six were Aboriginal, numbers that clearly reflect the marginalization and surveillance of these communities. Those who did not live with their parents boarded in the homes of other families (378 or 19 per cent) or, more rarely, shared apartments with other working women (98 or 4.9 per cent); only fourteen women asserted that they lived alone in apartments that they could afford on a single woman's wages; for 118 women information regarding domicile was not recorded in the case file. Young women were aware, however, that they could not live forever with their families of origin. A woman's ability to have a home of her own was dependent upon attracting the affection of a man with a dependable wage and a commitment to family life. One mother asserted that 'not having a man would be to always be poor.'[31] In this context, dating, with the perils it entailed, was not simply something 'girls' did for fun.

Sex and the Single Woman: How Unusual Was It?

Women told stories of pregnancy that reflected the economic imperative of dating and heterosexual mating for working class women. They admitted that they put up with behaviour that they did not like – including pressure regarding intercourse – in the hope that men would commit to them. They provided evidence that their relationships with the fathers of their children were long standing and ostensibly serious. They did not consider themselves particularly different from other young women who did not happen to get pregnant. They recognized that no woman 'gets herself' pregnant and exhibited anger and frustration when men were not held accountable for their sexual behaviour. They described boyfriends who pressured them to engage in intercourse with tactics that ranged from threats of withdrawal of affection to the use of physical force. They were painfully aware of – and critiqued – the sexual double standard. Social workers, however, clung to the belief that women alone were responsible for being sexual gatekeepers and condemned those women who had failed in their moral obligation to be chaste.

Evidence – even as documented by social workers who simultaneously insulted and categorized these women as promiscuous, delinquent, and neurotic – suggests that unwed mothers were unusual, not in experimenting with sexuality, but in failing to get married when they found themselves to be pregnant. It seems that a pregnant young woman's real crime, the thing for which she was punished, was not premarital sexuality, or even out-of-wedlock pregnancy, but her inability to keep the man who had fathered her child. As one American psychiatrist asserted in 1961, 'a girl in our society who starts a pregnancy with a man whom she is either unwilling or unable to marry has shown herself to be a disturbed personality. I think that we are entitled to look upon an illegitimate child as the living proof of his mother's severe emotional difficulties.'[32] The woman was responsible for the pregnancy, disturbed even when willing but unable to marry the father of her child, and incapable of adequate mothering. It would, perhaps, have been more realistic to construct unwed fathers as immature, and unwed mothers themselves recognized this contradiction.

The majority of these women had been involved in long-term, publicly sanctioned relationships, but when they became pregnant men could simply walk away from responsibility. In 45 per cent of cases (896 of 1,992) the young women claimed to have entered into sexual relations only 'under promise of marriage.' A shocking 5.7 per cent of women (113 of 1,992) claimed to have become pregnant as the result of rapes by men they were dating. In a further 32.3 per cent of cases (644 of 1,992), women asserted that intercourse resulted when, as one mother described it, she and her boyfriend 'lost their heads'[33] to passion. It is entirely possible that some women claimed engagement or at least long-term dating and betrayal in order to increase the sympathy with which their cases might be viewed by social workers. Mass circulation magazines that 'began appearing in the 1920s and multiplied in the decades following ... specialized in stories of love triumphant, love gone bad, and sexual transgressions punished.'[34] These stories provided the vocabulary and plot for tales of seduction and abandonment. In the majority of cases, however, incidental evidence – much of it provided by family and friends – suggests that relationships were stable, monogamous, acknowledged by family and community, and ostensibly permanent. Only 8.7 per cent of women (173 of 1,992) admitted that sexual experimentation had occurred with more than one partner, but even in these cases they asserted that sex had occurred in the context of committed relationships that had subsequently failed. In 8.3 per cent of cases (166 of 1,992), women refused to answer the questions asked of them, automatically forfeiting any support that they might have received from the CAS. This refusal provides powerful evidence of resistance to regulation and resentment of judgment (see fig. 3.2).

Young women sought recourse to court proceedings when boyfriends broke the promise that 'if THEY got caught, if she got into trouble ... if anything did happen ... that I would marry you.'[35] They expressed anger when they were condemned as promiscuous, delinquent, or maladjusted when they believed that their behaviour was both common and morally correct in the context of loving relationships. As early as the 1920s, young women expressed little shame in having indulged in intercourse 'under promise of marriage'; as one mother put it, 'we loved each other and it was ok as we planned to be married.'[36] Another mother vehemently asserted, 'It was all-right as

Figure 3.2: Stories of pregnancy

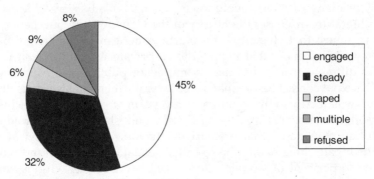

they were to be married.'[37] The majority had become pregnant, as some social workers were beginning to recognize by the late 1960s, in the context of 'friendship or love relationships which at the time are perceived as positive and good.'[38]

In this context, women expressed more shame – and anger – that men had fled than about the fact of pregnancy itself. One mother lamented in a case that came before the court in Toronto in 1952, 'It's ok as long as you don't get caught; I'm caught.'[39] The rule, according to another mother, was not to remain chaste but to avoid being 'caught pregnant.'[40] When women married boyfriends early in pregnancy, such an objective had been achieved. As Veronica Strong-Boag argues,

> girls were in the awkward position of being encouraged to desire boy-friends and eventually a husband without committing themselves to any premarital physical intimacy. Not surprisingly, under the pressure of their own and their boyfriends' desires, many had babies rather sooner than they had anticipated ... more often than not, they married the father.[41]

It should not be surprising that unwed mothers did not see themselves as sinners, psychotics, or self-conscious sexual rebels, but as unlucky and as betrayed by the men they (had) loved.

The evidence regarding sexuality that can be gleaned from the 1,992 cases of non-cohabiting women who sought child support under the *Children of Unmarried Parents Act* adds strength to the arguments of those who contest the radical nature of the sexual revolution of the late

1960s, suggesting instead 'how deep-seated and mainstream the origins of many of those revolutionary changes really were.'[42] Most of this literature discusses the history of the United States, but these case files suggest that change was a North American phenomenon. Beth Bailey argues that 'what people did in private was quite often radically different from what they admitted in public.'[43] To experiment with sexual contact before marriage, several American historians illustrate, was increasingly common in the years after 1920.[44] The Kinsey Report, *Sexuality and the Human Female*, published in 1953, provided substantial evidence that premarital intercourse was common in the United States long before the so-called sexual revolution of the 1960s. Over 50 per cent of women interviewed had not been virgins when they married; moreover, non-virginal brides did not regret their sexual experience which, in the majority of cases, was with the men they would later marry.[45] As one extensive longitudinal study of bridal pregnancy, abortion, and illegitimacy rates in the United States concluded in 1972, 'the sexual revolution has largely been concentrated among girls involved with males who will become their husbands,' and the 'image of an abstinent past and a promiscuous present is highly exaggerated.'[46]

Although no parallel study exists in the Canadian context, incidental evidence suggests that sexual activity before marriage was also increasing here. James Snell implicitly makes this argument. His data on divorce illustrate that a rising proportion of the women in divorcing couples between 1900 and 1939 had been pregnant before marriage.[47] Both rates of illegitimacy and the proportion of women who married under twenty rose slowly but steadily in Canada between 1921 and 1969, suggesting that sexual activity was beginning at a younger age for an increasing percentage of the population.[48] With regard to the population of Quebec at this time, Denise Baillargeon asserts that being pregnant on one's wedding day, despite the disapproval of society and the church, was not uncommon.[49]

If all that differentiated the unwed mother from her contemporaries was the irresponsibility of her male partner, it should not be surprising that these young women expressed resentment of the stereotypes applied to them by social workers. The construction of the unwed mother as neurotic was illogical in a context in which, while births out-of wedlock remained rare, many first marital babies were conceived before the wedding day. A critic of attitudes towards the unwed mother asserted that in Canada the vital statistics are not kept in such a way as to show what proportion of first-born children of married women have been illegitimately conceived. But in Great Britain, Australia and elsewhere, it has been established that it is something like one in four. Their conception conditions are in no material way different from those of other unmarried mothers. If we are to say with conviction that mothers of illegitimate children are psychologically abnormal and therefore unfit to raise their children, we must extend the charge to about a quarter of the married mothers of families.[50]

Hers, however, was a voice in the wilderness in the social work community. Pregnant young women continued to be caught in the contradictions inherent in 'the tendency to censure sexual behavior only when there are visible manifestations, and then only to censure one-half of the offending couple – the woman.'[51]

In a culture that emphasized couples and dating, that 'mandated sex appeal but prohibited sex,' the fate of unwed mothers 'dramatized the paradox' and contradictions all young women faced when they negotiated intimacy in heterosexual relations.[52] The culture that surrounded young women celebrated the erotic and suggested that women had to be sexy in order to attract the affections of men.[53] Although women were warned repeatedly in movies, novels, and sexual education classes that they did not want to 'be ruined,' popular culture also made it clear that sex was glamorous. From the 1920s onwards, 'sex became the central public symbol of youth culture, a fundamental part of the definition that separated youth from age.'[54] And the older generation expressed deep concern that this behaviour represented a threat to family and nation.[55] Rouged lips, new (short) hair, and (more revealing) clothing styles and public smoking were all outward symbols of troublesome change.[56] Necking, petting, and other forms of sexual experimentation were increasingly normalized within youthful culture. Romances and erotic adventures, as women were frequently reminded, were supposed to lead to marriage, but sexual negotiation, whether or not couples engaged in intercourse, began long before they entered the nuptial bed.

In this context of heightened emphasis on sex and romance, moreover, sexual negotiation was taking place away from the controls and limitations of home as women and men socialized increasingly as couples, on dates, in the anonymous world of the town or city. The case files provide overwhelming evidence that interaction with men took place largely away from home: at movies, in parks, at parties and amusements, at bars, in cars, and on the streets. Dating, and the freedom and anonymity it offered, changed the balance of power in courtship, with parents and kin exercising less control over the activities of the young courting couple and over mate selection. For women, however, changes in courtship rituals were a mixed blessing. While young women were subjected to less immediate parental supervision, dating required money. 'One had to buy entertainment, or even access to places to sit and talk. Money – men's money – became the basis of the dating system, and thus of courtship.'[57] With their limited wages and access to cash, working-class women became increasingly dependent upon treating as their means of enjoying the pleasures offered by the modern city. Most could also not afford to refuse the dating culture, as successful heterosexual mating was essential to a working class woman's future financial security.

This system was also, paradoxically, based on a presumption that women were responsible for setting sexual limits. As one observer acknowledged, the 'onus is placed upon the girl because throughout childhood and adolescence she is warned to be on her guard against men who, in the nature of the species, "only want one thing." It is no good looking to the man for help, once she has given way. If she does not heed these warnings, then she must accept the consequences of her actions.'[58] This placed women in a double bind that unwed mothers described eloquently in the *Children of Unmarried Parents Act* case files. Although the dating system implicitly endorsed at least limited physical and romantic contact, girls were expected to be the gatekeepers of sexual morality and young men could be, not only relentless, but violent, in their assertion that they should, as one young woman quoted her boyfriend, 'get what they paid for.'[59]

Although men were not taught to respect the boundaries that women set, women were bombarded with messages that warned of the consequences of failing to maintain one's virginity. Although only a minority of women became pregnant out of wedlock, the punishment of the unwed mother provided a lesson in sexual ethics for those who might be tempted into sin. As one (anti-)sex educator asserted in his 1930 sex manual for adolescents, 'bad girls,' even if they did not get pregnant, would ultimately suffer for their indiscretion:

> The first girl a boy thinks of for a petting party is not often the first one he thinks of for a wife. She may be all right for his good times but ordinarily

he does not want second-hand goods, or a woman who has been freely pawed over, for a sweetheart, wife and mother of his children.[60]

While his right to enjoy 'good times' and 'petting parties' was not challenged, the young woman with whom he would engage in such activity became undesirable, 'pawed over,' and 'second-hand goods.'[61] Such attitudes implicitly endorsed the right of men to walk away from pregnant girlfriends. In this discussion of the consequences of premarital sexuality, it was assumed that the wages of sin were to be paid entirely by women. Some social workers were beginning to recognize by the 1960s that there was a 'contradiction in encouragement of dating at an early age, the minimal controls placed on it, and the strong social sanctions (against unwed) pregnancy.'[62]

Pregnant young women recognized and contested this contradiction; as one mother put it in a letter of complaint to the CAS after her case was dismissed by them, whether or not 'you [CAS workers] know this, I did not bring this child into the world BY MYSELF.'[63] Women repeatedly asserted that it was boyfriends, not pregnant women, who should be ashamed of themselves. One mother fumed to the CAS that her boyfriend had promised that 'if THEY got caught' he would marry her and that 'THEY were pregnant, not just me [her].'[64]

While women recognized and contested this contradiction, men exploited it. They could use promises of marriage to elicit sexual favours that women otherwise might have been hesitant to bestow. Even when such promises had initially been made in good faith, men could and did decide that they weren't ready for marriage, leaving pregnant women to pay the full price for premarital sex. When girlfriends announced that they were pregnant, vague promises of marriage 'sometime in the future'[65] were tested; one putative father asserted that 'a single guy had a freer time and such promises were only made to be broken.'[66] Another father admitted that, although he had promised marriage, he hadn't really meant what he said: 'She gave it [sex] to him, and would have for others ... Was he to be burdened by this for life?'[67] Another father, while acknowledging that the woman had been in love with him and that he had told her they would marry if she became pregnant, claimed that the relationship was 'just a passing affair' and that he would 'head for the west coast before he would contribute in any way' for the baby.[68] In a context in which setting sexual limits was constructed as an exclusively female obligation, such irresponsibility should not be surprising since it was explicitly legitimated in public discourse. The sexual double standard, moreover, implicitly endorsed the power differential within the dating relationship itself.

Dating and Danger: Sexual Assault

Women bore responsibility for sexuality in a context in which they lacked control. It was not acknowledged that the nature of the dating system – women's financial dependence on men and a couples' new-found privacy – undermined women's ability to say no to intercourse and to other forms of potentially unwanted sexual contact. While women were reminded that pregnancy would be one's ruination, they often found themselves in situations in which they were vulnerable. In 113 of the 1,992 cases, women explicitly asserted – by using the terms rape or assault – that they had been sexually assaulted by the putative fathers of their children. In a culture in which rape was not discussed, this represents a surprisingly significant percentage of cases. Moreover, the use of force is suggested in 185 other cases, in which women used phrases such as 'I was overcome' or 'he made me do it' to describe their sexual encounters with boyfriends. In the process of outlining their previous sexual histories, another sixty-seven women asserted that they had lost their virginity as a result of rape by someone other than the putative father of the child. This suggests that one in five of these women had suffered some kind of sexual violence. These cases illustrate that forceful behaviour, what we now would call date rape, was an ever-present risk for young women, one that they understood and feared.

Stories of rape reveal the contradictions that all heterosexual women faced in negotiating their sexuality. It is striking, moreover, how clearly implicated the car – the great symbol of post-war masculinity – was in sexual power dynamics that disadvantaged women. Paradoxically, the very mobility that made the car an attractive location for intimacy also made it a site of conflict for women; in a literal and symbolic sense, women were not in the driver's seat.[69] Of the 113 women who described their pregnancies as the result of rapes, ninety (79.6 per cent) had experienced this violation in cars. One woman, who had dated the putative father of her child for six months, broke off their relationship pending his divorce. They had not, during this time, indulged in sexual intercourse. He convinced her, however, to go out with him one last time to discuss their future and, angered by her refusal to resume their relationship, 'he took her out into the country for a car ride and forced his attentions on her by tying her hands with a camera strap.'[70]

Another woman asserted that she and her ex-boyfriend had double dated on all but one occasion. On this particular date he had taken her, in a borrowed car, to the drive-in, where 'he did not ask her consent but went right at it.' After this traumatic event she refused all further dates with the man, but was unlucky enough to find herself pregnant.[71] A young woman who became pregnant in 1951 described her boyfriend's 'use of force' at the drive-in; she was disbelieved, however, because she had continued to date him. She asserted that intercourse only occurred 'on his insistence,' but she had no witness to prove this claim; she had continued to date him because, as a consistently and well-employed mechanic, 'he was a good prospect as a husband.' Frighteningly, she spoke extensively of the fact that most of her friends had also experienced 'pushy' behaviour from their boyfriends.[72] Another pregnant woman claimed that she had been at the drive-in with the putative father of her child, whom she had dated for some time but with whom she had not had intercourse, when he raped her. They had been necking from 'the time of the middle show and started to pet when he pushed [her] on the back seat, tore off [her] jeans and blouse, and put it in [her].'[73]

Such behaviour was, however, implicitly endorsed or forgiven by both the CAS and the police. A woman who had been raped in a car during a date had 'resisted by kicking, screaming and trying to get away.' She called the police immediately but was 'advised against pressing charges because she had a drink with him'; under pressure from the CAS, the putative father agreed to pay expenses pending adoption.[74] Another young woman produced her sister as a witness to her rape. They had been on a double date with two brothers and both sisters were forcibly confined in the car and raped. Only the elder of the two girls had the double misfortune to become pregnant. Although the putative father asserted to the court that 'she didn't object' and that there had been 'no struggle at all,' the sisters had immediately reported the rapes to both their parents and the police. Although rape charges were not instituted against the brothers, this evidence was taken as material corroboration of paternity.[75] In another case in which the young woman had formally charged her ex-boyfriend with rape, such charges were dropped on his agreement to cover her confinement costs and the costs of caring for the baby pending adoption placement. Compromises like these implicitly condoned violence against women.[76]

Victims of rape were disbelieved and humiliated by the CAS and the court. One mother, in discussion with the CAS, tearfully asserted that she had only had consensual intercourse with the putative father of her child, but that she had not been a virgin before meeting the putative father, as she had been raped two years previously. A recent immigrant who did not speak English well, she had been told by her employer that she might 'have to go back to Germany if she reported it [the rape]' to the police. The CAS, however, agreed with the putative father that her failure to report reflected her dishonesty. Although questioned in a degrading manner, she responded with anger. When she was asked how she could remember the date and detail regarding an event she had not reported, she said that 'she would never forget it as long as she lived.'[77]

The treatment to which women could be subjected is well illustrated in the cross-examination of one young mother by the lawyer representing the putative father of her child:

Q: Had you done anything to arouse him? Now, you didn't object to the kissing?
A: No.
Q: This went on for half an hour without objections, but you did object when he tried to put his hands on you ... You didn't think of getting out of the car ... He took down his clothes, or opened them, or unzipped them, and got your clothes up and had intercourse with you over your objections?
A: Yes.
Q: Are you telling us that seriously?
A: Yes, because it is the truth.
Q: Isn't it a fact you helped with the clothing?
A: Well I didn't (sobs).
Q: Didn't you have your hands on his penis long before?
A: No, I didn't.
Q: You deny that ... don't scream at me.[78]

The woman was expected to enforce sexual limits and, if necessary, to flee from the car, despite the fact that the boyfriend had taken her into the country, where she did not even know her way home. Collapsed in sobs, the woman refused to provide further testimony. A male friend of the defendant, however, asserted that he had bragged to his friends that he 'got her good.' The defendant also admitted to the intercourse itself. But his lawyer was successful in disproving paternity by asserting that the young woman should not have 'gotten in his car' and then 'claim[ed] that she was trying to avoid it.' Her evidence, the lawyer said, 'was simply not to be believed' and 'even if you accept it, what are the chances of a virgin becoming pregnant under these circumstances.'[79]

This case reveals the contradictions – not to mention the physiological myths about pregnancy – young women faced. The dating system suggested that women owed men at least some petting and kissing, but if you engaged in such behaviour, or even got in his car, you were asking for more. Dating put women in vulnerable situations, yet they were responsible for controlling the behaviour of men. When men were violent, women were still to blame. The sexual double standard enforced public silence about rape; it also ensured that women and men were denied the means to control the consequences of sexuality, again reinforcing the vulnerability of women.

Avoiding Pregnancy: Birth Control and Abortion

Social workers refused to acknowledge the challenges that women faced in preventing conception or terminating a pregnancy. Many social purity advocates in the early decades under study were opposed to birth control, even within marriage. Helen MacMurchy, for example, advised that the young should be told that birth control was unnatural, unreliable, and 'contrary to the higher instincts.'[80] Ironically, however, by the 1950s failure to prevent conception was cited by so-called experts on unwed pregnancy as evidence that the pregnancy was planned and deliberate and provided evidence, therefore, of neurosis on the part of the mother. Helene Deutsch went so far as to argue that 'the fact that she expected the man to take full responsibility for contraception shows that her infantile narcissism won the upper hand over proud self-reliance.'[81] This erased the pressure that young women were under to appear chaste and asexual; to plan to be sexually active would be considered to reflect the immorality of the mother, yet her failure to use contraception was constructed as proof of her neurosis and immaturity. This argument also ignored the fact that until 1969 birth control was illegal in Canada.

In this context it is not surprising that the women – and men – in these cases appear to have had little knowledge of birth control. As one contemporary American observed by the 1960s:

This lack of information and the confused attitudes it breeds gives rise to an alternative mythology which frequently justifies the failure to contracept. Girls cannot conceive until they are married, or until they have had a long period of sexual experience. Conception is prevented if intercourse is performed standing up. Boys aren't fertile until they are 21, or married, or if they masturbate. *Coitus interruptus* is a reliable method of contraception. Girls automatically go through an almost unlimited safe period. All of these myths are regularly trotted out as reasons why the couple did not need to contracept.[82]

While moralists and (anti-)sex educators failed to convince young people that all non-marital intercourse was sinful, they did succeed in limiting the access that couples had to both information regarding sexuality and to birth control itself.

Several cases illustrate these themes. One mother claimed that she had not believed that she was pregnant until quickening, despite the fact that a doctor had confirmed her pregnancy at five weeks. She asserted that her disbelief had stemmed from the fact that 'they had had sexual relations for a long time without using anything and nothing had happened. Mr. K was under the impression that he was sterile since his hernia operation and thus would not believe that he was the father.'[83] A putative father who admitted intercourse without the use of contraceptives nonetheless claimed that he could not be responsible for the pregnancy since 'he was very careful' and always 'withdrew early.'[84] Another man asserted that he could not be the father: 'I had intercourse with her but I couldn't finish. I penetrated her but I didn't reach climax.' He was deemed not to be responsible for the pregnancy.[85] Yet another young man claimed that he could not be responsible for his girlfriend's pregnancy because 'when intercourse took place I did not complete the act, and always had kleenex ready for this purpose.'[86] Social workers seem to have accepted such evidence as a contraindication of men's paternity.

Two men gave evidence, in defence of another putative father, asserting that they, too, had had intercourse with the woman and that her testimony could not be trusted. They claimed that they had 'taken turns with her' in the back seat of the car. They were unafraid of paternity suits being instituted against them because they had 'used precautions'; they claimed to have 'shared a French safe' by reversing and reusing it.[87] The pregnant woman in question denied the story as completely fabricated. Whether or not the men were simply trying to humiliate this woman and protect the financial interests of their friend, their story reveals a shocking ignorance about the proper use of contraceptives.

It is not surprising, given this abysmal lack of information, that by the end of the 1960s more liberal social reformers and social workers understood that lack of information about and access to contraceptives were causal factors in high rates of illegitimate pregnancy. One reform-minded American social worker argued that 'it is possible that if there were genuine opportunities for the dissemination of birth control information, there might be a marked reduction in unwanted, illegitimate pregnancies. The social work profession has taken too little interest in promulgating birth control programs.'[88]

Abortion was also illegal. During their interviews with CAS workers, 187 of the 1,992 women admitted having contemplated recourse to termination of pregnancy. There is little doubt that these numbers do not reflect the extent of illegal abortion, since if a woman were successful she did not require funds for childbirth or child-rearing and would not discuss her dilemma with state officials. Abortions, however, were not readily obtained. The cost of abortion was prohibitive; for the poor women in these cases, this was a very practical problem that limited their options. In the age of backstreet abortionists, moreover, the dangers of abortion were self-evident. The cases in which women had contemplated or attempted abortion reflect these themes. The women were afraid of the consequences – legal and medical – of abortion. The doctor of one girl testified that she and the putative father had come to him seeking advice on abortion. Although the doctor had refused to help them, the girl admitted that she had taken abortificants, but that, much to her dismay, they had failed, in the process making her extremely ill.[89] Another mother admitted that although the putative father had 'given her $60.00 for an abortion,' she had been 'too scared' to subject herself to the operation, arguing that, despite the pain and risk of childbirth, 'abortion was worse.'[90]

Many of the women seem to have contemplated abortion under considerable pressure from boyfriends who had much less to fear than they did. While 187 women admitted that they had considered abortion (and many of these talked of discussions with boyfriends), a further 131 asserted that boyfriends had attempted to force them to abort against their will and despite their concerns about health and safety. In a case that came before the court in Toronto in 1947, evidence was presented that the putative father had written to his girlfriend early in the pregnancy acknowledging paternity and suggesting that she get rid of 'the problem':

> It's too bad that we don't see eye to eye on this or there might be a good solution to all this, but I must say that I have no intention of marrying you. If you feel that you can get fixed up by medical attention then go ahead and I'll foot the bills. If you want medical attention it is a good time right away. I'm sorry that I'm not there to help you out at this time, but I wish you'd get the best care if you decide on the op.[91]

Ironically, these letters and his offer to pay for the abortion were not considered to constitute adequate evidence of paternity to justify court proceedings. Another putative father, who had promised his girlfriend that 'if she got into trouble I would marry you,' instead tried to force his now ex-girlfriend to abort, beating her and threatening that 'either the child will die or you will.'[92]

What were young women to do? They lacked control over the sexual exchange and access to the means of contraception. When they found themselves pregnant, boyfriends could – and did – abandon them and abortion was often not a realistic option. They were left with little choice but to reveal their pregnancies to families and friends. How did families respond to daughters in their time of need? Did working-class communities share the social work perspective that out-of-wedlock pregnancy marked a woman as 'second-hand goods'[93] or was there some understanding of the pressures and contradictions that women faced?

Family and Community Response to Pregnancy

Evidence from these case files suggests that parents and communities seem to have challenged some aspects of the sexual double standard; in particular, they did not accept the idea that women alone should pay the price for mutual sexual expression. The majority of women in these cases were not abandoned by their families or ostracized by friends and community. In fact, much of the evidence presented in these cases suggests that parents, friends, and community were quietly tolerant of sexual experimentation in relationships that were perceived to be marriage-oriented. In one case that illustrates this theme a landlord had found a young woman in bed with her lover. He had not intervened, he admitted in court, because 'it was not his business as he understood they were to be married.'[94] A mother asserted in court that the putative father of her child, to whom she had been engaged and who was a boarder in the family home, had been permitted to share her room. Not only did her parents claim that this was 'ok as they were to be married' but also the family was poor and this sleeping arrangement allowed the parents to rent the putative father's old room to another young man.[95]

Over half of the young women in these cases – a minimum of 1112 or 55.8 per cent – arrived at the CAS with their mothers or sisters, or sometimes both. Such actions suggest that families and friends, while potentially condemning premarital sexual relations, nonetheless believed that, at least within the bounds of committed and publicly acknowledged relationships, its consequences should be shared. The story of one young woman who arrived at the CAS offices with her mother exemplifies these complexities. Prior to the pregnancy, the woman had lived with her mother in an apartment (the father was deceased) and both had been working. She and the putative father were engaged, and her mother admitted that the young woman 'often slept with the defendant in her room in the apartment, although she did not approve.' When CAS workers asserted that the mother should have put a stop to this immorality, she rebutted that 'her daughter was 23 years old, and worked for her living, and could make these decisions for herself. I love her. And we needed both incomes.' After the birth of the child, the mother, daughter, and grand-daughter continued to live in the apartment together.[96]

Even when conflict had arisen over boyfriends, parents forgave daughters and provided assistance for them in their time of need. In seventeen of the 1,992 non-cohabiting cases there is evidence that women ran away with boyfriends against the will of their parents. However, in all of these cases the parents later allowed the daughter, now humiliated and deeply hurt, to return to live in the family home. In one case, for example, a seventeen-year-old girl fled her parents' home to live with her nineteen-year-old boyfriend. Her parents had expressed disapproval of the man for months while the couple dated. The mother of the child claimed that she had not been sexually active with anyone before the putative father (or anyone else thereafter), and her parents agreed that no conflict over boys had arisen before this relationship. The couple had lived together in a hotel for two months, during which time she became pregnant. She left him, however, when he asserted that he would not marry her. Moreover, he had been exceptionally violent. She had lost her front teeth during an assault, and had called her parents to take her home after being hospitalized. Her parents told the CAS that she was a 'good girl, who had fallen for the wrong man,' but that it was a mistake she 'would not be likely to repeat.' The mother was planning on keeping her baby, a plan for which they expressed their support.[97]

In theory, young women were required under the act to report their pregnancies to the CAS immediately. In fact, however, a minimum of 968 of 1,992 women were well advanced in pregnancy before reporting to the CAS. In the interim, they, in concert with their families in many cases, had attempted to convince recalcitrant boyfriends to accept responsibility for their actions and to enter into marriage. They told long and bitter tales of fruitless negotiations with putative fathers. It is striking that while public discourse focused on the culpability of unwed mothers, families exerted considerable pressure on putative fathers to 'accept responsibility for their actions ... to behave like men.'[98] One unwed mother's father went so far as to threaten the putative father of his daughter's baby with death; he brandished a butcher knife and announced that unless the putative father married his daughter, he would 'kill him.'[99]

The mother of another pregnant young woman asserted that she had accepted the father's word that he would marry her daughter:

> The admission R made to me was New Year's Eve, out in the kitchen. I asked him what you and he had decided to do, and he said that you were being married in 2 weeks. I said 'When do you expect the baby' and he said 'June, about the middle.'[100]

Despite this promise, within two weeks the putative father wrote a letter to his former girlfriend asserting that 'I have decided not to go through with our marriage.' Within a year, he disappeared entirely from the community.

In another case that came before the court in 1950, the couple's relationship had been on going for over two years. During the hearing the mother produced letters from her former lover that proved that paternity had not been disputed and that, initially at least, both parties had assumed that marriage would take place. Apparently afraid of impending responsibility, however, the putative father, on the pretence that he would later send for his girlfriend, had fled to Calgary:

Q: What discussion took place?

A: It was spoken of, we were going to get married and there was never any question of it not being his. As things occurred I told him everything that happened as it happened, like my doctor's visits and everything. I saw him every day and it was just like telling your husband something.

Q: He apparently had to be served in Calgary. Can you describe to the Court the circumstances surrounding his visit to Calgary?

A: Well, he drank quite a bit and he believed because of his environment and thought it was just a force of habit and by going away and making a new start and thought he would do better out there and he liked Calgary and by him going there I would come as well once he got a job and got settled and that would give us both a better chance to adjust.[101]

Instead, he refused to send for her, taunting her with the fact that the court had no jurisdiction over him once outside Ontario.

Repeated promises of marriage caused another young woman to withdraw charges against the putative father of her child. In a letter written in September 1944, when her baby was eight months old, her father told the court that 'my daughter has seen Mr. A and they have agreed to be married in January. So I have decided not to take action against him.' The couple did not, however, marry but the putative father did sign an agreement for support. Shortly thereafter he fled the jurisdiction. When he returned in 1947 the unwed mother's father wrote to the CAS seeking enforcement of the agreement: 'I had an accident and broke my back and it is not possible for me to work and give the support I did for the boy's care.' As late as 1950 the putative father wrote letters to the unwed mother alternately offering marriage and threatening that he would report her 'promiscuous' behaviour to the Department of Child Welfare and have their son taken out of her care:

You see I made you an offer in the last letter, just to refresh your memory it went something like this – If you were willing we could be married and by doing that we could give J a name which he rightfully deserves and one that is his proper name. Secondly, you would have a home of your own and you wouldn't have to work any more. I am willing to forget what I saw in the Lincoln Hotel here when you and this new boyfriend you have phoned me that Sunday morning. I have enough on you to have J taken away from you and unless I hear from you in regard whether you and I will be friends again or what you intend to do you are going to be very sorry. I am not threatening you but only trying to do what is right for J's benefit.[102]

The promiscuous behaviour to which he referred was the ongoing relationship the woman had entered into with a man whom she would subsequently marry. The putative father's threats illustrate that he was aware of the power of the state to remove children from the custody and care of 'unfit' mothers. Ultimately, when she called his bluff and they arranged to be married, he disappeared. When he returned to the city in 1952 she reopened proceedings against him. She asserted that 'Mr. A and I were not married as intended and I do not now wish to marry him so I am asking for partial maintenance for my son, born January 1944. Mr. A has never paid anything towards the maintenance of the child.' Not surprisingly, Mr A again skipped town and at this point all records in the case cease.[103]

Not only did the parents of unwed mothers evince considerable support for their 'fallen' daughters but also the parents of putative fathers were ashamed of men who refused to 'do right by their girlfriends.'[104] It was noted in one case file by CAS workers that 'his parents know of the situation and deplore the fact that he is still unwilling to marry her.'[105] The mother of one putative father paid the child support herself, despite her poverty. When her son joined the Armed Forces in an attempt to evade financial responsibility for the child that he admitted he had fathered, she asserted 'she hoped it would do him some good. He had never helped her or the girl in any way and perhaps the Army will make a man out of him.'[106] In another case, the putative father's own father asserted that the young man 'had had his fun and would have to pay for it.' The parents told the young man that unless he married his girlfriend, he could no longer live at home. When he fled, the father took the man's new address to the CAS in order to facilitate proceedings against his own son.[107] Another young woman lived with the family of the putative father of her child after announcing her pregnancy. Although the father resisted marriage initially, his family ultimately persuaded him to 'fulfill his obligation to the girl,' and the case was dropped upon the couple's marriage six months after the birth of the child.[108]

The belief that men should stand behind long-time girlfriends ensured that some putative fathers went to great lengths to preclude the possibility that their parents might learn that such girlfriends were pregnant. The case of one young woman, who had dated the father of her child for over four years and who had repeatedly been reassured that 'if she should get pregnant they would marry immediately,' illustrates this tactic. The putative father explicitly acknowledged that his parents, had they known about the pregnancy, would have insisted upon marriage. With this fact in mind, he had persuaded the mother of his child to move from Cape Breton to Hamilton. The move to Hamilton was intended to preclude the possibility that his parents would learn of the pregnancy. The young woman described her experiences to the CAS:

> I waited almost 2 months and he hadn't told them so I faced him with the issue and asked him what he was going to do and he said he didn't know what he wanted to do; he couldn't make up his mind and that he felt for several reasons he couldn't get married. He felt he was too young to get married, and he didn't want to accept the responsibility.[109]

He then returned to Cape Breton, leaving his pregnant girlfriend alone in a new city and unable to use family and community pressure to force him to accept responsibility for their child. This case is suggestive in two important ways. First, the woman clearly hoped to get married and to avoid having to tell her friends and family that she had had sex outside of marriage. Nonetheless, the father was also afraid to reveal the pregnancy to his family.

These cases suggest that attitudes towards unwed pregnancy – if not the sexuality that led to it – were less rigid and unforgiving in working class communities than in the offices of the CAS or in the court. Young women were not abandoned by their families. Young men were expected, by the parents of pregnant young women and often by their own parents, to take responsibility for the consequences of their (sexual) actions. Young men, however, could defy community standards with impunity and proceedings in the offices of the CAS, ironically, did little to change this dynamic.

Women, as this chapter illustrates, were under considerable pressure to 'perform' on dates, lacked control over the sexual exchange, and had limited access to and knowledge of contraceptives. It was, in this context, hypocritical to 'point the finger – in sorrow or in anger – at the unmarried mother.'[110] Yet fingers continued to wag and to point and in the offices of the CAS pregnant young women were deemed unintelligent, neurotic, unreliable, overly sexual, dishonest, and unfit

cases of illegitimacy, only the consent of the mother was required.[7] This consent could be granted by the judge, even against the express will of the parents, if such parents were deemed unfit to give consent, if the parents were imprisoned, or if the child were deemed neglected by the CAS and had been made a Crown ward.[8] Under the *Children of Unmarried Parents Act* this power was expanded and the child could be removed from the mother's custody solely on the basis of her poverty.[9]

An adoption order divested 'the natural parent, guardian or person in whose custody the child has been of all legal rights in respect of such child.'[10] The child became, instead, 'for the purposes of custody of the person and rights of obedience, to all intents and purposes the child of the adopting parents.' The child had 'the same right to any claim for nurture, maintenance and education upon his adopting parents as he would have were they his natural parents.' The child would be known by the surname of the adopting parents and had, with respect to his or her adoptive parents, equal rights of inheritance to children born in lawful wedlock.[11] Since the ties between the child and his or her natural parents were irrevocably severed by adoption, the relinquishing parent had no right to information about the child.[12] Moreover, the act made no provision for the adopted child to obtain information about his or her natural parents. The adoption process was shrouded in secrecy; the natural parent was symbolically erased from the child's life and all original birth records were sealed. In effect, as Katrysha Bracco argues, the 1921 statute introduced into Ontario law the 'statutory death of the biological parents and the rebirth of the adoptee.'[13]

The magistrate or judge could only grant an order for adoption if 'satisfied of the ability of the applicants to fulfill the obligations and perform the duties of a parent towards the child to be adopted.'[14] The child had to have 'lived for at least two years previously with the applicant and ... during that period the conduct of the applicant and the conditions under which the child has lived [had to] have been such to justify the making of the order.' Although it was not explicitly stated that judges had discretion in this regard, it appears to have been common that this probationary period be shortened. The status of the child during the period of probation was tenuous. Could the child be reclaimed by an unwed mother? This question, not surprisingly, was the subject of confusion, debate, and judicial wrangling in the years after 1921. Only in 1950 was it firmly established by the Supreme Court of Canada that 'before such final Order is made, the natural parents may be able to reclaim their child on application to the court.'[15] In 1951 this probationary period was reduced to one year in Ontario, a timing that appears not to have been coincidental.[16] The adopting couple, until the order was finalized, had the right at any time to return the child to the adoption agency, and the natural parents, in such a case, would potentially be considered financially responsible for the child until a new adoption placement was found.[17]

Although judges granted final legal approval to adoption proceedings, the records of the court provide little detail about the process by which an adoption was organized and secured. Judges relied heavily upon the recommendations of social workers. They did not have the resources, or the inclination, to directly supervise the details of individual placements. This ensured that the CAS was largely unsupervised and indirectly awarded the agency enormous discretionary power. Ostensibly, all adoption orders were to be forwarded to the Registrar General and statistics on adoption were to be maintained.[18] In practice, however, this was not done, and until the 1970s no reliable statistics on adoption were available in Ontario.[19] As June Callwood lamented in 1976, 'Canada keeps better records on its animal population.'[20]

In the absence of consistent formal records, the case files produced under the *Children of Unmarried Parents Act* provide one of the few sources of historical information about the means by which decisions regarding adoption placement were reached in the offices of the CAS. They also reveal the conflict of interest that permeated adoption proceedings when CAS workers controlled both access to support proceedings for unwed mothers and the most reliable source of babies for adoption by infertile couples. This conflict of interest was intensified by external demand for infants for adoption and by internal constraints at the CAS, both financial and ideological.

The Demand for Babies

Even before the passage of legislation it is clear that demand existed for babies for informal adoption and that adoption was believed to be desirable for illegitimate children. Ontario child reform leader J.J. Kelso argued that 'no unmarried mother can successfully bring up her child and save it from disgrace and obloquy. [But] the child, if adopted young by respectable, childless people, will grow up creditably, and without any painful reminders of its origins.'[21] There were, however, some popular fears that had to be overcome. Eugenic beliefs suggested that parents might be wary of adoption, since the sins and weaknesses of the biological parents could, according to these theories, be transmitted to their offspring. Ada Elliott Sheffied, director of Boston's Bureau of Illegitimacy, argued in 1920 that the 'children of unmarried parents, who doubtless make up a large number of adoptions, may turn out to show an undue proportion of abnormal mentality.'[22] Charlotte Whitton echoed this sentiment, asserting that unmarried mothers were usually of low intelligence and weak morality.[23]

However, these problems, child welfare professionals believed, could be mitigated through careful social work practice. Much effort would be put into matching an infant, on the basis of extensive psychological and intelligence testing,[24] with his or her adoptive parents. It should be noted that the major concern expressed regarding adoption placement was not the question of how to ensure that parents were fit and suitable, but to reduce the likelihood that adoptive parents would receive a 'defective' child. It was in this context that 1935 article in the popular *Parents' Magazine* argued 'that the danger of adoption has been largely obviated by scientific advance.'[25]

Adoption was also endorsed by the popular press; babies were described as 'securities' that promised 'investors' plenty of 'dividends' in the form of smiles and giggles.[26] Potential adoptive parents had pragmatic reasons for overcoming their eugenic concerns and embracing the 'smiles and giggles' rhetoric.[27] Illegitimate infants were 'the easiest to place since they [were] taken directly from the hospital to the adoptive home.'[28] The new adoption mechanisms were immediately put to extensive use. In 1930, Kelso noted that in the nine years since 1921 over 6,000 adoptions had been completed.[29]

While adoption was already popular in the 1920s and 1930s, demand for babies increased further in the immediate post-war and Cold War period. As Wayne Carp argues in the American context, 'parenthood during the Cold War became a patriotic necessity. The media romanticized babies, glorified motherhood, and identified fatherhood with masculinity and good citizenship.'[30] The childless were marginalized in new and unprecedented ways and childless couples 'sought adoption in record numbers as one solution to their shame of infertility.'[31] The infants available for adoption were 'by and large, those born to unmarried mothers.'[32] One American social scientist argued in 1956 that, in this context, white illegitimacy was a blessing for the 'involuntarily childless':

Over one in ten of all marriages are involuntarily childless. Since most of these couples desire to adopt a baby, illegitimacy is a blessing to [them]. Curiously, from their standpoint there are not enough illegitimate births because most of these couples must wait one or two or three years in order to adopt a baby, and some are never able to have one because there is [sic] not enough for all who want them.[33]

It was explicitly babies, not children, who were in demand. Under the influence of popular psychology, in particular the work of John Bowlby in the 1950s, parents sought custody of babies as early as possible. Bowlby asserted that 'on psychiatric and social grounds ... the baby should be adopted as early in his life as possible ... the first two months should become the rule.'[34] Many parents also wanted to maintain the fiction of the biological family to the wider world (and at times even with adopted children themselves) and this was facilitated by adoption of the infant as early in his or her life as possible. Not all babies, however, were desirable for adoption.

As one concerned American social worker observed, 'for every infant available we have about ten applicants, but we have few applicants who are willing to accept an older child or one with a handicap.'[35] This meant that, despite the demand for babies, a significant number of children went without homes when mothers were too impoverished to provide the specialized care they required. Only three children in the extant *Children of Unmarried Parents Act* files were explicitly described as handicapped and all were institutionalized. It was also admitted by social workers that 'another group of children who are especially hard to place are babies who come from mixed racial backgrounds ... Traditionally people like to adopt babies who look enough like themselves so that the child can at least appear to be blood related.'[36] Only one non-white child in this sample is known to have been placed for adoption. In this case the social worker asserted that

there may be some delay in finding a family who will accept the part Negro background. This child is not Negroid in appearance. He is quite attractive with a full little face, small regular features, ovile complexion, very dark brown eyes, medium brown hair that may curl. He is small but sturdily built. Therefore we feel he has a good chance of achieving adoption.[37]

Had he been more 'Negroid looking,' it is suggested, adoption would have been unlikely.

It is clear, however, that while to be considered desirable for adoption a baby had to be white and healthy, adoptive parents were less concerned about the ethnic background of children. Despite eugenic fears in the 1920s and 1930s about genetically inherited inferiority, the assumed cultural inferiority of non–Anglo-Saxon groups could be overcome, it was repeatedly asserted, through assimilation. Adoption offered the most complete and irrevocable form of assimilation possible. It is disturbing, but perhaps not surprising, that women who were not Anglo-Saxon, particularly those who were first generation immigrants, were very vulnerable to pressures to release their children for adoption. Not only would cultural assumptions in the CAS have ensured harsh judgment of the women's morality and mothering potential, but the financial situation of recent immigrants was likely to be more precarious than that of other unwed pregnant women. Often, these women did not have extended family in Canada to whom they could turn for help, and their communications with the CAS were fraught with difficulty if they did not speak English. Of 1,741 English-speaking and Anglo-Saxon never-married women, 380, or 21.8 per cent, released their children for adoption. By contrast, 173 of 251, or 68.9 per cent, of non–Anglo-Saxon or non–English-speaking women relinquished their children.

The demand for healthy white babies invited abuse. Evidence from the United States during this period illustrates the existence of a widespread and profitable underground market in white babies.[38] It was recognized, at least in the American social work community, that the popularity of adoption had created problems for those genuinely concerned about child welfare: 'One of the outgrowths of this imbalance between the number of couples who want to adopt and the number of babies available is a practice commonly referred to as the "black market" – the selling of babies for adoption.'[39] Workers in child care agencies asserted that 'many abuses have been reported around a mother's relinquishment of her child.'[40] Ironically, however, evidence from the United States also makes it clear that some of the worst cases of abuse of power with regard to adoption involved child welfare agencies themselves. It is possible that some welfare workers in Ontario were also corrupt.[41] Several young mothers hinted that the CAS was profiteering in the baby racket, asserting that 'babies had been sold to the United States without the consent of their mothers.'[42]

The vast majority of child welfare professionals, however, were not involved in such practices and they expressed deep concern about 'black market' adoption. Child welfare workers asserted that all adoptions should be regulated through children's agencies in order to prevent undue exploitation. However, they simultaneously admitted that 'agency policy is to have mothers of illegitimate children consent to having those children made Crown wards so that adoption may be facilitated and the process speeded up.'[43] They did not recognize that simultaneous control over adoption and affiliation proceedings placed child welfare workers themselves in a position of conflict of interest. This conflict of interest, moreover, was intensified by the financial constraints faced by CAS workers and by their ideological presuppositions about the delinquency and instability of unwed pregnant women.

Financial Constraints at the CAS

There is little doubt, as one critic of child welfare law put it in the 1970s, that 'behind the belief that adoption is a good solution is money. Adoption is the cheapest solution.'[44] And cheap solutions were definitely required. Until 1965 only a limited portion of the costs involved in placing and caring for children were covered by the provincial government; the rest of the money required by the CAS had to be raised through charitable donations and alternative fund-raising.[45] Adoption made it unlikely that a child would be in the care of the state beyond a few weeks immediately after birth. It was recognized in the social work and reform communities that 'with the combination of the stigma attached to illegitimacy, and the lack of means of support for the child,' many unwed mothers who opted to keep their children later left their infants in institutional care; these older children were then considerably harder to place for adoption.[46]

Social workers associated with child-placement agencies repeatedly lamented that 'again and again public and private agencies are obliged to take over the care of illegitimate children whose mothers have maintained custody of them.'[47] Such cases were cited as evidence that illegitimate children should always be released for adoption immediately after birth: 'All too often the child later becomes dependent. A number of these children might have been suitable for adoption had they been available for placement before having suffered the rejection and neglect that are so often the lot of the illegitimate dependent child.'[48] Although it is indubitable that change of guardianship was difficult for children who were released for adoption later in life, this denigration

of unwed mothers as neglectful erased the financial and social challenges that women faced in raising children alone.

Social workers may also have been motivated by the possibility that
some wealthy couples might complete the process of adoption with a
significant 'charitable' donation to the agency. The Hamilton CAS, for
example, admitted to one set of prospective, and very wealthy, adoptive parents in 1944 that 'a gift from them in such an amount as they
choose will be gratefully received.'[49] Did such a gift constitute payment for a baby or influence the selection of adoptive parents by CAS
workers? By contrast, court proceedings for paternity declarations and
child support were very expensive and, as social workers knew, were
often unsuccessful. Some contemporary social workers admitted that
financial constraints undermined their work. 'This is where the dollar
first rears its ugly head. Children's Aid Societies are entirely dependent for their adoption money either on community fund raising, gifts,
or contributions from the municipalities. This lack of funds has meant
a shortage of staff. Principles, too, have a way of getting tangled with
the budget.'[50]

Social workers were also aware that the limited costs required to
cover the costs of placing a child pending adoption could usually be
obtained from putative fathers, making adoption even more financially desirable for the CAS. Social workers used the threat of paternity
proceedings to scare men into maintenance agreements on the understanding that children would be released for adoption and that debts
would therefore be finite. Although men fled the jurisdiction to avoid
long-term child support, it was rarely worth sacrificing family and
community to flee the small, finite debts associated with adoption. In
fifty-one of 562 cases (9.1 per cent), men paid their debts with regard to
adoption in full without recourse to court proceedings. But when men
failed to pay, the CAS was ruthless about collecting money owed to
the agency.[51] In 511 cases, the CAS resorted to court proceedings to
force recalcitrant men to pay up, and they were overwhelmingly successful. In 438 of 562 cases (77.9 per cent), payment was ultimately
made in full. In thirty-seven cases (6.6 per cent) partial payment was
received. In three cases (0.5 per cent) fathers died before payment
could be completed. In twenty-two cases (3.9 per cent) payment was
suspended due to the inability of the father to pay, and only in eleven
cases (1.9 per cent) did men flee the jurisdiction (see fig. 4.1).

The summons process was used repeatedly and this process, with its
ultimate threat of imprisonment, was effective. Each time a man was

Figure 4.1: Payment to the CAS in adoption cases

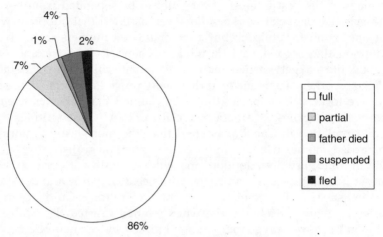

summoned into court he could be forced to pay a small sum towards his debt to the CAS; unlike in cases involving long-term child support, the quantum of the debt did not increase over time, and eventually the debt would be eradicated through small and partial payment. Many putative fathers realized it was simpler to pay debts voluntarily than to repeatedly be summoned into court.[52] Fathers must have felt considerable relief when they received notice that adoption placements had been obtained and that their responsibility had come to an end: 'We wish to advise you that your child has now been adopted. Therefore, it is no longer necessary that you make payments into the court for the support of the child.'[53] The ability to close a file also had significant financial implications for the CAS, but the conflict of interest in their position was not acknowledged. Moreover, encouraging fathers to pay costs for adoption further reduced the choices of unwed mothers themselves, empowering men to influence the decisions of mothers.

Ideological Commitment to the Adoption Mandate

Ideological constraints were also operative in the CAS. Unwed mothers were constructed as delinquent and unstable, unable to be good mothers. One Canadian social worker critical of the adoption mandate pointed out that the description of the unwed mother as sick mandated removal of the child: 'If the mother is abnormal it follows of course that she is not a fit person to raise her own child. Obviously, then, it becomes in the best interest of the child to be separated from her.'[54] The majority of social workers, however, asserted that adoption was not only good for children but also for unwed mothers themselves. Adoption, they argued, gave the mother a chance to start over and lead a 'good' life – to get married and raise legitimate children for the state.

Social workers acknowledged that many unwed mothers expressed a desire to keep their babies, but they claimed that this was itself a symptom of sickness.[55] American social workers, whose writings had wide circulation in Canada, asserted that 'the more healthy, normal unmarried mother has usually faced her situation realistically, has a plan in mind, usually adoption, and will stay with her decision. She can see her child as a human being, with needs, growing and developing, and she is willing to make the best plan for him.'[56] Guidance from the social worker was essential when women resisted the 'realistic' solution to unwed pregnancy: 'When blocked by her neurotic needs, the unmarried mother will frequently be unable to reach a sound decision to relinquish her child unless the social worker takes a firm stand.'[57] The social worker had to be prepared to face considerable opposition from the unwed mother, but it was necessary that such opposition to relinquishment be overcome. As American social worker Florence Clothier asserted,

> social workers, like physicians, must be prepared to reach a decision as to what will be best both for the baby and for the mother, and then to work actively toward the carrying out of that program. The physician decides what medical procedure will be best for his patient and does everything in his power to carry it out, even though the operation or the medication may involve suffering for the patient. It behooves the worker to formulate a tentative plan for the separation and to get in as much as possible of the preliminary work of carrying out this plan before the baby is born. This preliminary work, of course, will include case-work treatment aimed at making it socially and psychologically possible for the mother to give up her baby.[58]

Popular beliefs echoed such sentiments. A 1966 editorial in *Maclean's* put it this way, 'Normally the best thing for the unmarried mother and for the fatherless child is for her to give up the baby to a home with two parents. Parenthood is a job for married couples.'[59]

It is, of course, highly ironic that this same unwed mother would be viewed as a good mother if the father of her child were willing and able to marry her. After all, relinquishment of infants for adoption was the second-best solution to illegitimacy, with social workers advocating marriage of the offending parties as the best solution to an unwanted pregnancy (except when this would necessitate an interracial marriage). In cases in which marriage was not possible, usually because the father refused to help the mother of his child, the woman who had been encouraged to wed, and who was assumed, if she wed, to be a good mother, was constructed as neurotic. It would have been more realistic, perhaps, to construct unwed fathers as immature, but this would not have provided a justification for relinquishment for adoption.

In the social work journals, only one Canadian voice offered open critique of this hegemonic discourse. Svanhuit Josie, a child welfare worker from Ottawa, lamented in 1955 that 'it seems to me that casework with the unmarried mother has come to mean the process of convincing her that it is impossible if not absolutely immoral for her to plan to keep her own child. She must be made to face the "reality" of the situation, which means to give it up for adoption.'[60] Josie argued that 'social workers do not admit that they encourage the mothers, and they emphasize that they only want the best for the mother and child. But I see encouragement in telling the girl how many good and loving families are willing to take her child and that most of these families are rather wealthy and can give the child everything, even the best education.'[61] Her critique, however, prompted a harsh, immediate rebuttal from the supervisor of the Unmarried Parents Department of the Toronto CAS, who asserted that most mothers keeping their children 'were emotionally sick people' and that the social worker therefore 'trie[d] to be of assistance in helping her assess the realities of her situation.'[62] The extant case files provide considerable insight into how 'assistance' to the unwed mother was provided.

Convincing the Unwed Mother

Young women were subjected to unrelenting pressure to conform to the adoption mandate. This did not go unnoticed by unwed mothers themselves. One distraught mother asserted that 'all social agencies are anxious that all unmarried mothers give up their children.'[63] Another mother, under interrogation in the court, echoed such sentiments:

Q: What are your intentions with regard to the child?
A: I am going to keep her and bring her up to the best of my ability.
Q: Has anyone ever explained to you that in the best interest of the child it would be better to give it up?
A: Too many people have told me that.[64]

As this exchange attests, unwed mothers did not always give social workers their complete cooperation. But they were vulnerable. CAS workers tried to convince young women of the necessity of adoption by describing the financial and social challenges that awaited them as single mothers.

CAS workers had a responsibility to ensure that mothers were aware of the financial difficulties that they would inevitably confront raising children alone, but lurid descriptions of abject poverty were used to dissuade mothers from keeping their infants. The Canadian Welfare Council advised social workers that

the mother should know that if she keeps her child she may be beset by many difficulties of which she can hardly be aware before experiencing them. She may be censured by relatives and neighbors; she will have, in all probability, acute difficulty in supporting herself and her child; she may jeopardize her opportunity for a marriage later on.[65]

Young women were routinely warned that the woman who insisted on keeping her child had 'less opportunity to meet appropriate men and future husbands.'[66] The Welfare Council asserted that issuing such dire warnings did 'not disregard the unmarried mother's right of choice, but with more understanding of the complications of the problem, the caseworker is able to approach the situation more objectively and help the unmarried mother arrive at a realistic decision.'[67] This 'realistic' decision was to relinquish the child; the possibility of challenging the poverty and stigma faced by single mothers was not considered.

The high pressure, and at times unsavoury, tactics that CAS workers could use to convince women to place children for adoption are well illustrated in a case that came before the court in Toronto in 1959. Although this case may have been extreme, it reveals the potential for abuse inherent in the allocation of conflicting powers to a single, unregulated, agency. The woman in this case had entered into an agreement with the putative father of her child through negotiations handled by the CAS. The putative father had agreed to pay the $700 costs on the assumption that the child would be placed for adoption immediately after birth. After delivery, however, the mother decided to keep the child. With the financial aid and support of her parents, she hired a lawyer to challenge the agreement. Her lawyer argued that the father had implicitly admitted paternity by signing the agreement (although he had not made an explicit written admission of paternity), that the mother had been coerced by the CAS into accepting a parsimonious settlement, that she had been unduly pressured to place the child for adoption, and that the agreement could not be binding, particularly since the mother had explicitly refused to sign consent to relinquishment papers. Lawyers for the defence asserted that their client had complied with the terms of the agreement, that the agreement was binding and final, and that the putative father had never admitted paternity. They claimed that he had 'signed the agreement with the CAS under duress, and on their promise that the child would be adopted.'

The father had much greater financial resources than did the mother. He worked at Mount Sinai and was a foreign student doing postgraduate work in medicine; she was a secretary. He claimed that the mother, and the CAS, had blackmailed him since he wanted to avoid publicity. He had, however, manipulated the informal proceedings with the CAS to his own advantage. While refusing to admit paternity, he offered to pay confinement expenses and costs for the child pending adoption. If the mother did not agree to this, he asserted that he would give her nothing and, since he had not admitted paternity, collecting ongoing support from him would require recourse to the court. He threatened not to 'pay a cent' if she kept the child, but to return to his homeland to avoid any such responsibility.

The mother claimed that she had become pregnant only because he had 'refused to use precautions' and had given her inaccurate information regarding the safe time in her cycle; she had trusted him because of his medical expertise. When she became pregnant, he continued to have regular intercourse with her, but threatened that 'he would lie about everything if called into court.' He had advised her instead that he was willing to pay for her to have an abortion in Montreal. She had refused, as 'it would be dangerous and she might lose her life.' She was angry because he was relatively well off and had gone on holiday in Europe during her pregnancy, yet had refused to give her any financial assistance. She was heartbroken that he had been so uncaring when 'he could afford to help me out and I needed some moral support, kindness or something.' She claimed that the CAS had tried to coerce her into turning the baby over for adoption and that they had a couple ready and waiting to accept the child. She also claimed that she had not been informed that the agreement was permanent or binding, but had assumed that it covered maintenance temporarily and that it could later be varied. Under vigorous cross-examination she asserted:

> Q: You stated that you had – in answer to your own counsel's questions – been pressed to put your child up for adoption.
> A: That's right.
> Q: By whom?
> A: Mrs. M., the representative of the CAS ... Both before and after the birth, and even after the 26 May when Judge B gave me custody of the child, and she still tried to tell me that it was the best thing to give the child up for adoption ... The CAS said that this money – I should accept it – otherwise Dr. M. might go away and I wouldn't get anything.

Called to the witness stand, Mr. B, a second CAS worker, inadvertently revealed the methods of influence that could be used upon unwed mothers to encourage them to place their children for adoption:

> It was made clear to me by Dr. M. that if there was a possibility of effecting a settlement for a fixed amount of money there was a possibility of this settlement being negotiated, if there was no possibility of effecting a settlement of a fixed amount then he was not interested in a settlement or an agreement of a continuing nature. Now this was made quite clear to Miss R. It was made clear to Miss R. the alternatives that there is a provision under the *Child Welfare Act* whereby an application can be made for an affiliation order. It was made quite clear to Miss R. that this was a service made available to her by the agency should she choose to avail herself of the service. We discussed the possibility of corroborative evidence, and in my considered opinion there was no evidence.
> Q: (posed by the lawyer of applicant) And therefore most of your discussions were how this desired object of Miss R's was going to be accomplished, how she was going to provide for the child, where she was going to stay, how it was going to affect the child and so on, right?
> A: Yes.
> Q: And would it not also be fair to say that in these discussions you implied or suggested to Miss R. as far as you could see, you found it diffi-

cult to see how she could keep the child and be fair to herself and the child ...

CAS workers had emphasized to the mother that she would live in poverty should she raise her child alone and that the 'reasonable' approach to the problem was to release the child for adoption. When this tactic failed, they resorted to threats, asserting that if she insisted on pursuing her lover in court she would not only lose, but would be humiliated in the process:

Q: You discussed with her whether or not there was adequate corroboration. You felt that there was no adequate corroboration.
A: I saw Miss R. had yet to provide corroboration. There was no intention at this point at all that Miss R. was desirous of taking this thing to court.
Q: Well the question of corroboration I suggest is a legal matter, whether or not there is corroboration – you discussed with Miss R. that in your opinion there was no corroboration, is that right?
A: That is correct.
Q: So you were advising her legally about the fact that there was no corroboration?
A: Well, let's say that I was.
Q: Well, then is it not true that in the CAS's handling of these cases that they usually handle the cases in which the applicant doesn't have a lawyer and the Children's Aid Society takes them under their wing and looks after them, isn't that right, and the CAS doesn't like a private lawyer. I suggest that Mrs. M implied to you that she hoped the child would be adopted ... and that she would be able to get Miss R. to agree to the said adoption.
A: Yes.

Miss R had obtained no legal advice at the time of the agreement, and had expressed her desire to keep the child. CAS workers knew, as her lawyer put it, that 'if the mother intends to keep the child then the agreement is not adequate.' The mother was subjected to a constant barrage of pressure to place her child for adoption, since a 'suitable family had been found for the child.' She was forced to get a court order confirming custody, at considerable expense, despite the fact that she had never signed consent papers for adoption. She was threatened that support would not be forthcoming and that it would be difficult, if not impossible, to raise the child herself, and was informed, without legal counsel, that she had inadequate evidence to take her ex-boyfriend to court.

CAS workers dismissed Miss R's corroborative evidence. She had several friends who were willing to attest to the long-standing and exclusive nature of the relationship between the parties. Moreover, CAS workers admitted under oath that the putative father had given a social history for adoption and that 'they would not normally accept such information if they did not believe the putative father to be the actual father of the child.' If they believed him to be the father of the child, why were they unwilling to go to court on Miss R's behalf? The answer seems to lie in three facts: court proceedings were expensive, this white baby, born of educated parents, was exceedingly desirable for adoption, and (wealthy) adoptive parents had been found for the child.

They also taunted the young woman with evidence of her previous sexual indiscretions. The trump card with which they threatened Miss R was the fact that she had previously given birth out of wedlock in 1949. Her evidence regarding the circumstances under which this child had been released for adoption is also illustrative of the pressure for relinquishment:

Q: When I inquired if you had a child previous to the one in question, you said yes and also that you had given up the child. To whom?
A. I don't know. When these people came to me I was quite young. I didn't even see the baby. They said the best thing was for the child to be adopted.
Q: Who are the people?
A: I don't know, but all this happened in the hospital, through the Children's Aid Society.
Q: Did you on that occasion sign any papers?
A: I signed. A lady came in and I signed my name to a paper. That's all. Nothing was read to me. I didn't see the child or anything and that's the reason I want to keep my child. I feel I have a right to keep my child. I know what it is like to give up a child.
Q: Would you explain that?
A: There are things that go on in your mind. You think about it. Sometimes you wonder if the child is alright.

It is ironic that Miss R had the fortitude to challenge the CAS because of her previous experience, yet this experience was used against her in court.[68] CAS workers may have perceived her to be particularly unfit as a mother precisely because this was her second illegitimate pregnancy. They asserted that a woman who had given a child up for adoption before certainly understood the consequences of the agreement that she had signed in this case and that the agreement was valid. The court concurred. Although the presiding judge softened the blow by asserting that 'my sympathies are with the mother,' he deemed that there had not 'been any undue influence on the mother at the time she agreed to accept this amount, and no unfair advantage seems to have been taken of her.'[69] He did not define what would, in his estimation, constitute undue influence or unfair advantage.

Under considerable pressure from CAS workers, as well as, in many cases, ex-boyfriends, it is not surprising that 553 of the 1992 women who had not cohabited with the fathers of their children (27.8 per cent) opted to relinquish their babies for adoption.[70] In fact, the compelling question is how the rest of these women managed to avoid relinquishment. The characteristics of the women who opted to release their children for adoption may provide some answers to this question. Statistically, the women who relinquished their babies were more likely to be young, to be non-Anglo-Saxon and unable to speak English, to be unemployed, and not to have the support of parents than were their peers who were successful in refusing adoption. It is striking that the average age of women who released their children for adoption was 19.6 (this average is for the entire period from 1921 to 1969). This is significantly younger than the average age of the non-cohabiting women who sought help from the CAS: 22 in the 1920s and 1930s; 26 in the 1940s; 23 in the 1950s; and 21 in the 1960s.[71] This suggests that younger women were more vulnerable. They lacked financial resources of their own.

Evidence also suggests that non-Anglo-Saxon women and women who did not speak English were particularly vulnerable; the 'good' mother was discursively constructed as Anglo-Saxon and English-speaking. Moreover, families who had immigrated recently were often less well established financially and therefore less able to provide material support for babies. A disproportionate number of white, ethnic minority, and non-English-speaking women released their children for adoption. Of the 553 non-cohabiting women who released their children for adoption, a minimum of 173 were either non-Anglo-Saxon or had limited ability to converse in English. Only in 251 of the 1,992 cases involving never-married women was it noted that young women were non-Anglo-Saxon or non-English speakers. But 173 of 251, or 68.9 per cent, of non-Anglo-Saxon or non–English-speaking women relinquished their children for adoption. By contrast, of 1,718 English and Anglo-Saxon never-married women, 380, or 22 per cent, released their children for adoption. Black and Aboriginal women (of whom there were a total of twenty-three) whose babies were not considered desirable for adoption, did not relinquish their children, with only one 'part-Negroid' child considered acceptable for potential adoption.[72]

Women who released their children for adoption were also less likely than their peers to be gainfully employed. While 1,130 of the 1,992 never-married women who sought help from the CAS worked in the exploitative female job ghettos of the modern economy, 427 of the 553 women who released their children for adoption were among the 865 who were unemployed. Women's jobs did not provide adequate wages for comfortable living, but at least a young woman who worked for wages could contribute to the family economy in order to help support her own child. Those who did not work were vulnerable if parents could not afford another mouth to feed.

Women who lacked financial resources of their own were very dependent upon their families of origin. Although the majority – 1,112 or 55.8 per cent – of the 1992 never-married women who appeared in the CAS offices arrived with their mothers or sisters to provide emotional support, only 24.4 per cent – 135 of 553 – of the women who relinquished their children for adoption were so accompanied, suggesting that these women lacked some of the social and emotional supports evident in other cases. The problems such lack of support could create are well illustrated in a case involving a woman who was a recent immigrant to Canada. Her boyfriend, who admitted paternity informally, had married since she had become pregnant and did not earn enough to support two families. The CAS warned him that he had 'entered into this marriage knowing full well that he had a responsibility to Miss K and that his marriage or any obligations since would have no bearing on the matter.' But he threatened that if called to court he would deny paternity and abscond. Both the mother and the CAS took his threats seriously. Although Miss K expressed a desire to keep her child, she was unemployed, uneducated, had minimal command of English and was only nineteen years of age. She had no family in Canada to help her out and her prospects for supporting her child unassisted were grim. Ultimately, she accepted her former lover's offer of $120 and gave her child up for adoption.[73]

In the majority of the cases mothers did not leave any explicit record as to why they elected to relinquish their children for adoption, but it is clear that economic considerations were paramount for numerous individuals. As one mother described her dilemma, 'I'd like to keep her, if I could, but without money I just can't.'[74] An unwed mother might not share the social work perspective that she could be a proper mother only 'by relinquishing the child.' She might not agree that 'if you love your baby you will give him up' because this is 'best for our babies, best for the lovely couple who would be the best people to have our baby, best for our family and best for society.'[75] Most, however, realistically acknowledged their limited financial resources; they sought help from the CAS because they believed that the financial resources of the fathers of their children should be made available for child support. When it became clear that the CAS would not assist them in obtaining such support, they were desperate.[76]

The financial and social challenges that unwed pregnant women faced – and the pressures to which they were subjected at the CAS – were recognized by the Supreme Court of Canada in 1970 in a case that reflects many of the themes evident in these case files. Sylvia Elaine Mugford sought an order for 'production and delivery of the infant David John Mugford' born to her out of wedlock.[77] The child had been made a Crown ward and had been placed for adoption, but the final adoption order had not yet been granted. Her application was dismissed by the Juvenile and Family Court of Carleton County, but her right to custody was ultimately confirmed by the Supreme Court of Canada.

The young woman, on learning that she was pregnant, had moved to live with a married sister in Ottawa. She consulted the CAS with regard to the future of her child and two female social workers both affirmed that the mother had been 'tense and upset,' 'depressed, without much self-defense or self-assurance' and 'in a state of indecision as to what should be done about the child since she would have no way of keeping it.' She was nineteen years old and her parents did not know that she was pregnant. She signed consent to adoption papers, but shortly thereafter was so distressed by her actions that she informed her parents of her predicament and sought their help in regaining custody of her child. The child had been placed in an adoptive home for only a few weeks, but the CAS informed the mother that 'David has adjusted well to his new environment and we cannot disturb this arrangement. However, you can feel assured that he is receiving plenty of loving care, and he will be given every opportunity to grow into a healthy and happy adult ... I hope you will be able to adjust and make a new life for yourself.'

The Supreme Court, however, determined that there was 'no evidence that the mother had deserted or abandoned the child' or that Sylvia was 'unmindful of her parental duties.' Instead, it held:

> While she at length consented to making the order whereby her child became a ward of the Crown, she was motivated solely by a sincere desire to do what she thought was then in the best interests of her child despite an almost overpowering desire on her part to keep him and be a mother to him. It was virtually an act of self-denial and required a strong effort on her part to suppress her innermost feelings towards the little human being to which she had just given birth. This becomes evident not only upon a consideration of her testimony given at the hearing but upon perusal of her letters. Her vacillation, upon which such undue emphasis was placed by the learned Juvenile and Family Court Judge, can surely be understood by anyone who takes a penetrating look into this woman's sorry and helpless plight, she being most desirous of keeping her baby yet not wanting to expose him to a life of penury and misery. Any doubts as to her true motives must surely be dispelled by the immediate and positive steps taken by her to recover custody when the kind and sympathetic understanding of her parents prompted them to come to her aid.

This case illustrates the social pressures which might encourage a woman to relinquish her child for adoption, the difficulty with which such a decision was made (and the regrets that might plague many women), and the reluctance of the Children's Aid Society to give due consideration to the rights of the unwed mother.

Few unwed mothers in the cases heard under the act, however, would have had the resources available to Sylvia Mugford. How many other mothers were informally told that adoption arrangements could 'not be disturbed' and that they simply had to 'make new lives for themselves'? Women were vulnerable, particularly if they were young, unemployed, unable to call upon the support of family or friends, or unable to speak English. Many potentially loving mothers were encouraged to relinquish their children for adoption in the hope that the adoptive home would provide materially for the child in a way that it was impossible for the mother herself to do; women sought to protect their children from potential 'penury and misery.'[78] CAS workers, understandably, shared this concern for the financial welfare of the child, but little consideration was given to the possibility that the financial prospects of the mother herself might be improved. The mother was convinced to give up her baby because it was 'best' for him or her, but did the adoption mandate work for mothers or for children?

After Relinquishment

As Svanhuit Josie asserted in her 1955 critique of the adoption mandate, social workers had not answered the questions, 'How much harm does the relinquishment do to the mother?' and is 'the adoptive child ... as happy with his adoptive parents as [he would be] with his own mother and relatives?'[79] Evidence suggests that relinquishment was extremely difficult for mothers and that little effort was expended in services to the unwed mother after she had released her baby. Perhaps more disturbingly, although it was recognized in the social work community that 'for the child, [adoption was] as good and as bad as the kind of adoptive parents selected,'[80] the rapidity of placements and the failure to conduct post-placement assessments suggest that the best interests of adopted children were not always adequately protected.

Despite rhetoric that emphasized that releasing a child for adoption was the first step in the rehabilitation of the unwed mother, few services were provided to her in the aftermath of relinquishment to ensure such 'rehabilitation.' As a report on the operation of maternity homes in Toronto confirmed in 1960, 'Children's Aid Societies' services are discontinued following court proceedings for wardship of the child, or signing release of the baby for adoption.'[81] Instead, the unwed mother was told to get on with her life and to forget about the baby. This exhortation to forget, however, was deeply ironic, for

> according to social work theory at the time in order for a girl to make a decision about her child she had to develop a loving attitude to it. True maternal love could mean keeping the child, but wasn't it also 'selfish and unmotherly' to sacrifice her baby's welfare and stable future by keeping an illegitimate child in a one parent situation'? The right choice was not difficult to fathom.[82]

But what was a mother to do with all that maternal love once her child was relinquished for adoption?

The decision to give a child up for adoption was difficult, and relinquishing mothers experienced a profound sense of loss that has been eloquently described as a feeling of being 'haunted by fear for their child's welfare, [and of] guilt both for abandoning their child and for continuing to love and long for him.'[83] Mothers who have relinquished children for adoption assert that not knowing how they have fared is the most painful aspect of the loss of the child. In repeated studies it has been found that women 'yearn for contact with or knowledge about their children.'[84] These emotions are also illustrated in the records of the *Children of Unmarried Parents Act*. One mother asserted that 'there are things that go on in your mind. You think about it. Sometimes you wonder if the child is alright.'[85] Several described being 'haunted by the[ir] bab[ies].'[86] Others spoke of the yearning to 'know that she was ok, that she was happy, that my decision was good for her.'[87] In this context, it is not surprising that a minimum of fifty-six of the mothers who released their children for adoption later sought information from the CAS regarding the welfare and/or placement of their children.

Their concerns were dismissed, however, and they were told to get on with their lives, that they had no right to any information, and that their relationships with the children had been permanently and irrevocably severed. Women who sought court orders to obtain information about their children were told that it was 'not useful or just to submit two families to upheaval that would result from granting the application (to have the adoption file opened).'[88] Not only did CAS workers assert that women had no right to such information, but also they could not have answered the questions about the welfare of children as very little was known about how children fared after placement.

One Canadian critic lamented as early as 1947 that

> whether the illegitimate child will grow to be a healthy, happy and useful citizen depends largely upon the skill and care used in placing him for adoption in the first year or two. At present people are clamoring for babies and will go to almost any extreme to obtain one for adoption. The baby of illegitimate birth needs the law's protection from the hazards of an undesirable home. And in Canada they are not getting that protection.[89]

In the rush to remove the child from the unwed mother, what measures were taken to ensure that he or she was placed in a loving and appropriate home? In the early decades, efforts were made to test babies, not parents.[90] With the decline of eugenic theory, however, emphasis was increasingly placed on matching children with loving and capable parents. The child, even when born of economically disadvantaged parents, could be accepted without question into the ranks of a middle-class family and be raised 'by a couple prejudged to possess all the attributes and resources necessary for successful parenthood.'[91] Social workers at the time agreed that 'the responsibility involved in placing a child in an adoptive home is a grave one. The child is defenseless and the power of the adoptive parents is almost unrestricted. The placement will determine the future course of the life of the child.'[92] But how could determinations about the fitness of parents be made, and what were the 'attributes and resources necessary for successful parenthood'?[93]

As more insightful workers recognized, 'there are no rule of thumb methods that the social worker can use to judge the suitability of a home for receiving an adoptive child.'[94] Social workers agreed that 'moral integrity, ability to support a child, good health, and adequate housing are all factors one can immediately perceive as being necessary' in prospective adoptive parents.[95] In practice, such ill-defined criteria left considerable scope for discrimination. 'Unmarried people,' along with the 'mentally ill' and 'alcoholics' were 'obviously disqualified.'[96] As Veronica Strong-Boag argues in her recent study of adoption in Canada, demand exceeded the baby supply, and 'in such high stakes [decisions], education, money and powerful ethnic and racial identities made a difference.'[97] The discretionary and amorphous nature of the decision-making process made it difficult to challenge.

Perhaps the most disturbing aspect of the discrimination evident in adoption placement is cultural. Incidental evidence suggests that almost all of the adopting parents in the *Children of Unmarried Parents Act* case files were English-speaking, white, Anglo-Saxon, and well assimilated into mainstream Canadian culture. Babies, however, while white, were often those born to poor mothers of non-Anglo-Saxon descent. Adoptive parents, albeit unwittingly, participated in a process of forced and irreversible cultural assimilation. Adoption also reinforced class hierarchies. It is incontrovertible that children were, as Strong-Boag puts it, 'rarely transferred to the care of others when material circumstances of biological kin [were] good.'[98] Although social workers were clearly motivated by a sincere (and easily understood) desire to improve the material circumstances of illegitimate children, material well-being is not the only issue that is important in ensuring that children have happy childhoods.

Adoption placements were also often made rapidly and without follow-up or supervision as required under legislation. Under the *Adoption Act*, adoptions were not to be formalized until a two-year period had elapsed; after 1951, this period was reduced to one year. Adoptive families were supposed to be supervised and evaluated during this period. But the volume of cases with which social workers were faced precluded such ongoing observation of adoptive homes. It seems to have been routine for judges to approve that the CAS ignore such formalities asserting that 'it is to the advantage of the said child in every respect that the period of residence be dispensed with.'[99] Social workers asserted that the probationary period was too long and that the insecurity of the placement undermined bonding within the adoptive family. It was common practice to do all possible to 'shorten the time required. All agencies agree that careful investigations are necessary, but feel it would be wonderful if the procedure could be speeded up.'[100] In 1960 the Social Planning Council of Metropolitan Toronto went so far as to assert that the ability of the unwed mother to change her mind with regard to adoption should be abrogated. She 'might delay placement' or 'demand the return of her child with disastrous consequences for the adopting parents and child and doubtful advantage for the unmarried mother.'[101]

This critique of adoption procedures is not to be understood as criticism of the childless couples who sought babies or as a denial of the fact that adoption could provide children not only with financial security but also with happy homes and family lives. Adoptive mothers asserted that 'love-lines, not blood-lines, make motherhood' and that 'true parenthood is a stewardship which has no necessary relationship to physical parenthood.'[102] They constructed motherhood, for themselves and to the wider community, as a matter of choice and loving care, not biology, chance, or intuition. In a society in which it was increasingly argued that all children should be wanted and planned, adoptive families were seen as giving children 'better than normal child's chance. For they (adopted children) go to homes that desperately and genuinely want children.'[103] Adoptive parents were encouraged not to hide the fact of adoption (although the details regarding the biological family were not to be discussed or revealed), but to use the 'chosen-child' story to explain the adoptive family to the child. This story focuses on the desire of the parents for a child, and the positive qualities of the adopted child that allowed him or her to be 'picked' by the adoptive parents.[104] The danger in the chosen-child story is that it did not answer the question as to why the birth mother did not 'choose' her child and rendered invisible the discrimination and poverty that forced mothers to relinquish children against their own desires. The chosen-child narrative thereby reinforced the cultural mythology that the children of unmarried parents were unwanted by their biological mothers and reinscribed the discursive construction of the 'good' mother as middle-class, white, Anglo-Saxon, and legally married. It also became a circular argument; if adoptive parents 'chose' children, while unwed mothers produced them by accident or chance, relinquishment was legitimated as the common sense solution to out-of-wedlock pregnancy. Certainly, adoptive parents wanted children; but the assumption that unwed mothers did not denied women choice.

The myths surrounding adoption could raise questions for children. A minimum of thirty-three adopted children sought information about their birth mothers before reaching the age of sixteen. One child, born and adopted in 1960, started writing letters to the CAS in 1971 requesting information about her biological parents. Although it is unclear what response she was ultimately given, she wrote eleven letters of inquiry between 1971 and 1977.[105] While adoption placements may have been happy and successful in this and other cases, such quests for information about birth parents reveal that 'adoption raises subtle and imponderable questions from the child's point of view.'[106] It may be that it is the secrecy surrounding adoption that is unsettling, not the fact of adoption. But adoption in Ontario was shrouded in secrecy, and sealed records were only opened when the petitioner could convince the court that he or she had 'good cause' for doing so. The courts, however, did not articulate a standard of good cause, making access extremely difficult.[107]

Adoption myths also reinforced a very traditional view of family life. As Julie Berebitsky asserts in her recent study of adoption in the United States, since the 1920s the cultural discourse about adoption has 'been about the future, meaning, and social function of the family.'[108] Adoption, by separating biological from sociological parenthood, has the potential to transform our ideas about family life.[109] But adoption as practised by the CAS reinforced the 'sexually satisfied, playfully compatible heterosexual couple with "planned for" children living in an "emotionally healthy" home as the ideal and only legitimate family.'[110] The conflict of interest inherent in the fact that the CAS controlled both access to child support from putative fathers and the adoption process was not recognized. Moreover, while adoption facili-

5

'Haunted by Bills':
Lone Motherhood and Poverty

Non-cohabiting mothers who defied the adoption mandate were denied adequate means to maintain their children in decency and were then blamed and punished for the poverty in which they found themselves enmeshed.[1] Combining childcare with paid employment outside the home was extremely difficult. Unwed mothers had little choice but to work for wages, but were then condemned as being 'bad' mothers because they were not at home with their children. Wages for women were low, and childcare was expensive, difficult to find, and not always reliable. Given these conditions, it is not surprising that many women relied on friends and family for survival; they shared housing and called upon relatives to assist with day care. They also sought child support from the putative fathers of their children. As modern social workers recognize, 'paternity and child support arrangements are an essential component of family stability,'[2] but the *Children of Unmarried Parents Act* was ineffective as a child welfare measure. In this context women's dependence on men was reinforced, as the most obvious solution to poverty was to have access to a male wage. A new relationship with a man, however, remained a fragile solution to the problem of poverty. It is not surprising that a number of illegitimate children, through no fault of their mothers, ended up in the care of the state. Living with poverty, prejudice, and threats to custody took tremendous courage. One mother admitted that 'it's going to be hard I guess, but that's something I'll have to make up my mind to accept. I know I will be poor.'[3] The resilience and determination of mothers is clearly revealed in these case files.

The Challenge: Simultaneous Work for Wages and Childcare

Svanheit Josie, an Ottawa social worker who was outspoken in her criticism of coercive adoption regimes, outlined the problems faced by the unwed mother who kept her child. In a critique of the law published in 1950, she wrote,

> They cannot pay for adequate care of their children. There are few positions open to them where a child would be acceptable to an employer ... What is the girl to do? Few if any private social agencies have the necessary funds to subsidize unmarried mothers in maintaining their children for any length of time. Public day nurseries such as are available in some countries are few and far between in Canada.[4]

For most of the non-cohabiting women who kept their children, it was imperative that they work for wages. In seeking waged employment, however, unwed mothers faced numerous challenges: wages for most women were inadequate to meet their day-to-day needs and those of their children;[5] working mothers were, in popular literature, scapegoats for many social problems;[6] and combining paid work with childcare was extremely difficult in a world without public, subsidized day care.[7] This classic double bind was intensified for unwed mothers who were under the constant surveillance of the CAS. An unwed mother could be deemed unfit purely because of her poverty,[8] but her inability to be an at-home mother also brought censure upon her and raised the prospect that she would be considered negligent.

Finding employment was the first step in successful survival as a single parent. The women who kept their children were accustomed to hard work. They had, for the most part, been employed before pregnancy and relied upon this experience in supporting their children. Of the 1,992 non-cohabiting women who sought help from the CAS, 1,130 (56.7 per cent) worked in the exploitative female job ghettos of the modern economy in the period immediately before their confinements. While 77.2 per cent of women who relinquished their children for adoption had been unemployed before confinement, only 178 of the 1,439 women who kept their children had been unemployed before their pregnancies, suggesting that the experience of employment, and the knowledge that they could earn at least a limited wage, gave women some confidence that they could manage to provide for their children. Most returned to jobs similar to those they had held before pregnancy; they worked in factories, as domestic servants, secretaries, waitresses, in retail, as laundresses and hospital aides, bank tellers, telephone operators, dressmakers and hairdressers, janitors, and informal childcare workers. Moreover, they returned to work immediately after confinement, often to the same jobs, with the same employers. One woman, whose employer described her as 'essential to his business,' reported that she had returned to her supervisory position at a local diner within five days of confinement.[9] Only five women of the 1,992 who were single and pregnant reported being fired once their pregnancies became too obvious; thus, the majority of employers seem to have been more concerned about retaining hard-working employees than about women's so-called moral failings. Even those who had not worked before confinement sought work thereafter; of the 178 women who had not been working when they became pregnant, but who kept their babies, eighty-three had paid employment by the time their children were one year old. Their greatest challenge was not finding work, but finding work that paid a living wage.

Despite very high rates of employment, there is no doubt that single mothers were seriously economically underprivileged. Much of this disadvantage is explained by the poor wages that women earned in the labour market. Few had employment benefits, such as health care coverage, pension plans, or regular holidays. And in casual forms of employment, jobs were tenuous. To this day it remains true that, 'although more women have entered the labour market, they enter in a disadvantaged position. The majority of jobs open to women ... are low paying and offer inadequate or low benefits and thus cannot lift women and their children out of poverty.'[10] Women who sought support for their illegitimate children were aware of their limited earning capacity. One mother pointed explicitly to the inequities at her workplace. She and the putative father did the same job, packing at a candy factory, but he earned $22 a week while she was paid $12.50 a week, yet she paid the expenses for the child and he evaded payment under the order by claiming poverty.[11] As one woman asserted during a hearing in which she sought an increase in child support payments from the father of her twins, 'He didn't tell me how much he was earning. Women's wages are not as much as men's wages and I support the two children.'[12] Mothers in these cases asserted that poverty was an ongoing, constant stress in their lives. Studies of unwed mothers in other jurisdictions have also found that 'the first ranking problem voiced by the women was in the area of financial support. They were primarily concerned with how they were going to meet the everyday living expenses of their babies and themselves.'[13]

Although these women knew that employment was essential to their survival, they also recognized that employment outside the home remained stigmatized for mothers. Popular magazine articles and scientific studies that sought to determine 'the effects of maternal employment on children' had wide circulation. Rarely, however, did such studies 'consider the effects on children of the non-employment of mothers.'[14] The very nature of the inquiry assumed that a mother working while her children were young was a problem. Working mothers, it was asserted, must expect 'repercussions in the children's emotional, intellectual or moral development and the incidence of juvenile delinquency or school adjustment problems.'[15] Psychiatrists speculated that working mothers were maladjusted, that they sought 'to escape maternal responsibility or (had) a pathological drive to compete with men.'[16] In this context, for many mothers, despite the necessity of paid employment, 'going out to work' must have raised 'doubts as to whether she [would] be able to combine job and home, and be a good mother.'[17] In a society organized around the 'complementary' roles of male bread-winning and female domesticity, unwed working mothers were susceptible to negative stereotypes regarding their ability as parents. They were placed in a classic double bind: to work was necessary for the material support of their children, yet not being in the home ensured that they would be censured as 'bad' mothers.

Unwed mothers protested this double bind, and the surveillance and judgment to which they were subjected by social workers at the CAS. As one mother asserted when her social worker questioned her decision to find paid childcare for her son: 'I have no choice but to work ... I am a loving mother to my son.'[18] The threat inherent in surveillance – that children would be removed from the custody of the unwed mother – must have been the source of considerable consternation and fear for overworked unwed mothers. Whatever her doubts, however, the single mother had little option but to work. In all of the speculation regarding the impact of employment on children, one fact was consistently ignored: 'among the seriously underprivileged the economics of the situation leave little free choice as to whether the mother should or should not seek outside employment.'[19] But when a mother was working, who would look after her child, and how, on limited wages, would she pay for childcare?

The difficulty of finding reliable childcare, at a reasonable cost, intensified unwed mothers' financial problems.[20] Publicly funded, accessible day care was not available and finding reliable care, often during non-standard hours, was a barrier to employment.[21] One mother, whose employment prospects were better than most, as she was a trained nurse, lamented this problem in a letter to the CAS in 1959. Her landlady was willing to care for her child during the daytime, but the only available work was covering the night shift.[22] As recent studies have confirmed, combining work with 'personal or family responsibilities' remains difficult for single mothers, and 'the labour force activity of female lone parents is affected by the presence of young children' and the paucity of adequate, affordable childcare.[23] Providing respectable and loving care for the child was not only a central concern of any parent, but was of particular importance to unwed mothers who were haunted with the possibility that they might be deemed unfit.[24] Mothers knew that they were vulnerable, ironically, both because they worked and because their work was inadequately remunerative.

In the context of this double bind, it is not surprising that the majority of mothers who were successful in overcoming the obstacles before them had material and emotional support from their own families. In particular, unwed mothers looked to their mothers and sisters for help with housing and childcare. Over one-third – 480 of 1,439 – of the women who kept their babies lived with their parents in the period immediately after the birth of the child; a further 206 of 1,439 lived with other relatives, in particular married sisters; 74 women shared accommodations with another, unrelated female adult described as a friend; a further 89 lived in boarding arrangements in which mothers paid their landladies to care for their children; and 62 children were boarded separately from their mothers. Only 59 women provided conclusive evidence that they lived alone with their children in the first few years after confinement. In the remaining 469 cases women were not forthcoming with information about their housing and childcare arrangements.[25] Sharing shelter could potentially reduce the cost of living for a young mother and her child, for in 'solving her problem of shelter she may in fact help in solving some of her other problems. Living with a family member, or a friend, may mean that there is someone to care for her baby during the day.'[26]

The presence of parents who would, as one mother put it, 'stand by [the woman] in every way'[27] made an enormous difference not only in the options available to the unwed mother herself but also in the material and emotional future of her child.[28] Supportive families could greatly widen the options available to distraught young women. One poverty-stricken widower whose sixteen-year-old daughter bore a child out of wedlock in 1945 took both mother and child into the family home, although he was already burdened with the care of eleven dependent children. He argued that despite the hardships his family faced, the pregnancy was a 'family problem and adoption was undesirable.'[29] Another set of parents responded to the suggestion of the putative father that the child be released for adoption with anger: 'We don't give up our own children.'[30]

However welcome such familial support was, it did not provide a long-term solution for women's poverty. Unwed mothers knew that as their parents aged, multigenerational cohabitation would become more difficult; they expressed appreciation for the help given by parents and family and a simultaneous desire to move on, to marry, and to establish homes of their own. One mother, for example, lived with her parents for several years after the birth of her illegitimate son. She worked, as did her father, and her mother provided childcare. When her father had an industrial accident and broke his back, it was no longer possible for him to work. The mother became the sole support for her aging parents. She continued to live at home, although she had a serious boyfriend who regularly stayed the night. When her father died, she married her boyfriend, quit her job, and her mother came to live in her new home.[31] She did not believe that such family support should in any way reduce the obligation of the putative father to provide support for his child, but was unsuccessful in obtaining financial aid from him.

Mothers who did not have family support frequently had to board out their children. Placing a child out, as more astute social workers occasionally recognized, did not reflect a lack of interest on the part of the mother, but was a realistic response to the contradictory demands of employment and lone childcare. As one British social worker admitted, 'some mothers place their babies soon after their birth, while they are looking around for a room to which they can take the child, and a job where they can earn enough money to support it.'[32] In such cases mothers paid a set amount per week for the care of the child in someone else's home; a minimum of sixty-two of the women in this sample were forced to board out their children. Often they were able only to

spend weekends with their children because of employment responsibilities.[33] Boarding homes could vary widely with regard to the quality of care that the children received. At best they were homes in the true sense and boarding-home mothers could express considerable concern ·
about and affection for their charges. At times, however, they did so in a manner invasive of the rights of mothers. For example, one boarding-home mother wrote to the CAS that one child who spent Sundays with her mother suffered from neglect. 'The environment was not good, that R. [the mother] went to work on Sunday and the child played in the street or went to call on her father who is in the neighborhood.' She recommended that the mother should only be allowed to take the girl on outings or to visit her at the boarding-home. Although the CAS seems not to have imposed such restrictions on the mother, the boarding home system could mean that mothers endured not only long absences from children but also an additional layer of surveillance.[34]

The moralistic policies of the court at times directly contributed to the need for women to place their children in the temporary care of boarding-home mothers. For example, one mother, who bore her child in 1946, had been involved with a married man. His wife sued him for non-support and he was placed on probation, 'one of the terms being that he must stay away from Miss H.' When he began cohabiting with the unwed mother, in defiance of the court order, he was jailed for thirty days and lost his job. Upon release, he once again resumed cohabitation with his wife, although they separated within months; after this separation they reached a support agreement that allowed the father to live with his lover and their child. In the meantime, however, the child had been boarded out for eleven months since the mother could not afford to support the child on her own.[35]

Moreover, and undoubtedly a source of great concern for mothers, boarding homes could be very mercenary operations. For example, one distraught young mother, who had limited earning potential because she had only a Grade 8 education, was trying to support her baby alone. Her parents were unable to assist her financially and could not provide her or the baby with a home; thus, she was forced to board the baby while she worked. When the putative father of her child failed to make payments under their agreement, she found herself unable to pay this board and wrote to the CAS in desperation:

I don't like to be forever complaining to you about the matter, but right now I am at my witsend as to know what to do ... As of today I am boarding her in a private home for the summer and I don't have a cent to pay the lady for her care, and won't have until I receive some of the money that's owed me by Mr. J. The lady won't keep her for more than a couple of weeks without being paid and I don't know what I am going to do with her then. It isn't that Mr. J can't afford to pay and I don't see why he isn't doing so. There is so much money in arrears that would be a godsend to me now and I can't understand how he is getting away with not paying it. There's something wrong someplace.[36]

Her plight, sadly, was not unusual.

The Limitations of the *Children of Unmarried Parents Act*

The *Children of Unmarried Parents Act* did little to alleviate women's poverty. Only a small proportion of non-cohabiting unwed mothers received financial support from the fathers of their children. In fact, it would be reasonable, as one British contemporary observed, to regard 'the whole question of paternal maintenance as an academic consideration. Affiliation Orders are seldom, if ever, made for a sum that would actually keep a child, and they are easily evaded by determined men.'[37] The out-of-wedlock father was believed to be, as one prominent American social worker put it in 1954,

> pretty much an adjunct to the problems and complications surrounding the central fact of illegitimacy. That he had a part in creating the situation was, biologically speaking, incontestable; but beyond that his chief importance was considered to be his capacity to give financial assistance and the question of his willingness or unwillingness to do so. To a marked degree he was considered a potential but probably unreliable resource to be ignored, appeased or bullied as the occasion required.[38]

Such a critique of unwed fathers, however, ignored the extent to which the policies of child welfare agencies themselves rendered men 'pretty much an adjunct' and 'unreliable.' After all, of the 1,992 men involved with non-cohabiting women who sought support through the Children's Aid Society, the overwhelming majority were not interviewed because the mother was disbelieved (508), disappeared (401), denied their paternity and agreed only to pay costs pending adoption (203), or convinced social workers not to pursue support by claiming that girlfriends were 'promiscuous' (409). Only 291 men admitted paternity and agreed to support their children. Of these men, 88 continued to admit paternity and to recognize, if not fulfill, their obligations under agreements with the CAS; 203 later denied paternity and, of these, 160 were ultimately successful in having the agreements overturned by the court. Only 43 of 1,992 non-cohabiting women obtained orders for support through court proceedings funded by the CAS, and 2 others when they went to court at their own expense. In total 133 of 1,992 – a mere 6.7 per cent – were successful in obtaining agreements or orders for child support under the provisions of this legislation. In the context of pervasive disbelief of the unwed mother, paternal maintenance, despite its acknowledged centrality to women and children's survival, was rendered largely an 'academic consideration.'[39] Furthermore, even once an order was obtained against a putative father, collection was not guaranteed.

Even in the small minority of cases – 133 of 1,992 – in which non-cohabiting mothers were successful in obtaining agreements or orders of support against the putative fathers of their children, the act failed to alleviate their poverty. Orders that were granted were based not on the needs of the mother and child but on the father's 'ability to provide and [his] prospective means.'[40] The putative father could not be required to pay beyond his means, but without such money, the mother might find her child dealt with as a 'neglected child.'[41] The means of men could also change over time and the unwed mother who was receiving child support lived with the constant fear that, should the father of her child marry, have other children, or lose his job, the award could be renegotiated in court. The court also failed mothers by refusing to collect arrears until a significant amount of money was owed to the mother; this meant that men could refuse payment with impunity. Provincial reports boasted that the new legislation provided an efficient means of obtaining support for unwed mothers, but what was seldom acknowledged was that in the majority of accounts for which collection was successful, money was owed not to a mother but to the CAS for the care of an infant pending adoption.[42]

In determining support orders, judges were to 'take into consideration the ability to provide and the prospective means of such father.'[43] In theory, this was an equitable way in which to determine support. In practice, however, many of the working-class men who were called into court earned insufficient wages to support two households. In the absence of some other supplement for the mother's inadequate wages, such a policy made unwed mothers and their children very vulnerable.

The mother's needs – and those of the child – were irrelevant to the determination of support. One judge explained this fact to a distraught mother who was concerned that the order would not allow her to support her child: 'It's not a question of what it takes to keep them. It's what this man is able to pay.'[44] Men who were unemployed or burdened with extensive 'legitimate' obligations would not be ordered to pay support to an unwed mother, whatever the evidence of paternity and the prospects of the mother and child.

Men had to be employed for collection to be possible. Many of the men in these cases faced intermittent unemployment or underemployment and few earned wages that would allow the support of two households. One maternal grandfather, who had assumed responsibility for the child of his daughter, complained about the failure of the father of his grandchild to obtain employment. In a letter dated in 1954, he wrote:

> The mother of this child is unemployed at the present time, and my wife and I have to stand all the expenses of raising this child. I can see no reason why this man should be unemployed. It was stated at court that he was a mechanic, and I feel that he should be compelled to work, the same as I have to, and accept this responsibility as ordered by the Judge.[45]

The grandfather repeatedly wrote to the CAS complaining that 'the provincial government is responsible for carrying out this judgment ... why is this not being done?'[46] Men could also refuse to divulge information about their employment or lie about the amount of their earnings. As one CAS worker noted, putting too much pressure on such men could be counterproductive: 'Mr. B would certainly not co-operate to the extent of telling us what his earnings are, and if we approach his employer, disclosing the agency's name, he might easily lose his job.'[47]

Married men who had sired children during extramarital affairs were perceived to owe their first responsibility to their legitimate families. The court always asserted that 'a man's first responsibility [is] to his own [legal] family.'[48] This could mean that women were told that no support was possible 'because this man cannot afford it.'[49] Ironically, after enduring the pain of paternity proceedings and succeeding in obtaining an order for support, twenty-one of 133 women were told that, although men should pay them money, no payment was possible because of men's obligations to their legitimate families. This did not relieve the poverty of the mothers; neither did the CAS cease surveillance of them.

In fact, and ironically given the judgment imposed on unwed mothers, the CAS and judges expressed much sympathy for married men who had 'made mistake[s], but who didn't want to hurt their wi[ves]':[50] 'The unmarried father who has a wife and children of his own is in a particularly unenviable position. Marriage is out of the question. Should he tell his wife about his indiscretion? What if he keeps it secret and then she finds out about it? For the moderate earner it would be difficult to explain where the missing money was going every week.'[51] Men, it appears, could be expected to 'sow a few wild oats.'[52] Unwed mothers, however, had no such protection from social sanction or poverty and vehemently denounced men who had deceived them by feigning bachelorhood.

One woman ended her affair when she learned that her lover was already married. By this time, however, she was pregnant. When he then claimed to the court that he could not afford to pay child support because of his obligation to his legitimate wife and children, she expressed scorn and anger. He had 'thought nothing of spending large sums on treating her.' Furthermore, he had

> represented himself as a single man when they were going together, and spoke of marriage to her when he knew very well he was married. She wonders why the maintenance of his children should concern him so much more now than then. Too, she feels that he is free to go and do as he likes after he has paid the $4.00 and she has much more to pay and the care too. She says that if he gets out of paying this it is only increasing his spending money.

She asserted to the court and to the man's legal wife that the man would simply use this spending money to 'get another girl in trouble.' When his wife left him, however, it did not improve the unwed mother's prospects for support, since the wife was awarded $15 a week in maintenance. The father evaded payment in both cases with regularity.[53] Although women expressed anger with men who had deceived them, CAS workers were contemptuous of women who had engaged in affairs with married men and such behaviour was taken as evidence of a woman's promiscuity, not of a man's dishonesty, a fact that clearly reflected the sexual double standard.

For moral and economic reasons, the court was hesitant to impose obligations on men who had previously existing families. While the concern not to undermine the standard of living of pre-existing children is understandable, the impact of non-payment on equally innocent illegitimate children was not considered. Judges routinely reduced payments when husbands said that missing money had aroused suspicion in their wives, and they allowed payment schemes that facilitated deception, at the expense of unwed mothers who needed regular support. As one judge asserted in a case in 1960, 'I am not going to make an order that will place a burden upon you and perhaps result in your wife finding out about this.'[54] When wives did find out about illegitimate children conceived during the time of a marriage, trouble often ensued. A social worker described one such case:

> It seems to us that Mrs. S is trying hard to keep her marriage and her home together but she finds it very hard to accept that her children must do without things in order to send money to London. She, quite naturally, resents Miss R, seeing her as a woman who came between her and her husband and tried to break up their marriage. She finds it hard to understand why the law should uphold this woman's claims against her (as she sees it).[55]

Although the court refused to do so, the CAS recommended in this case that payments to the unwed mother be halted in order to aid in the sorting out of the putative father's 'marital difficulties.' Little thought appears to have been given to the ramifications that 'halting payment' would have on the innocent illegitimate child.

Even in cases in which men were employed and unmarried, the unwed mother always faced the prospect that support payments might be reduced. If the putative father lost his job, if he became ill, or if he married and fathered legitimate children, a variation of the original order could be obtained. At times mothers expressed disbelief regarding the claims of fathers with regard to poverty. One mother, for example, who during a bout of illness had received no support, responded to the putative father's claims of illness with sarcasm:

> I can fully understand the position of Mr. K right now. I can still remember the time when I had to pay my doctor's bills totaling $585, besides bringing up a small baby. But as Mr. K has shown himself to be very considerate when the baby or I were sick, I will give him another 6 weeks to

get over the loss of his appendix ... Trusting that the above will please him, and hoping the doctors will not find another appendix for the next 12 years.[56]

Sometimes, however, reductions in payments appear to have been accepted as reasonable by all parties. The men who came before the court worked, overwhelmingly, in poorly paid occupations and many faced periodic unemployment. Partial, but regular, and even intermittent, payments could be evidence of a sincere desire to do right by children. Some mothers explicitly recognized that other commitments prevented full payment and that this did not necessarily reflect a lack of interest on the part of fathers. One mother, whose child had been born in 1955, was granted $5 a week in support. In 1959, the putative father in this case, who had been paying intermittently, was summoned to account for the accumulation of arrears under this order. In the interim, he had married and had a young son who was hospitalized with polio. He was working in a bakery, earning only $59 a week, and his wife was unable to work as they had two other young children at home. When questioned by the judge, the putative father agreed to sell his car, which the judge deemed a luxury since he lived within walking distance of work, and to pay $1.50 a week, a sum that all parties agreed represented the maximum this man could afford. The mother of the illegitimate child was herself working and when the judge told her that 'I think that this boy might not be able to pay the amount of this order when he is married,' she responded that she would be happy 'as long as he can just pay some.' This reduced amount was paid regularly until the child reached the age of sixteen.[57] As a nurse, the mother in this case earned a better wage than many of the other single mothers to come before the court. She also had support from her own family. For mothers without such resources, however, a reduction in an award might mean the difference between independent survival and loss of custody of a child.

Mothers resented the fact that payments would be reduced because men had added to their obligations while knowing that their illegitimate children required continued support. One indignant mother asserted, 'Could you please explain to me why it is that he can afford to support a wife and child but *CANNOT* send $7/wk for the support of his *daughter* that is his *first* responsibility?'[58] Another mother put her anger very bluntly in a letter to the court in 1950. He ex-lover had been ordered to pay her $4 a week, but was very unreliable in doing so:

H goes free. He wasn't married when he first had his payments but now he is married and he has excuses and gets away with it. It sure looks to me that you are not all working for the child welfare ... Pay for a few months then miss and until time for a court case then pay a few more months and stop again ... He [the baby] would sure go hungry if he had to depend on the welfare of H to help him ... I make only a small wage and my health is not as good as it should be and I had to take housework to pay my debts. Yet H can't pay his small part and I can ... I think myself he enjoys defying the law and making a joke of the whole concern.[59]

This mother explicitly pointed to the irony that while she was scrutinized by the CAS and at risk of being considered neglectful due to her poverty, the father of her child was not so judged, even if he used money intended for his 'legitimate' family in wasteful ways: 'If I neglect my child what would happen to me for it? Sure is a good government we got. He has money for drink but not for food or clothing for his child.'[60] At times, social workers seemed to have recognized the problems this policy created for unwed mothers, but they continued to insist that legitimate families, whenever acquired, had first claim on men and their resources: 'We realize that the situation has been difficult for Miss P but Mr. D's first responsibility is to his wife and legitimate child.'[61]

As the previous cases illustrate, perhaps the greatest problem that custodial mothers faced with regard to collection was the fact that the court made minimal, and ineffective, efforts to enforce payment. Once a court order was made, the CAS would write letters to negligent fathers reminding them of overdue payments. If men still refused to pay and remained within the jurisdiction, they could be summoned into court to account for their failure to abide by orders. They could present evidence of legitimate reasons, such as unemployment or marriage and the birth of legitimate children, to explain non-payment or to justify a reduction in ongoing payments. Collection procedures, however, were easy to evade. Most importantly, men were not immediately called to court when they missed a payment under an order. The policy of the court was to allow arrears to accumulate to a minimum of $100 before court action would be taken:

It is our policy not to move to enforce payment on arrears on agreements and orders until the arrears reach a substantial amount, $100 or more. To make applications to enforce payment on smaller amounts for the thousands of open cases in our files would clutter the County Courts of the Province.[62]

Although this made sense from the perspective of the court, men were thus afforded a means of evading payment for long periods of time. It also reflects a clear understanding by the court that significant sums had not been paid to deserving mothers. While to the court the amounts under $100 seemed insignificant, for mothers these monies represented their means of survival. It is also ironic that the $100 threshold was not imposed in cases in which men owed money to the CAS under adoption agreements.

Some men responded to letters of reminder from the court with small payments, secure in the knowledge that as long as some payment was made in response to the letter, court action would not be undertaken. In one such case the CAS representative 'advised the Court that since the making of the Order the defendant would send in one or two payments and then stop, a reminding letter would be sent and one or two more payments would come in and so on.'[63] A father who repeatedly and brazenly ignored a court order could be jailed, but in practice this was rarely done since to jail the father precluded further payment under the order and because those most determined to evade payment simply disappeared before they could be incarcerated. Evidence from the case files suggests that only three of the 133 putative fathers who owed support were jailed, despite high rates of non- or partial payment. In part, this is because jailing men could be counterproductive, not only for the unwed mother but also for a man's other dependents. One father expressed this concern in a letter to the court: 'Should you wish to have me sent to jail for days because I cannot pay the full balance do so, but remember that there are 3 small children and one woman who will have no money or support during or immediately after this time.' His wife also wrote: 'What purpose will be affected in putting my husband in jail? It will cause great anguish to myself and my children, who are old enough to sense anything wrong at all. I can't see what business he would have at all if his clients find out he is in jail.' They also threatened that if he were jailed, they would thereafter leave the jurisdiction of the court and the intermittent payments the unwed mother was receiving would cease.[64]

As the court was well aware, many men simply voted with their feet and fled the jurisdiction. If a woman could not provide the court with a current address for the putative father, little attempt would be made to track him down. It was realistically acknowledged that spending public money to find men was wasteful of community resources since 'even if the parent is located, he may be unable to pay child maintenance.'[65] Any man who left the province effectively evaded a court order. Mothers also had to remain in Ontario to be eligible. One mother, who had returned to Montreal so that her parents and family could help her to raise her illegitimate child, discovered that she had thereby forfeited her right to support from the baby's father.[66] Such women, in effect, had to choose between the support – housing, assistance with childcare, and companionship – that they could obtain from out-of-province families and the possibility of economic support from recalcitrant putative fathers. It is hard to disagree with the assertion of a contemporary critic of British social policy with regard to illegitimacy that 'the law asks little indeed of the father of an illegitimate child and it enforces less.'[67]

Custodial mothers who became frustrated with the cat and mouse game of collection under weekly orders could settle, if men remained in the jurisdiction, for a lump-sum payment. This represented a desperate attempt to try to get at least some money from men who had evaded orders. One mother, who had been granted an order of $5 a week in permanent maintenance, had received payment only on three occasions and each of these times only when the putative father was summoned into court. In total, in four years she received only $100, less than one-tenth of the $1,040 due under the order during this time. Frustrated with this process, she agreed to accept a full settlement of $1,500. The putative father still failed to pay and after a further six months she accepted a lump sum of $500. Although this man had successfully evaded payment under the order for almost five years, once this smaller finite sum was agreed upon he immediately paid in full.[68] Ironically, however, although a woman might have accumulated large debts while payments were in arrears, she did not receive the lump sum in its entirety once a settlement was reached and the putative father made payment to the court. One CAS worker explained this policy to a mother who was concerned that she had not received the money due to her:

The money is payable to the Provincial Officer and may be disbursed in 3 ways. You may have a monthly sum, bearing in mind that the settlement must be extended as long a period of time as is possible. You may call upon the fund perhaps 3 or 4 times a year for money you would require for the child's clothing, medical care etc. or the money may be deposited with the public trustee, bearing interest at three percent, and held as a trust fund for the child.[69]

For women earning minimal wages, payment of child support was crucial to family survival, and non-payment or worry about non-payment, created enormous difficulties and stresses for custodial mothers. The repeated letters of one mother to the Department of Public Welfare illustrate these problems. Her twins, born in 1947, were entitled to support from their putative father at the rate of $10 per week. The father, however, paid only intermittently under this order and the mother worked at a variety of cleaning jobs to support her children. Her children were in ill health, yet she could not afford medical care without assistance: 'I do not take my children to clinics, which are free, because I cannot get off work to do so, therefore any medical attention is costly. I still cannot see why my children have to *wait* for THEIR money so I can give them necessary medical care.'[70] As another mother lamented in a letter to the office of the CAS, 'Mr. C is responsible for B until he is at least sixteen years of age *unless* my financial status improves a great deal in which case I shall be only too pleased to have no further dealings with Mr. C.'[71] A maternal grandmother wrote to the CAS in 1961 complaining about a putative father who had made no payments under the order of the court: 'It is getting on five years now since the child was born. My daughter has done a wonderful job of providing for her, but she can't now work due to ill health. Don't you think that under the circumstances it is about time that he showed he is a man and helped her out a bit?'[72] As another mother put it while complaining to the CAS about the failure to collect, 'I only receive payment when the pressure is put on him. He knows that he can send any amount that he feels like ... I only survive because of the help of my mother.'[73]

Mothers suffered emotional distress as they watched their children grow up in poverty. The budget of one mother appears to have been typical; she earned $27 a week, but paid $12 a week for her own room and board, and a further $12 a week for the room, board, and care of her child with their landlady. Without support as ordered by the court, she had $3 a week for transportation, health, insurance, and all other incidental expenses.[74] Under such conditions, one unwed mother described her life as 'going without clothing and living on oatmeal';[75] another asserted that she had little opportunity for any social life, relaxation or 'normal living.'[76] The double burden of single parenthood and long hours of work ensured that mothers felt that they were denied the opportunity to raise their children as they would have desired. One mother described her circumstances to the CAS in a detailed letter in 1954. The putative father of her child was paying only intermittent support and she was in dire straits trying to support her child:

> I am working now six days a week from 7am to 7pm and Sunday I go for three hours as a waitress and still I earn not more than $150 a month. How long can I do this only a make a living for us and be a good mother too ... I am not a street girl, even if I have a child and were not married ... My girl will be 8 in November and she has to come after school to the nursing home where I am working and wait there until 7pm when I can go home with her ... Please do help me. I moved to a small town as everyone said it would be cheaper, but still I cannot keep up and I am so tired ...[77]

Another mother asserted that after eight years of supporting her child alone she 'was getting a little weary now. For some years we have lived in one room – we have advanced now to an apartment and to us it is a palace. We wouldn't even entertain the thought of living in a house or owning a piece of land like G (the putative father). As nice as it might be, it is beyond our dreams.'[78] Another complained that she was tired of the priority that was given to the concerns of putative fathers at the expense of their children. In a letter to the CAS, she lamented that the agency had 'given Mr. K a lot of consideration. I wonder if the court will give me some consideration for a change.'[79]

Obtaining an order of support under the *Children of Unmarried Parents Act* required women to submit to humiliating questions and procedures, and even when successful, collection was often intermittent and unreliable. Because of prejudices in the CAS and in the court, only 133 non-cohabiting women successfully obtained orders of support against the fathers of their children and most of these women received only a small portion of the money that was theoretically owed to them. Although not all files are complete, a minimum of 48 of 133 men obtained amendments to orders reducing the quantum of original orders of support; in 21 of these cases women were told that payment was not possible because of men's 'legitimate' obligations. A further 13 negotiated lump-sum payments. At least 51 men disappeared, and 11 clearly made partial, but intermittent, payments on orders. In 7 cases the outcome is not clear, but in only 3 cases of 133 is evidence incontrovertible that men paid the entire amount due under an order. (See fig. 5.1.)

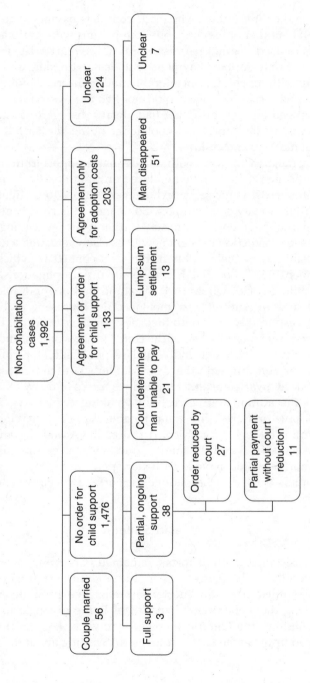

Figure 5.1: Payment outcomes in non-cohabitation cases

One of the three fathers who made complete payment had wanted to marry the mother of his child, but both parents were underage and her parents refused to grant permission for her to marry. The father maintained not only support payments but also an ongoing and close relationship with his child, even after the mother married another man. He was adamant that his child would not live in poverty; he was the son of an unwed mother, his father had always disregarded support payments, and he had first-hand knowledge of the hardship this inflicted on both mothers and children.[80]

In the majority of cases, without adequate support from the putative fathers of their children, women faced an uphill battle in maintaining their families. It is inadequate, however, simply to castigate men for their failure to pay child support. Some men, it is clear from case files, made partial payments only to stay further court proceedings, or abandoned the jurisdiction to begin new lives elsewhere, unencumbered by responsibility for their children. But in a context in which many of these men were poor and had other financial obligations, including other children with whom they lived and had ongoing relationships, partial and intermittent payments could represent real efforts to behave responsibly and to do their best for their children. It is important to critique the emphasis of the court, social workers, and the wider community on exclusive individual responsibility for child maintenance. The concern 'with the absent father's fault and irresponsibility ... displaced awareness of the limited resources of many absent fathers and of the administrative costs of "making them pay."'[81] Mothers would have preferred direct and reliable support to having to coerce recalcitrant fathers through court proceedings, and the apparatus of control – the CAS and the family court – was expensive to maintain. Such monies would have been better spent providing direct support for mothers. Such direct economic support, however, was next to nonexistent.

State Support

Social assistance, in all its forms, remained parsimonious and degrading throughout the period under study. Until 1956, unwed mothers were excluded from the most comprehensive program targeted at improving the welfare and standard of living of single mothers and their children, the Ontario mothers' allowance. As one mother was informed in 1945 when she wrote the CAS asking about the allowance, she was categorically 'not entitled for a child born out of wedlock.'[82] When reform was implemented in 1956, officials were careful to insist that 'the putative father is not to be relieved of his legal and financial responsibility.' Indeed, the mother was required to visit the local CAS to attempt to procure payment from the father; until this was done, the mother did not become eligible for the allowance. As well, a two-year waiting period, specific to unwed mothers, was instituted, to ensure that the mother was 'fit' to care for the child and that she did not continue her 'improper' sexual practices.[83] Of course, during those two years, without other forms of support, the unwed mother might well be forced by poverty to release her child for adoption.

Moreover, once they were officially eligible for the allowance, unwed mothers had to apply for such help and were often refused; within the first year of eligibility, only 133 unwed mothers in the province received benefits.[84] Of the 607 non-cohabiting mothers who kept their children after 1956 (1,439 kept their children over the entire period, but for those before 1956 this legislation was irrelevant), only four can be proven to have collected the Ontario mothers' allowance, suggesting that this legislation remained largely irrelevant to unwed mothers who had not cohabited. Moreover, even for these few, the allowance was inadequate to meet the basic needs of families; as astute observers recognized, 'no family groups who receive Mothers' Allowances are able to live on them in health and decency if the allowance is their sole source of income.'[85]

Municipal welfare, without universal provincial standards or criteria for eligibility, was also inadequate, and opposition to state financial assistance for single mothers remained strong. Single mothers were routinely accused of 'living off the hog.'[86] Such assertions, however, reflected a profound prejudice and lack of knowledge about the actual conditions faced by unwed mothers. Relief, for some of these mothers, prevented absolute starvation and homelessness, but unwed mothers, like other welfare recipients in Ontario, were stigmatized and denied adequate assistance to live in anything resembling comfort or decency. Throughout the period under study, except during the crisis of the 1930s, Ontario experienced rapid economic growth and relative prosperity. It was not, however, a prosperity that was equally shared. In fact, as K.J. Rea argues, 'it [is] surprising how little the actual distribution of income ha[s] changed since the 1930s.'[87] All welfare was means-tested and humiliating and failed to lift women and their children out of poverty. Michael Katz argues that 'welfare will never be satisfactory. It cannot escape the contradictions between its goals – deterrence, compassion, discipline and control.'[88]

Welfare in Ontario was undergoing dramatic transformations in terms of delivery and bureaucracy, 'from an uncoordinated structure of private charity, houses of refuge, and local poor relief into one of our most complex and controversial bureaucratic structures.'[89] Throughout these changes, however, welfare 'failed to provide its clients with minimally adequate standards for meeting their basic human needs.'[90] Rents, which skyrocketed in the post-war period, absorbed much of the relief budget, leaving families with inadequate resources to meet their nutritional needs. Clothing, health care, eyeglasses, schoolbooks, dental care, and recreation were outside the welfare budget entirely. Many of the unwed mothers who were dependent on welfare lived in substandard housing, often in single rooms, and went hungry themselves in order to pay the rent and to fill the bellies of their children. Family allowance payments, enacted after the war by the federal government, were universal but inadequate as the sole support for a family. Evidence from 174 case files illustrates that a significant number of unwed mothers did receive some charitable or welfare assistance, although the source of such income is not always explicitly detailed. Women spoke of 'waiting in line for food'[91] at charitable institutions, of 'groveling for the dole,'[92] and of being 'hungry and afraid, day after day.'[93]

Welfare provisions remained parsimonious because of deep-seated societal concerns that to allow welfare recipients to live in comfort would be to discourage the work ethic; thus, inadequate provisions provided a constant reminder that 'continued effort on their part [was] expected.'[94] In the case of single mothers these attitudes completely negated the childcare work they were performing in the home. In an era in which women were encouraged to be stay-at-home mothers and to be financially dependent upon husbands, the child-rearing work of single mothers was invisible and unvalued. Single mothers were explicitly accused of not working and were told to seek day care and paid employment. It was believed that 'by going out to work [they] can adjust more quickly, meet other people, and possibly marry.'[95] But day care was not readily available and following such advice would not, in any case, relieve women of public censure. As late as 1965, the minister of public welfare, Louise Cecile, publicly stated that working mothers 'were neglecting their most important role of all' and 'condemning several thousands of children in Ontario' to possible delinquency because of their 'disregard for their offspring.'[96] In this context, it is ironic that inadequacies in welfare provisions were explicitly intended to force recipients into the workforce.

Some improvement was evident in the late 1960s in popular and governmental attitudes towards welfare. In the context of the 'dramatic spillover effects'[97] of U.S. President Johnson's War on Poverty in the Ontario legislature, the attack of the opposition New Democratic Party on Louise Cecile, and calls for the department to shed its 'neanderthal views ... [of] welfare recipients as unregenerate and undeserving,'[98] the government was forced into (limited) action. Both at the federal and the provincial levels, governments committed to their own wars on poverty in 1965. As critics asserted even at the time, however, 'despite grandiose rhetoric, Canada's war on poverty contained a fair amount of "window dressing."'[99] The major federal program to emerge out of the war on poverty was the Canada Assistance Plan, which received parliamentary assent in July 1966. Although this measure was passed with great fanfare, it 'failed to alter, in any fundamental way, longstanding approaches to the needs of the poor.'[100] Under the Canada Assistance Plan, the existing category-based programs were eventually to be eliminated and a national standard achieved for welfare. However, the definition of basic needs for welfare recipients was left in the hands of the provinces and pre-set minimums were maintained.[101]

In 1967 the consolidation of category-based benefits was achieved in Ontario with the passage of the *Family Benefits Act*. For the first time, this meant that unmarried mothers were not singled out as undeserving, but maximum payments under the *Family Benefits Act* remained inadequate. There is no doubt that the availability of even minimal welfare as a basic right (and not something for which women had to beg and to prove themselves worthy) contributed to the decline in the relinquishment of illegitimate children for adoption in the 1970s. Such changes in welfare policy, however, came too late for the majority of women in the *Children of Unmarried Parents Act* case files. Parsimonious welfare policies, moreover, reinforced women's dependence on men.

Obtaining Access to a Male Wage

In a world of poor wages, problems with childcare, unreliable paternal maintenance mechanisms, and limited welfare assistance, cohabitation or, better, legal marriage offered a woman her best route out of poverty. As contemporary observers have noted, it is still true that 'marriage remains a major source of economic security for women with children, especially if they have few job skills. In fact, many divorced and unwed mothers escape welfare (and poverty) only through marriage.'[102] Dependence on a man, however, as these women were aware, was a risky venture. Cohabitation put women in a difficult legal position and even after legal marriage men were not responsible for children who were not biologically related to them.

Cohabitation imposed no legal obligation upon the new partner to support either the woman or her children; however, most women found that cohabitation improved their standard of living. Cohabitation offered immediate economic rewards but without the security offered by legal marriage and at the risk, moreover, of having further illegitimate children. Yet despite its risks, cohabitation was common: 286 of 1,439 single mothers (19.8 per cent) entered into cohabitation relationships while still under the supervision of the CAS. Cohabitation sometimes allowed mothers the luxury of conforming to societal ideals by retiring from the paid workforce. For example, one mother, who had brought her relationship with the putative father of her child to an end when she learned that he was already married, refused to give her child up for adoption, despite the hardships she knew would be attendant upon raising the child. Her ex-boyfriend, however, who already had to pay $15 a week in support to his estranged wife and child, was less than dependable in making payments for his illegitimate daughter's support, paying on average less than $4 a week on an order for $7 a week. The mother lamented that she could not 'support her daughter on her own' and had found a job in a factory and made arrangements to have her child cared for by her landlady each day. In 1948 she entered into a cohabiting relationship and expressed happiness that she would no longer be obligated to work in the factory. In 1950, when the child was five years old, she legally married her 'husband,' who had obtained a divorce from his first wife. Given the tenuous legal status of cohabitation, it was not until the relationship was formalized that the mother released the putative father of the child from any further financial responsibility. In her letter to the CAS, she described her new husband as a 'man in good financial standing' and asserted that he thought of her daughter 'as his own.'[103]

It is striking that, despite the supposed outcast status of the unwed mother and the dire warnings of social workers that keeping the child while single resulted 'in a young woman remaining single longer and permanently,'[104] 434 women of 1,439 (30.2 per cent) entered into legal marriage within the first two years after the birth of an illegitimate child. Many others probably did so in ensuing years, as the CAS tended to supervise women and keep records about their ability as mothers most intensely in the first few years after confinement. This suggests that illegitimacy, contrary to middle-class diatribes against premarital sexuality, did not make a working-class woman undesirable or 'pawed over' or 'second-hand goods.'[105]

Even legal marriage, however, did not impose any obligation upon the husband to support the illegitimate child, although marriage did make him liable for the support of his wife. Without formal adoption proceedings, illegitimate children (unless the biological children of both parents) remained outside the new family unit. Cognizant of the stigma attached to illegitimacy, it is not surprising that mothers expressed relief when husbands adopted their children. Evidence is clear that in a minimum of 211 cases husbands adopted children as soon as possible after marriage. One husband explicitly stated a desire to 'make the boy one of the family.'[106] Although from a feminist perspective the dependence of women and children on men was problematic, for unwed mothers themselves such outcomes were economically most advantageous. Other mothers were not so lucky.

Losing Custody to the State

Without adequate wages, day care, family support, affiliation orders, welfare, or a new relationship with another man, mothers who had initially kept their children could later easily find themselves in circumstances that precluded maintaining the family under one roof. Many children moved in and out of boarding homes or state care as the ebb and flow of economic circumstances dictated.[107] One mother, for example, placed her child first in a boarding home and then with the CAS while she awaited the arrival of her mother, a German citizen, who emigrated to Canada to care for the child while the mother worked to support the family.[108] Another mother worked in a series of low-paying jobs, with her child in the care of her landlady, for eighty-five weeks. When she lost her third job, however, and with the putative father having fled the jurisdiction, she released her baby for adoption, although she asserted that this occasioned 'great distress.'[109]

Even women who were successful in raising their children alone were haunted by the possibility that they would be forced to release them into the care of the state or lose custody involuntarily. One mother had received very limited payment under the order of the court. The putative father used every means possible to evade his obligations: 'Under oath, in court, he acknowledged paternity. Now, through his lawyer, he questions this. I cannot afford further counsel. I am trying desperately to keep our son.' The putative father continuously resisted payment: 'He (the representative of the CAS) will write two or three weeks after my letters. Two or three weeks after that Mr. M will reply. Possibly, two or three weeks from that time Mr. M will appear in court with another request, or reason or lame excuse. However, my son cannot be put in a suspended animation state. Every day he requires care.' The mother intermittently placed her boy with the CAS when funds were too tight for her to pay her landlady for childcare. The man ultimately returned to his legal wife and the court 'suspended the order on the basis that his wife resents him paying money for Miss M's child.' No other means of support, however, was provided for the mother, who lamented in a letter to the CAS in 1957, 'I'm haunted by bills even in my sleep ... Must I give up my son?'[110]

Not only were women encouraged to release their children for adoption immediately after birth to avoid such scenarios, but the CAS also had the power to deem any child left in their care as being neglected. In this context, leaving children, even temporarily, in CAS facilities was a last-resort option. To leave a child for too long, whatever the financial circumstances that dictated such a course of action, was to risk losing custody. Social workers routinely asked, 'How long does an agency continue a child in care before it decides enough is enough? At what point does it designate itself the child's advocate and try to secure an involuntary surrender from a mother?'[111] It was a 'vexing question' to determine at what point a parent who had left a child voluntarily in the care of the state 'may be considered to have deserted the child.'[112] It is clear, however, that in some cases CAS workers used the power of 'child protection' to remove illegitimate children from the custody of mothers who could simply not afford to support them, whatever the wishes of such parents. For example, one mother was described by the CAS as 'a girl of slightly sub-normal intelligence who is employed as a waitress and earns on average $9.50 per week from which she has made some contribution toward the support of her child. She has tried to interest relatives in G without success. Her mother is dead and there is no family home to which she can take him.' After three years, during which the mother consistently visited and attempted to pay for her child, the CAS sought ward action. They removed the child from the custody of the mother, not because she had been a disinterested or neglectful parent, but simply because 'this child is born out of wedlock and his mother is unable to maintain him.'[113]

Tragically, this was not an isolated case; a minimum of 67 of the 1,439 (4.7 per cent) never-married women who initially kept their children ultimately lost custody to the state. Such outcomes, importantly, were racially specific. Of 1,718 white, apparently Anglo-Saxon women, 17 (1 per cent) lost custody of their children to the state; all of these women had left their children in the care of the state intermittently due to poverty. Non-white, non-Anglo-Saxon women were subject to such tragic interference in their lives even when they did not resort to using state facilities in times of financial desperation. Black women and women of non-Anglo-Saxon descent were also at increased risk of being deemed unfit: of 14 women of colour, 4 (28.6 per cent) lost custody of their children to the state involuntarily; of 251 non-Anglo-Saxon women, 37 (14.7 per cent) lost custody of their children in this manner. Those at greatest risk of losing custody of their children, however, were Aboriginal women. In a pattern repeated across the nation, all 9 women in these files who were described as being of First Nations descent lost their custody of children when they were deemed 'unfit' mothers. These children were not adopted into families but placed in residential schools.

The case of one child, who was removed from her mother's home at the age of three, is illustrative. The mother was described by her CAS worker as having a 'history of immorality and consequent neglect of B. She is at present living immorally with one WW.' While for white women cohabitation might be viewed as the inevitable result of divorce being expensive and inaccessible and therefore was understood to provide evidence of stability in a mother's life, in this case cohabitation was constructed as immorality. One CAS worker was very forthright that the issue of race was directly connected to the perception that this mother was 'unintelligent, inadequate and incapable,' stating that 'these people [First Nations men and women] are none too reliable.'[114] At all stages of proceedings at the CAS, racism was rampant. The derogatory comments that were so common in the files about non-white women had ideological, as well as material, consequences. The 'good' mother was explicitly constructed as Anglo-Saxon, and these cases both reflected and reinforced such notions. (See fig. 5.2.)

The 'good' mother was constructed as not only being Anglo-Saxon

Figure 5.2: Outcomes of CAS custody hearings for mothers and children by race (%)

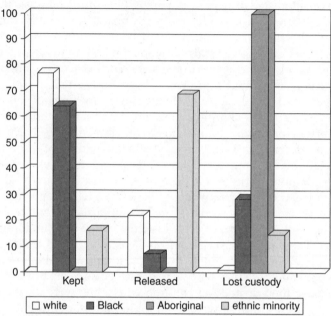

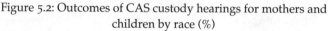

but also as not being poor. The fact that single unwed mothers remained poor, despite the passage of the *Children of Unmarried Parents Act*, had consequences beyond the material lives of those most intimately affected by the legislation. In fact, the ineffectiveness of the legislation ensured the circular nature of the stereotypes it embodied; single mothers were 'poor' mothers, figuratively and literally, and were therefore deserving of punishment and social denigration, not material aid. The poverty of unwed mothers, in turn, reinforced the emphasis on adoption in the CAS.

In the face of poverty and ostracism, single mothers struggled to make decent lives for themselves and their children. Their efforts should be respected. In a cogent critique of American social policy, Rose Bernstein described the barriers an unwed mother faced and still faces:

She may need public housing not because of some mysterious ingredient in her marital status, but because she cannot afford private housing. She

may need day-care services because, like many working and unsup-
ported mothers, her earnings do not allow her to provide adequate substi-
tute care for her child. She may need public assistance because, like other
poor people, her income is inadequate for her and her child's needs. She
may need a helping hand and emotional support because, like other solo
parents, she carries the burdens of parenting and homemaking unassisted.[115]

By blaming the unwed mother for the poverty in which she found
herself, society absolved itself from seeking solutions to the very real
problems that all single mothers faced and, at the same time, legitimated the adoption mandate. It also reinforced the sexual double standard and the discursive construction of the 'good' mother as Anglo-
Saxon, middle class, and legally married. Blame reflected and
entrenched an ideology which 'legitimate[d] women's dependency (on
men),'[116] yet, as the Children of Unmarried Parents Act case files illustrate, dependence on men was fragile and contingent, and collection of
child support from fathers was only viable when men had money. This
problem has not been eliminated. Margrit Eichler critiques current law
and argues that 'if further reform of the family law is proposed as a
solution to the problem of female and child poverty, we must ask ourselves what this avoids doing.'[117]

Generous state support was and is essential to the independent survival of single mothers; evidence of this fact, with which social workers
were routinely confronted in these cases, did not lead to improvement
in welfare provisions or increased sympathy for unwed mothers in the
offices of the CAS. Important family law reform, however, did emerge
from the Children of Unmarried Parents Act. The problems that illegitimacy created for the cohabiting mother were the subject of extensive
professional and public dialogue by the 1960s and contributed significantly to pressure for the liberalization of divorce law.

6

'Known as MRS S':
Cohabitation and the *Children of Unmarried Parents Act*

The majority of women who attempted to obtain child support through the *Children of Unmarried Parents Act* had lived with the fathers of their children in family units largely indistinguishable from married families. One journalist asserted in 1962 that 'nobody knows how many Canadians are involved in that type of conjugal relationship which doctrinaire Christians deplore as "living in sin."'[1] The *Children of Unmarried Parents Act* case files cannot answer the question of how many Ontario couples cohabited, but they do illustrate an extensive use of informal marriage as an alternative to divorce and remarriage within working-class communities. The cases provide important new evidence about the ways in which ordinary couples constituted and reconstituted family relations and evaded and challenged legal definitions of marriage. They also illustrate that women, and often the fathers of children as well, believed that cohabitation was equivalent to marriage. The law, however, did not support this belief.

Although social work journals, until the late 1950s, rarely discussed the plight of the informal wife, the mother in a once-functional family was treated differently in the offices of the CAS than was the single unwed woman. The informal wife was rarely disbelieved and, in the majority of cases, orders for child support were instituted against fathers. This, however, did not solve the problems of the woman and her family. Although fathers in these cases were much more likely to pay the support as ordered by the court than were men who had not cohabited with the mothers of their children, the act was nonetheless inadequate to meet the basic needs of women and children. The quantum of orders depended upon the means of the father, and many had obligations to legitimate families as well. Women who had lived in long-term marriage-like relationships were more likely than other single mothers to have multiple offspring, a fact that made sole support even more challenging. It is not surprising that many entered into new cohabitation relationships which, of course, were subject to the same potential insecurity as the relationships on which child support applications were based. By the 1960s, not only social workers but also the general public began to recognize the contradictions inherent in this situation, and an unforeseen result of the legislation of 1921 was to provide evidence of the need for divorce law reform.

Informal Wives, the Law, and Social Work

Evidence from the *Children of Unmarried Parents Act* case files clearly illustrates that 'cohabitation is not new ... [and was] most common amongst couples where at least one party had been married before.'[2] Although the particular concerns of cohabiting families were not explicitly referred to in the *Children of Unmarried Parents Act* and no separate provisions were made for such mothers, in practice, the majority of women who made use of the legislation were, in a functional sense, deserted or separated 'wives.' Of the 4,023 cases found, 2,031 involve couples who had been cohabiting at the time of conception. The proportion of cases involving cohabitation, moreover, did not vary significantly between decades or over time: cohabitation cases constituted (377 of 763) 49.4 per cent of the total cases extant for the 1920s; (435 of 853) 50.9 per cent of the cases for the 1930s; (399 of 805) 49.5 per cent of the cases in the 1940s; (484 of 951) 50.8 per cent of cases in the 1950s; and (328 of 651) 50.4 per cent of the cases extant for the 1960s.

Many couples had been cohabiting for a significant period of time. Although not all women stated the duration of their cohabitation relationships, for the 1,583 cases in which such information is extant, the average period of cohabitation before relationship breakdown was 7.7 years. The longest enduring cohabiting relationship found in these case files was an informal marriage that had lasted twenty-seven years before the 'husband' deserted with another woman. The mother was fifty-three years old. She had been previously married, but her legal husband had deserted her after only five years of marriage and she was left with the responsibility of caring for two young children. Within the first year after this desertion, she began cohabiting with the father of her illegitimate children; they had five children together, all of whom were known by the surname of their father. The two youngest children were under sixteen, and she sought, and received, support for them. The support ceased upon the children coming of age, however, so she faced a future of poverty.[3] Her story is illustrative in several ways: she was older, with multiple children, some of whom were born of legitimate relationships that preceded cohabitation, she was believed by the CAS and granted support, but she remained impoverished.

Contrary to the eugenic stereotype that 'unmarried mothers are mostly young, and they have previously been delinquent or immoral,'[4] cohabiting mothers were significantly older than non-cohabiting mothers, a fact that reflected their experience, not as previous delinquents, but as mothers who had often been legally married and who, during cohabitation, had been accepted in their communities as married. For cohabiting women, mean ages were 30 in the 1920s; 29 in the 1930s; 32 in the 1940s; 30 in the 1950s; and 28 in the 1960s.[5] The average age of women at first marriage in Canada in the 1920s and 1930s was 24.5 and 24.2, respectively; in the 1940s, 24.9; in the 1950s, 23.6; and in the 1960s, 22.6,[6] reflecting the fact that many of these women had previously been married.

The majority of cohabiting women not only were older but also had multiple children. In 843 of 2,031 cases (41.5 per cent) women had legitimate children from previous relationships; overwhelmingly, these children lived with their mothers in the relationship of cohabitation and were maintained, at least in part, by the new 'husband.' Not only did many women have legitimate children but also, not surprisingly, they produced multiple offspring during extended relationships of cohabitation. In 1,711 of 2,031 cases (84.2 per cent), women had more than one child born of the cohabitation relationship. Only 103 women (5.6 per cent) had one child (from all relationships). The average number of children per family (including legitimate and illegitimate offspring) declined over time from 4.2 in the 1920s to 3.7 in the 1960s (these numbers do not include the legitimate children that men had from relationships that pre-dated cohabitation); the largest family in this sample had eleven children, all but one of whom were illegitimate.[7] Not surprisingly, women expressed considerable concern about their ability to provide for multiple children.

It is clear from these case files that working-class couples entered into extralegal cohabitation as an explicit – and affordable – alternative to formal divorce and remarriage. In Ontario, until 1930, a divorce could only be obtained through a private member's bill in the federal Parliament, ensuring that it was effectively available only to the very wealthy. After 1930, couples could divorce through proceedings in the provincial divorce court, but fault requirements remained stringent in order to deter marital dissolution. Moreover, divorce remained prohibitively expensive and, without much property to protect or divide, many couples simply separated without legal sanction.[8] The evidence in these cases provides overwhelming support for the assertion of James Snell that 'the cost of divorce was high, and that alone was an insurmountable barrier for many people.'[9] Without the money to procure a divorce, often with young dependent children and without access to a living wage, it should not be surprising that women looked to cohabitation as a source of financial support and, one would assume, companionship.

By the 1950s there was some public acknowledgment that 'generally speaking, common law unions involve couples who don't marry because they can't, one or both of the parties involved already being married to someone else ... they are decent everyday people who find themselves trapped in impossible marriages from which there is no escape, and subsequently start living with another mate as a means of some kind of happiness.'[10] The case files vindicate these assertions. Women did not see themselves as rebels abandoning marriage and family but as excluded from formal marriage against their will and desire. In 875 of 2,031 cases, women could not marry because the men with whom they lived were legally married to someone else. In 932 of 2,031 cases, couples could not marry because the woman was still legally tied to her former husband. In only 219 of 2,031 cases, would marriage have been legally possible. (See fig. 6.1.)

Cohabitation was a reasonable response to marital breakdown in a context in which divorce was expensive and difficult to obtain and in which, for women with children, self-support was precarious. There is no evidence in these files to suggest that a significant number of women self-consciously rejected marriage. In fact, cohabiting women considered themselves to be married and often unabashedly assumed the title of Mrs and presented themselves to the community as legal wives. Women attended church and school functions, made friends in their communities, and lived ordinary lives; the legal ambiguity of

Figure 6.1: Marital status of cohabitants

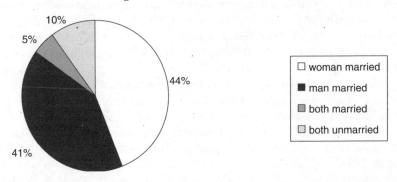

their relationships remained invisible as long as cohabitation continued. One minister wrote to the CAS, supporting the claim of a deserted
'wife' from his parish, that 'until they broke up, I had no idea that they
were not legally married.'[11]

In 735 of 2,031 cohabitation cases (36.2 per cent), evidence is extensive that women were known by the names of the men with whom
they had cohabited. Women repeatedly chastised CAS workers and
court officials for refusing to address them by their 'married' names: 'I
am known as *MRS. S* in Guelph, and it will cause embarrassment to
my children if you insist on addressing mail to me as Miss L.'[12]
Another mother wrote to the court to 'respectfully request that any
cheques be made out to me in the name of U rather than F as I have
been using and known by this name for 14 years, and my children also
use the surname U.'[13] During cohabitation most men also referred to
their partners as 'my wife.'[14] In 501 cases (24.7 per cent), men either
explicitly used this term in their discussions with the CAS or in written
documents that were provided as evidence of cohabitation by mothers.
Children also assumed the names of their fathers; in 1,123 cases (55.3
per cent), evidence is clear that children were so known. Cohabiting
women considered themselves to be married and therefore deserving
of the same aid and respect as any other deserted wife. The law, however, did not protect the interests of the informal wife.

The legal disadvantages of cohabitation became apparent when such
relationships ended, either through death or separation. Neither the
cohabiting wife, nor her children, had any rights intestate to the estate
of the husband/father. The cases adjudicated under the *Children of*

Unmarried Parents Act involved relationship dissolution, not death. Women in such circumstances, however, were equally vulnerable. Since cohabitation was not legally recognized, women were not able to divorce or to seek alimony and the *Deserted Wives and Children's Maintenance Act*, under which legally married women could apply for support without a formal divorce, did not apply to informal families. Women in informal marriages had no claim for personal support or alimony against 'husbands.' And support for children was not automatic but dependent upon a woman's ability to establish paternity through demeaning affiliation proceedings. The order, when granted, imposed obligations of support on the putative father, but it did not give him any status with regard to his child.[15] Neither did the child have any claim, beyond maintenance, against his or her father. By the 1950s these contradictions, and the problems that informal wives faced, were explicitly acknowledged in social work literature.

Before this time, however, social work journals were surprisingly silent about cohabitation. Stereotypes that erased the existence of the informal wife dominated discussions of unwed pregnancy and the rhetoric of individual pathology rendered invisible the fact that stringent divorce laws made cohabitation inevitable. Simplistic ideas about the etiology of out-of-wedlock pregnancy dominated professional and public discourse and social work and psychiatric literature condemned the unwed mother as young, unintelligent, delinquent, and maladjusted. These preconceived notions, however, did not in any way reflect the lived experience of cohabiting mothers. Ironically, in fact, cohabiting mothers often exhibited precisely the traits of 'restrained heterosexuality, domestic monogamy and honest motherhood'[16] that were so venerated in social work discourse. Although social work literature did not discuss the plight of informal wives, it was implicitly acknowledged that the 'delinquent girl' model of unwed pregnancy was inadequate to describe the circumstances of cohabiting mothers. As one author admitted when describing the sample with which he claimed to have proven that the average 'girl' pregnant out of wedlock was a sex delinquent, 'no cases were used in which the unmarried mother was living with the father of her child in a stable home and family relationship, since such cases frequently are actually a marriage in the true sense of the word and differ little or none from legal marriage situations.'[17]

This recognition that dominant social work ideas did not describe cohabiting mothers became explicit in the late 1950s. The language of judgment of the unwed mother was transformed in the post-war period and social workers described unwed mothers as very young, overly sexual, and psychologically disturbed:

> The commonest type of unmarried mother is the impulse ridden charac-
> ter. This is the childish, irresponsible, pleasure seeking girl who with little
> thought as to future implications yields to temptations ... her personality
> structure is flimsy and she is not capable of making adequate plans for
> herself or her baby.[18]

But such denigration of the unwed mother fit uneasily with evidence that cohabiting women had successfully raised children in stable home environments and had simply been unable to marry because of the cost of divorce. It was increasingly argued that cohabiting mothers were different: 'So here emerges the first clear subgroup among illegitimate children. Around 40% of them are born to couples living stably together but debarred from marrying by the still existing marriage of one or other partner.'[19] Such families were not decried as dysfunctional, but were particularly vulnerable to poverty in the case of relationship breakdown. As British social worker Virginia Wimperis admitted, the 'evidence we possess at present about the children of these unions is, on the whole, surprisingly encouraging ... [But] if the union should break down, the family is in a much less favorable position than a legal family.'[20]

Adoption was not to be advocated in cases in which mothers had proven themselves worthy and capable. Moreover, older and multiple children were difficult to place, even should social workers view an individual mother as less than competent. In a context in which 'helping the mother with her decision regarding plans for her baby, casework [was] generally geared to relinquishment,'[21] social workers were clearly not providing necessary services to the cohabiting mother. Although social work literature acknowledged the plight of the informal wife, solutions to her problems were rarely discussed. The *Children of Unmarried Parents Act* case files, however, provide extensive detail about the challenges that awaited the cohabiting mother after relationship breakdown.

Surviving Cohabitation Breakdown

Like non-cohabiting women, cohabiting women faced daunting challenges once they found themselves to be sole parents. They had to find the material means to support themselves and their children, and, simultaneously, they had to care for their dependent youngsters. They faced the prospect that wages for most women were inadequate to meet their day-to-day needs and those of their children, [22] and, unlike non-cohabiting mothers, they were likely to have been removed from the workforce for a significant period of time, as most had been house- wives while cohabiting. In going back to work, they also faced public denigration as working mothers were, in popular literature, scape- goats for many social problems. [23] Combining paid work with childcare was challenging, although the children of cohabiting women were often older than the babies born to non-cohabiting women and these mothers could rely on school, and sometimes older siblings, to provide childcare. They also relied on the wages of older children to aid in fam- ily support.

Of the 2,031 cohabiting women, only in 347 cases did mothers explic- itly state that they had been employed outside the home during their cohabitation relationships. In 467 cases, evidence with regard to employment was not extant in the case file. In the majority of cases, however, mothers asserted that they had been housewives and that they thought of childrearing and homecare as their full-time occupa- tions; 1,217 women – well over half – made this assertion. Women rec- ognized that finding paid employment was essential to their survival, but they found the prospect of job-hunting daunting. Mothers explic- itly told social workers that 'finding a job would be hard ... I haven't much experience since living with G.' [24] Another mother lamented, 'I am 45. What employer will want me?' [25] Mothers also expressed con- cern about the life change that employment would represent for chil- dren who were accustomed to having mothers in the home. As one mother put it, 'My boys have always known me at home ... who will care for them as I have?' [26]

Evidence suggests that women were correct in their assertion that work might be difficult to obtain for the older woman with limited experience and a long period of having been out of the workforce. While the majority of non-cohabiting women had little difficulty find- ing work in the exploitative female job ghettoes of the modern econ- omy, fewer cohabiting mothers reported paid employment within the first year after the breakdown of their cohabitation relationships. Of the 1,217 women who described themselves as housewives, only 311 found paid employment while under the supervision of the CAS. By way of contrast, of the 178 never-married women who had not been working when they became pregnant, but who kept their babies, eighty-three had paid employment by the time their children were one year old. For both groups of women, however, finding work that paid a living wage was almost impossible. Of the cohabiting women who were successful in finding employment, details of such work were recorded on the standard questionnaire in 392 cases. They worked in dead-end, poorly remunerated sectors of the economy – in factories, as secretaries, waitresses, laundresses, hospital aides, bank tellers, telephone operators, hairdressers, janitors, casual cleaners in private homes, and in retail.

The most notable difference between cohabiting mothers and noncohabiting women in terms of their employment choices is that only seven cohabiting mothers worked as domestic servants (all of them before the 1950s); in comparison, eighty never-married women found employment in this sector (again, largely before the 1950s). This undoubtedly reflected the fact that domestic service required women to live in, a requirement hard to reconcile with the obligations – and housing needs – of multiple children. Like non-cohabiting mothers, cohabiting mothers expressed frustration that they had limited earning potential in comparison to men. One mother asserted when angry that her former 'husband' was paying only part of the money owed to her under an order of the court, 'He earns twice what I do, I work as many hours and have the care of the kids besides ... why can he not pay? The children still need to eat and have a home.'[27]

For mothers who were employed, finding reliable childcare was challenging. Unlike young women who were still living at home when they became pregnant, cohabiting women could rarely return to their homes of origin after relationship breakdown. While 406 of 1,439 (28.2 per cent) non-cohabiting women who kept their children lived with their parents in the months immediately after the birth of children and another 206 (14.3 per cent) lived with married sisters, only thirty-seven of the 2,031 (1.8 per cent) cohabiting women returned to their homes of origin and a mere five found shelter with married siblings. Significantly, all but three of the forty-two women who were able to call upon their families in this way were among the minority of cohabiting mothers who had only one child. This suggests that for women with multiple children the number of dependants made it impossible for wider kin to provide housing and support. This is not surprising, given that families of origin were often already living in marginal economic circumstances. This also does not preclude the possibility that grandmothers and sisters might have provided informal help with childcare while women continued to live on their own with their children. In thirty-three cases, explicit mention was made by mothers of help of this nature being provided by families of origin.

More common, however, was women relying either upon the unpaid childcare work of older daughters so that mothers could seek employment or upon the paid labour of older children to supplement family income. Of the 658 cohabiting women who were employed immediately after relationship breakdown, 111 cited the childcare work of daughters, either full time or in the hours before and after school, as essential to their ability to balance the conflicting demands of paid employment and at-home motherhood. Mothers expressed some concern that such arrangements were fragile; as one mother asserted, 'My daughter wishes to marry, but who will care for my son?'[28] In another 203 cases, mothers cited the earnings of older children as essential components of the family budget. Some, however, were troubled by the obligations this imposed on children. 'My son (age 16) had to leave school,' lamented one mother. 'I had hoped for better for him.'[29]

In a context in which only 658 of 2,031 women were gainfully employed (and another 203 had employed older children), and in which co-residence with families of origin was rare, cohabiting women faced enormous fiscal challenges. A social worker in one case attested that 'the girl's rent is being paid by the city, but she is in debt and lacks necessary food etc. for the children. The children need clothing badly and she cannot get it on the money she has.'[30] In this context, the *Children of Unmarried Parents Act* was an important, if not entirely reliable, source of support.

Collecting Support: The *Children of Unmarried Parents Act*

Although in 103 of 2,031 cases (5.1 per cent) involving cohabitation the outcome of applications is unclear, evidence is strong that, unlike non-cohabiting mothers, cohabiting women were believed by social workers and were supported in their attempts to obtain child support from the fathers of their children. Women provided case workers with letters addressed to 'Mr and Mrs' and rental agreements signed by the mother and father to provide material evidence of cohabitation; they also brought friends and family, including older children, to the CAS offices to corroborate their stories. Only eighteen women of 2,031 (less than 1 per cent) who had cohabited with the fathers of their children were disbelieved at intake at the CAS. By contrast, of the 1,992 women who had not cohabited with the fathers of their children, 508 (25.5 per cent) saw their cases dismissed at intake. This means that of the 2,031 cases involving cohabitation, 2,013 advanced to the stage at which social workers initiated contact with the putative fathers.

Again, in stark contrast to cases not involving cohabitation, few cohabiting fathers disappeared in advance of service of notice by the CAS. While 401 of 1,992 men (20.1 per cent) who had not cohabited with the mothers of their children disappeared, only 42 of 2,031 men (2.1 per cent) who had cohabited with their 'wives' and children could not be located. Cohabiting men were older and had stronger ties to their communities and employment than did non-cohabiting fathers. They also had meaningful relationships with children with whom they had lived since infancy. Many of these men happily admitted to paternity; 1,242 of 2,031 men (61.2 per cent) admitted paternity and entered into agreements for child support. This contrasts starkly with men who had not lived with their children, only 291 of 1,992 of whom (14.6 per cent) admitted paternity (and 203 of these later recanted such admissions during court hearings).[31]

Significantly, moreover, when cohabiting men denied paternity they were not believed by social workers. Although 615 of 2,031 cohabiting men (30.2 per cent) denied paternity when interviewed informally by social workers at the CAS, in 543 of these cases, social workers disbelieved the denials of fathers. When CAS workers went to court on behalf of the 543 cohabiting women whose 'husbands' denied paternity, judges supported all such applications. In 72 of 2,031 cases (3.5 per cent), cohabiting women had their cases dismissed by the CAS when men denied paternity in informal interviews. Two of these women hired lawyers to challenge the decisions of the CAS and, of these, one was successful in obtaining child support. (See fig. 6.2.)

Of 2,031 cohabiting women who sought child support under the auspices of the *Children of Unmarried Parents Act*, therefore, 1,786 (87.9 per cent) were awarded child support either through an informal agreement with the putative father or via court proceedings. Of the non-cohabiting women who used the same mechanism to seek child support, only 133 of 1,992 (6.7 per cent) were awarded it. It is ironic, in this context, that no cases involving child support in cases of cohabitation appear in the law reports of the province for the entire period of 1921 to 1969. (See fig. 6.3.)

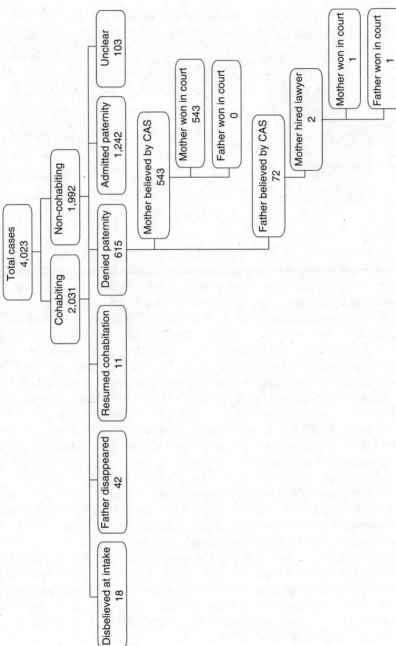

Figure 6.2: Outcomes in unreported cohabitation cases

Figure 6.3: CAS response in cohabitation cases

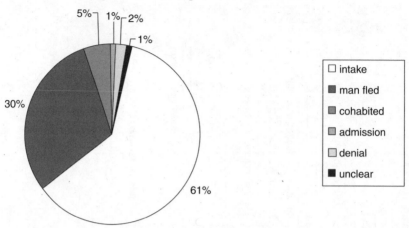

As women quickly learned, however, obtaining an award for support did not guarantee that money would be received. Despite the willingness of both the CAS and the court to support cohabiting women's applications, and despite the fact that most men admitted paternity, the effectiveness of the *Children of Unmarried Parents Act* was limited. As in cases involving non-cohabiting mothers, orders that were granted were based not on the needs of the mother and child, but on the father's 'ability to provide and prospective means.'[32] This undermined the purpose of the legislation in providing economic support for the illegitimate child and rendered the mother vulnerable. In a context in which many of these men worked in marginal occupations – and, perhaps more importantly – many already had legitimate wives, and sometimes children, to whom they owed support (and whose claim on the husband's income was always considered primary) – the amount of awards was usually insufficient to meet the needs of cohabiting women and their children. Furthermore, if a man's circumstances changed, or if he returned to a legal wife, married (in cases in which he was legally able to do so), lost his job, or if his means were reduced for some other legitimate reason, the award could be reduced or abrogated altogether. As was also the case with regard to non-cohabiting women, men could and did use non-payment, and the reluctance of the court to seek arrears, to vitiate awards. The policy of the court was to allow arrears to accumulate to a minimum of $100 before court action would be taken.[33]

In determining support orders, judges were to 'take into consideration the ability to provide and the prospective means of such father.'[34] In an attempt to protect the interests of children, the court came to assert that cohabitation was almost equivalent to marriage. For example, in 1953, Judge Helen Kinnear awarded a twenty-three-year-old waitress support for the two children born of an informal union. The father of the children, a painting contractor of considerable means, had returned to his legitimate wife and was supporting her, his three children aged twenty-two, nineteen, and eleven, and the illegitimate son of his twenty-two-year-old daughter. The judge asserted that the nature of the union was irrelevant to the question of support: 'The evidence clearly shows that if the child had been born in wedlock, he would have enjoyed a high standard of living. It shows too that the applicant is unable to support the child herself.'[35] In theory, this was an equitable way in which to determine support, and in practice, in this case, the unwed mother received significant ongoing support as the father of her children had a large and thriving business and did not wish to undermine his own standard of living by leaving the community.

For many mothers, however, the 'taking into consideration the ability to provide and the prospective means' of the father precluded the possibility of an award that would provide the mother with adequate means for survival. One father who consistently made payment for his three children came before the court requesting a reduction in the order (that had been made for $3 a week per child). He earned $71 a month, but paid $18 for his room, $16 for his board, $6 for transport to and from work, $2.12 for insurance (under which his former 'wife' and children were the beneficiaries), $3 for laundry, and $5 for tobacco. This left $19.88 per month, but under the order he was to pay $36 in support. Not surprisingly, the court reduced the award.[36] As the letter of one father illustrates, poverty often prevented payment, and not surprisingly, men placed priority on providing for women and children with whom they lived: 'Just how do you expect me to pay upkeep of that babby and also her bills. i have a wife and a little girl of my own to take care of ... $54 a week don't leave me very much to do it on ... but i meant to do my best for the babby.'[37] The amount of his payments was reduced, and he continued to provide intermittent support until the child reached the age of sixteen.

Not all men, however, were equally honourable, and some who had initially agreed to pay for children became frustrated with how the payments were affecting their standard of living and that of the fami-

lies with whom they were cohabiting. Over time, they either disappeared entirely or abused the leniency of the court with regard to
payment. For example, one father, whose new legal wife was pregnant, asserted in the court hearing that he could not afford support. He
argued that 'he loved his wife and didn't want her suffering for his
mistakes, and he could see no sense in depriving one more child, along
with the three that were before the court.' Shortly thereafter, without
making a single payment under the order, he fled the province, leaving
his informal 'wife' of seven years with the lone responsibility for their
three children.[38] Another mother expressed her frustration with the
marriage of the putative father (and the reduction in payments that the
court had allowed based on this marriage) by crashing his wedding
with the baby in her arms. He complained to the CAS that she continually phoned him at home and harassed him about payment, but they
expressed little sympathy for his plight. He was told that 'he should
carry out the agreement and catch up on the arrears and then if the
woman was still bothering him the Court might be able to do something about it.'[39] Instead, he disappeared.

Men could also evade payment by transferring legal ownership of
property into the hands of relatives. For example, a putative father
who had cohabited during a period of separation from his wife admitted paternity and was ordered to pay $15 a week in support. Later, rec-
onciled with his legal wife, he signed over all his property to his grown
son (it is perhaps noteworthy that it was not his wife whom he trusted
in this way) and deliberately remained unemployed. His rental prop-
erties earned an income of over $300 a month, but the property was no
longer his and the court was powerless to act. The unwed mother in
this case never received the money due under the order. The father
brazenly ignored the judge's inquiry as to when the transfer of property had occurred: 'Did you sign this property over subsequent to the
date that you were served to appear at this hearing?'[40]

As was the case with non-cohabiting mothers, fathers who wished to
evade payment had little difficulty in doing so by abandoning the
jurisdiction, placing property in the hands of trusted relatives, or simply refusing to send payments and waiting for the court to intervene to
enforce payment. The policy of the court not to enforce arrears until
they reached a total of over $100 ensured that 'husbands' could avoid
making payments. One mother asserted that her ex-'husband' paid
under the award only when summoned and threatened with jail: He
would 'send in a payment, stop, a reminding letter would be sent, and

then he would stop again ... the court waits to collect, but my children still need support.' Each time he appeared in court he paid the lowest amount the court would permit, and then would immediately stop paying the support again, waiting for arrears to mount and for further court appearances. The mother became increasingly frustrated and angry that she had to miss work (and not be paid) in order to give the same evidence over and over again against the father of her children. She noted that he 'enjoyed making it all a joke.'[41]

It was in this context that some mothers accepted lump-sum settlements in lieu of long-term support (and the hassles of collection that it entailed). One mother, for example, who had been granted an order of $7 a week in permanent maintenance, had received payment on only three occasions and each of these times only when her ex-'husband' was summoned to court. In total, in four years, she had received $210, less than one-fifth of the $1,456 due under the order during this time. Frustrated, she agreed to a full settlement of $1,200. She still did not receive the money owed to her and six months later agreed to a lump-sum settlement of $500. Although this man had consistently evaded payment by pleading poverty when summoned into court (which the mother had vehemently contested, stating that he had given all his property to the legal wife with whom he had reconciled), once the lump-sum payment was agreed upon, he immediately paid in full.[42]

While men had fiscal power, women could pressure them to pay support by threatening to withdraw access to their children. Cohabiting fathers were routinely informed that 'all children born out of wedlock belong entirely to the mother and the putative father has no rights at all in the matter.'[43] Mothers could use this control of access to encourage men to make payment as ordered by the court. One mother, for example, wrote to the father of her child, with the assistance of a social worker at the CAS:

> You have absolutely no rights of access to my children at any time or place. You are hereby requested to stay away from and do not watch and beset, molest, approach, come upon, annoy or accost my children in any way. Further, take warning that if you should fail to comply with the above request I shall immediately obtain judgment against you under the Criminal Code of Canada.

When he paid the child support due under the order, however, she reinstated his informal weekly visitations with their children.[44]

Men who knew their children and who were allowed to continue to be involved in their lives had a positive incentive for payment and a disincentive against leaving the jurisdiction; mothers who received payment regularly also had less reason to deny informal rights of visitation. It is striking that of the 877 women who were successful in collecting support (either in a partial but on-going manner or in full as ordered by the court), 657 (74.9 per cent) granted the fathers visitation rights. These men lived with the constant knowledge, however, that mothers had the right at any time to revoke their consent to visitation.

For some fathers, denial of access caused deep emotional suffering. For example, one father asserted in court, 'I am the father, I love that child.' He promised that he 'would work at washing dishes in order to help his child.' For eleven years he faithfully paid $7 a week for the child's support and visited him regularly. In 1966, however, when the boy was fourteen years old, the mother decided to move to the United States with her son. She was getting married and was unconcerned that the boy's father would not be able to afford the trip to see his child.[45] Another father wrote to the CAS asking what could be done to allow him access to his child. The mother was now cohabiting with someone else 'and has taught M to call Mr. M and recognize him as father and not to know me at all.' He was told that this was fully within her rights, and that he must nonetheless continue to make child support payments.[46] The sense of loss such fathers experienced was poignantly expressed by another man whose informal 'wife' had left him and who had been denied access to their son:

> At last I can say that the bitterness is over and I am now not anxious to see E but wish her well and compliment her and her family on the fine care they have taken of my precious son. I long for him every day and sincerely want what is best for him and hope that I can catch up on my back pay as soon as possible and arrange to see him soon ... I am doubly sure that I will never again make that mistake of bearing any children that can ever be taken away.[47]

This letter suggests that the father perceived catching up on his back pay and seeing his son again as interconnected events.

Paradoxically, access issues could also render women vulnerable. When men were abusive or domineering, women who used this tactic to collect money were forced to continue contact with fathers they would rather have dismissed from their lives (and from the lives of their children). One mother, for example, who had been repeatedly assaulted by her 'husband' before the breakdown of the cohabitation relationship, had hoped that access to the children would encourage their father to pay support. Instead, on three occasions she had to seek the help of the police to force the man to return the children to her custody, and on a further five occasions the police were summoned for her physical protection.[48] Violence was not an uncommon problem. A minimum of 197 of 2,031 (4.8 per cent) cohabiting women had been repeatedly assaulted by the fathers of their children and claimed that violence played a role in the breakup of their relationships. In one case, CAS workers went so far as to use a pseudonym for the mother in all correspondence because of the violence of her former partner. Her file was marked 'HER address to be kept CONFIDENTIAL,' and it was noted that he had twice attempted to murder her.[49]

Another mother enlisted the help of the CAS in forwarding a warning to her former partner: 'You have no legal right there and I must ask you to refrain from bothering Mrs. W or her children in any way, otherwise this may lead to a breach of the peace.' The man had been besetting the children at school, approaching the house in a drunken state, and threatening bodily harm to the mother and to their four children.[50] In a further case, the CAS wrote to a father explaining the conditions under which the mother had permitted access:

> Mrs. K has called us complaining about your coming to the home drunk in the middle of the night and expecting to see the children. Under no consideration could that be called reasonable access. Mrs. K does not have to allow you to see the children, but she is quite willing that you can have them if you come and get them and return them at a reasonable hour, that you do not drink when you are with them, and that you do not, for any reason, come into the house.

When he failed to comply with these conditions, threatening her and entering her home in a drunken state, she denied further access.[51] One mother explicitly pointed to the power that men claimed over women when they exercised access to children: 'He feels that he has a right to my person because he supports the children and his visits are in the main an effort to get to me and not to visit the children.'[52]

But denying access, even for reasons related to personal security, could result in men's refusal to continue to pay support. For example, one mother, who had a legitimate son by a previous marriage and a daughter born out of cohabitation, attempted to keep her family together. The relationship had ended because the man was abusive, but she tolerated ongoing drunken interference in her home in the hope that her ex-'husband' would thus pay support. Her social worker described her dilemma:

> This man comes to her home in an intoxicated state and she does not want him to do this. He annoys her landlady and puts her in an awkward position. If she allows him to see the baby for a short time he stays much longer. One night recently he hit this girl because she would not allow him in. At Christmas time he was very good and gave additional money for the baby and for her and her own son by marriage and she had the man for Xmas dinner to repay his assistance. However, he brought liquor to her home and was very drunk while there and she could not deal with him.

When, after too many such episodes, she denied him access to their child, he fled the province. She was caught in a no-win situation. She refused to allow him to see the child in order to protect herself and the baby from potential violence, but once he had been denied visitation rights the putative father lost interest in supporting his infant. The mother lacked the resources necessary to support two children on her own. By 1949, she had been forced to place her daughter in an Infant's Home. Her son went to summer camp while she worked, hoping to earn sufficient money to reclaim both children in the fall. In 1954, however, both children were made wards of the Children's Aid Society. This young mother had lost custody of her children solely because of her poverty.[53]

As this case illustrates, the sympathy of social workers for the plight of informal wives did not solve the material problems they faced in raising their children alone. Problems of collection were endemic under the *Children of Unmarried Parents Act*. Of the 1,786 cohabiting women who were awarded support, 274 (15.3 per cent) received the full support as awarded; 603 (33.7 per cent) received ongoing partial or intermittent payment (either because men had other obligations and/ or because they sought to evade orders); 405 (22.6 per cent) negotiated lump-sum settlements after long struggles to receive the support as awarded by the court; 390 (21.8 per cent) men disappeared after having made only minimal – or no – payments; 103 (5.8 per cent) men transferred property to a relative to evade payment; and in 11 cases the payment outcome is unclear. (See fig. 6.4.)

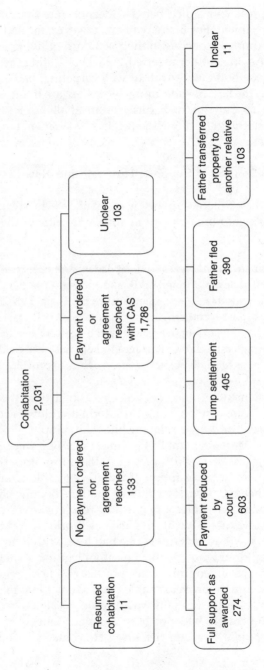

Figure 6.4: Payment outcomes in unreported cohabitation cases

This represents a much better collection rate than for women who had not cohabited. For many women, however, the end of cohabitation marked a dramatic decline in their standard of living and that of their children. As one mother asserted, while cohabiting 'her children lived in an $18,000 home with wall to wall carpeting, had a brand new car every year, the best of everything. Now they are living in an apartment and don't have any of the luxuries of life at all. I don't have money for food and clothing, let alone the niceties.'[54] Women, however, had limited options.

Other Sources of Support: The State and New Relationships

Few sources of state support were available to cohabiting mothers after relationship breakdown. In 1952, one critic of the law argued in *Chatelaine* that

> the Canadian Armed Forces paid dependents' allowances to common law wives and children during WWII, and there are common law 'widows' collecting pensions ... A common law wife is paid the federal family allowance ... In several provinces – Alberta, Saskatchewan, Manitoba and Alberta – a woman impoverished by the death of her unmarried mate may be granted mother's allowance to help raise her children, although regulations as to eligibility vary from province to province.[55]

Such supplements to income, however, other than the federal family allowance, were available only to informal widows; women who had been deserted or whose relationships had simply broken down were not eligible. Moreover, until 1956, informal wives were excluded under the *Ontario Mothers' Allowance Act*, the most important provincial mechanism for child support. In that year, following more than a decade of heated discussion, unwed mothers became eligible.[56]

This change was, at least in part, the result of adverse publicity generated by one case. During the Second World War, Marjery Pearson applied for a widow's pension. She had lived with John Dunn and they had two children who were technically illegitimate. Both Pearson and Dunn were estranged from legal spouses, and neither had money with which to secure divorces to enable them to enter into marriage. In 1943, after Dunn's death, Pearson was refused an allowance under the act because the couple had not been married. John Flett, a local judge, made the public aware of her case. 'He contacted labor, charity, and women's groups, threatened to print a booklet of articles supporting his position, and wrote letters to the premier, attorney-general, and other provincial notables.' Advocates of change were accused of seeking to 'bonus immorality.' In their defence they asserted that, in a context in which divorce was beyond the means of the average couple, 'the living together of two persons who could not get married is not always and necessarily immorality.'[57]

When Ontario's *Mothers' Allowance Act* was reformed, officials were careful to insist that 'the putative father is not to be relieved of his legal and financial responsibility.' The mother was required to visit the local CAS to attempt to procure payment from the father; until this was done, the mother did not become eligible for the allowance. As well, a two-year waiting period, specific to unwed mothers, was instituted, to ensure that the mother was 'fit' to care for the child.[58] Once they were officially eligible for the allowance, unwed mothers had to apply for such help and were often refused; within the first year of eligibility only 133 unwed mothers in the province received benefits.[59] Ironically, moreover, while in 1958 the two-year waiting period was abolished, unwed mothers with more than one child were simultaneously deemed to no longer be eligible for assistance, a fact that dramatically reduced the pool of formerly cohabiting women who were eligible for support under the legislation.[60] Not surprisingly, evidence from the case files suggests that few separated informal wives benefited from the amendments to the act. Of the 1,173 cohabiting mothers whose cases files are extant for the period after 1956, only 47 (4 per cent) can definitively be proven to have collected the Ontario mothers' allowance. Even for the lucky few, the allowance was inadequate to meet the basic needs of families.[61] Even mothers receiving maximum state support, therefore, were nonetheless obligated to work for wages. This is ironic, given that the original intent of the act had been to prevent worthy widows from being compelled to work outside the home for wages.

As was the case also for non-cohabiting mothers, municipal welfare was inadequate. Evidence from 311 case files involving cohabitation illustrates that a significant number of unwed mothers did receive some charitable or welfare assistance, but the detailed budgets they prepared for social workers confirm that while relief might prevent starvation, recipients were subjected to intense interrogation. Nor did the amount of welfare allow women – or their children – to escape poverty.[62] Although the application process for welfare was made less onerous in

1967 when the consolidation of category-based benefits was achieved in Ontario with the passage of the *Family Benefits Act*, maximum payments under the *Family Benefits Act* remained inadequate. Parsimonious welfare policies reinforced women's dependence on men.

Not surprisingly, after the dissolution of a cohabiting relationship, a woman's best route out of poverty was often to cohabit with someone else, either informally, or when possible, in legal marriage. Dependence on a man, however – as women who had experienced failed cohabitation relationships (and often failed marriages) knew – was a risky venture. A 'common-law relationship' imposed no obligation upon the new partner to support either the woman or her children. For many women who had previously cohabited, legal marriage was impossible as they were already married and unable to afford divorce. Despite its risks, it is not surprising that cohabitation was common: 503 of 2,031 cohabiting women (24.7 per cent) entered into new relationships of cohabitation while under the supervision of the CAS. Most expressed relief to CAS workers that new unions would allow their standard of living to improve and perhaps facilitate their return to former roles as housewives and full-time mothers.

For example, one separated woman lived for nine years with a lover who was twenty years her senior; he, too, was separated and had four children by his marriage. Their nine-year union produced two children, one born in 1946 and the other in 1948. In 1949 the relationship broke up. He claimed that the break-up was the result of interference on the part of her family; she asserted that she had told him to leave their home because of his heavy drinking and his resultant failure to support the children adequately. She was granted support at the rate of $7 a week, but by 1956 she had given up trying to collect the money that was owed to her. His failure to pay is not surprising given the reason she claimed had caused their separation. It is also instructive to note that she had entered into a new relationship of cohabitation. While she had cleaned houses to support herself and the children while on her own, she now once again referred to herself as a housewife and she was pregnant with the child of this union.[63] Her responsibility for the children of the union, his failure to provide child support, the low wages that she could earn in the job market, and the lack of state-funded alternatives to ensure the well-being of her children ensured not only her poverty but, ultimately, her dependency on a new man.

Another mother, separated from her lawful husband, had borne two children, one in 1950 and the other in 1954, in an informal union that lasted over twelve years. She eventually left her lover because he 'drank and beat both me and the kids.' Her husband, from whom she had been separated for three years before she entered into this relationship, obtained a divorce on the grounds of her adultery. She would not have been able to afford such proceedings herself, as she was a waitress and her earnings were meagre. Despite the fact that she was divorced, in 1965 she entered into a second informal union with a man with whom she worked. She did not marry him because he was separated but not divorced. Regardless of the informality of this relationship, the Children's Aid Society representatives referred to the man as her 'new husband ... a man well accepted by the family group,'[64] reflecting increasing acceptance of cohabitation as an institution in many ways equivalent to marriage. Ironically, new informal spouses were under no obligation to provide for illegitimate children not borne to them, nor were they required to support women should relationships fail in the future. Women, however, were at risk of bearing further illegitimate children during cohabitation.

For these reasons, whenever possible, women formalized new relationships through marriage. For women who were separated from lawful spouses but not divorced, however, serial cohabitation remained more common than remarriage. Only 204, or 10 per cent, of cohabiting women entered into legal marriages during the period of supervision by the CAS. Marriage provided women with greater security than did cohabitation. The legal husband was required to support his wife should the relationship break down in the future, and any children who might be born would be legitimate. However, the court was adamant that while husbands might be expected to play some role in the support of their wives' children, this responsibility remained primarily with putative fathers, ensuring that the problem of support for illegitimate children was not necessarily resolved through legal marriage.

CAS workers expressed concern that new husbands might resent illegitimate children and that requiring them to support children they had not fathered might impede happy marital relations. Their response to one man whose four children were living with his ex-partner and her new husband, and who therefore asserted that he should no longer be obligated to support the children, is illustrative:

That is not enough to keep one and yet the man has not paid. How can this woman keep four children on $10 a week in Toronto – that couldn't be done in China – defendant said that Mrs. I was married some time ago and he believed her present husband was willing to look after them ... Mrs. I's husband is not liable for the support of these children and it seemed that this defendant wanted to get out of his responsibilities completely ... How can this woman live happily with this man while asking him to support the children of another man?[65]

After receiving infrequent support from the father of the children, the mother accepted a lump-sum settlement of $700, a small fraction of the $5,200 that was due under the order. Although the putative father had claimed unemployment and poverty when summoned into court, when the settlement was agreed upon, he paid the sum in its entirety. Ironically, given the fears of the CAS, the woman's new husband wished to adopt the children and thereby take on formal responsibility for their care. The family was then reconstituted as a legitimate household.

Adoption by new husbands seems to have been common. Of the 204 once-cohabiting women who entered into legal marriage, 174 husbands formally adopted illegitimate children. The fact that 'even after an affiliation order the man [putative father] was still a stranger in law ... [who] had no rights to access to the child nor any other claim upon the child'[66] facilitated family formation because no impediment stood in the way of the new husband adopting the children. By the 1960s it was increasingly recognized, not only among social workers but also by the general public, that facilitating remarriage and the formalization of cohabitation relationships would offer needed protection to the vulnerable.

Changing Public Attitudes towards Cohabitation and Divorce

As early as the 1950s there was some public discussion of the challenges faced by informal wives. In a long and sympathetic article published in Chatelaine in 1952, a fictional description of the plight of one such woman was provided for Canadian (female) readers. The explicit intent of the article was to mobilize ordinary, caring Canadians to think about the problems inherent in stringent divorce laws and to encourage them to overcome the prejudices and moral censure that were applied to cohabitation. As the author wrote, it might be 'difficult for the average married woman who has gone through the familiar and orthodox pattern of courtship and marriage to imagine how an "ordinary girl" could become a common law wife. Yet the social workers with whom I talked told me of case after case,[67] which should arouse sympathy, not denigration. The circumstances 'of a girl we'll call Mary,'[68] described in the article, reflect closely the stories told by informal wives in the *Children of Unmarried Parents Act* cases:

Mary attended church regularly and taught Sunday school. When she was seventeen she took a bus to Toronto where she found a job as a waitress in a restaurant. A few weeks later she met Sam who was 21 and a truck driver and they were married shortly afterward. They set up housekeeping in one small room, where they had two children in two years. Sam didn't earn enough to support his family properly ... His drinking lost him his job, and they were forced to go on relief. In the summer of 1948 Sam went West to find a job on the wheat harvest. For a while he sent home part of his pay, but soon the money stopped and so did his letters. Mary placed her children in a day nursery and took a job once more as a waitress. She never heard from Sam again ... One day a man we'll call Mike Fennery, from Mary's home district, dropped into the restaurant. Mike – in his late thirties and employed as a bricklayer – began walking home with her from the restaurant in the evenings ... She began looking to him for companionship and protection, not only for herself, but for her children. One evening Mike told her that he loved her, and asked her if she would marry him after getting a divorce from Sam ... She knew that he would be able to give her children the type of home that she would never be able to afford. Mike bought a new bungalow and he took Mary out to see it one Sunday afternoon. She compared it with her shabby little room, and when Mike asked her to go and live with him there, pointing out the advantages there would be for the children, she accepted. She decided that as soon as it was possible she would sue Sam for divorce, but in the meantime she would live with Mike ... Today the Fennerys are respected members of their suburban community; Sam's children are known to their playmates as the Fennery kids, and Mary is the mother of two more children, proud of her clean and tidy home and her steady, hard-working 'husband.' She made a few half-hearted attempts to trace Sam at first, but soon gave it up, although she still talks occasionally of a future divorce and legal marriage with Mike.'[69]

A leading article published in 1961 in *Canadian Welfare* also explicitly pointed to the legal problems faced by separated young women who were forced into cohabitation by the inaccessibility of divorce proceedings. The author, Phyllis Haslam, contested what she deemed to be the common moral condemnation of the cohabiting woman and the public belief that there was no excuse for such women 'to live "common law."' 'Where,' she queried, would social workers or ordinary citizens 'suggest she live. Her husband was not supporting her. In the particular town where she lived she was not eligible for relief. She had no job ... So what would you do?'[70] In this context the plea for services for the cohabiting mother was transformed. While it was still asserted that 'social workers are long overdue in focusing their skill and their concern on the repeating unwed mother,'[71] reform of divorce law was now viewed as more important to the cohabiting mother than any programs that social workers might offer. Women were not, after all, lacking parenting skills, they were simply excluded from an institution that could provide them with protection and security.

Historians now recognize that 'one of the primary objectives of promoters of reform (of the divorce law) was to solve the problem of "stable illicit unions" by allowing persons whose marriage had irretrievably broken down to destroy the "empty legal shell" of that marriage, thus enabling such persons to give legal validity to their currently functioning relationship.'[73] The *Children of Unmarried Parents Act* was one of the primary mechanisms by which informal families engaged with the state, and the types of cases reviewed in this chapter provided important evidence that convinced social workers, and ultimately the public, that liberalization of the divorce laws was necessary, not because marriage was believed to be unimportant but in order to facilitate the formalization of existing, legally unrecognized, but stable, unions. Given the moralistic origins of reform, it is ironic that the most important long-term effect of the *Children of Unmarried Parents Act* was to encourage the liberalization of divorce law.

Conclusions

This study of the *Children of Unmarried Parents Act* adds new dimensions to our understanding of the origins – and limitations – of the Ontario welfare state. Importantly, the themes that emerge in this study – that unwed mothers were subjected to intense judgment and interrogation in the offices of the CAS, that the procedures mandated by the act were amorphous and amenable to extralegal regulation of young women, that the legislation failed as a child welfare measure, and that the treatment of mothers was sharply differentiated based upon the circumstances surrounding pregnancy – are not evident when reported cases are reviewed. The most basic assertion in this text is that formal law reports are an inadequate historical source with regard to quasi-legal proceedings such as those created under the *Children of Unmarried Parents Act*.

The case files produced by CAS workers, however, provide extensive detail supporting the assertion that non-cohabiting women were denigrated, disbelieved, and denied the means to support themselves, and their children, in decency. They were also, far too often, denied choice. The procedures gave extensive discretionary power to the Children's Aid Society. The *Legitimation Act*, the *Adoption Act*, and the *Children of Unmarried Parents Act* failed as child welfare legislation. As measures that regulated women's sexuality, however, the acts were successful. In fact, the acts both reflected and reinforced the discursive construction of the 'good' mother as Anglo-Saxon and legally married;

while her child might be considered worthy of social investment, the unmarried mother herself remained 'illegitimate.' The unwed mother – and her exclusion and poverty – continued to provide an object lesson in sexual ethics; legal marriage was an essential component of acceptable motherhood. In unforeseen ways, however, fractures and challenges to this discourse emerged. Indeed, ironically, given the moralistic origins of the child welfare package of 1921, the most important legacy of the *Children of Unmarried Parents Act* was to provide evidence of the need for divorce reform.

By the 1970s, attitudes towards illegitimate children were again under scrutiny. Echoing the attitudes of early-twentieth-century reformers, the Ontario Law Reform Commission argued in 1973 'the most common term is "illegitimate child" but we feel that this is unnecessarily opprobrious. If our recommendations are accepted the term will disappear from the language of the law, and ultimately, we hope, from common parlance.'[1] Affiliation proceedings were abolished on 31 March 1978,[2] and the designation 'illegitimate' was formally removed from Ontario law in 1980.[3] Since that time, the *Children of Unmarried Parents Act* has largely been forgotten. This, however, is unfortunate. The limitations of earlier legislation continue to reverberate through the present day: 'It is one thing to abolish the legal consequences of illegitimacy, and quite another to allow a person to take advantage of such abolition, for there remains the problem of establishing paternity.'[4] The *Children's Law Reform Act* sets out presumptions of paternity (based on cohabitation) and provides for the use of blood tests. It does nothing, however, to address the poverty of children for whom paternity is not established. Moral judgment of the unwed mother, and punishment of her child, continues. Deadbeat dads are castigated, but women who are sole parents 'by choice' remain 'illegitimate' and unworthy. The formal legal equality of the illegitimate child remains largely theoretical; children living in single-parent, female-headed households in this country continue to be poor, and poverty precludes true equality of social opportunity.[5]

The burdens of single parenthood are not inevitable or unchangeable, but are deliberately sustained by social policy. By exploring the regulation of unmarried mothers in a specific time and place, this book elucidates the contradictions evident when reformers express a desire to improve the social conditions of children but continue to condemn the mothers who bear them. A central assertion of this book is that the poverty of children will not be overcome unless the social conditions in which their mothers labour are addressed. The normalization of the two-parent household, the inequality of men's and women's wages, the inaccessibility of affordable childcare – these are the structural factors that condemn single mothers to poverty. Economic policy continues to function as a means of controlling the sexual behavior of women. As Sharon Hays writes, single mothers are 'effectively punished for having children out of wedlock or for getting divorced' and fear of poverty 'reinforce(s) all women's proper commitment to marriage and family.'[6] Moral judgments of mothers shaped the historical response to child poverty and these ideas have yet to be effectively challenged.

The solution to the problem of poor mother-led families is not 'making men pay' or forcing mothers to work in dead-end jobs, as the evidence from the *Children of Unmarried Parents Act* files attests; nor is it to force women into new relationships of dependence on men. Those who seek to reduce the costs of welfare are concerned, not with poor women's dependency, per se, but with their dependence on the government. They insist that women should be dependent, instead, on individual men. They abhor not the fact that poor single mothers are poor but that they are single. As the *Children of Unmarried Parents Act* cases illustrate, this concern, this obsession with so-called morality, has a long history. The study of the treatment of unwed mothers and their children should illustrate that privatizing the costs of reproduction represents an abdication of our communal responsibility to ensure the well-being of all children. It also denies women choice. In this context, this book is explicitly political in intent. It is hoped that by exploring the historical construction of ideas surrounding lone parenthood current misconceptions will also be challenged. Reform that seeks simultaneously to punish errant women, control female sexuality, and improve child welfare will not work. To eliminate child poverty, we must also make a social commitment to deconstructing the belief that mothers can be categorized as 'illegitimate' on the basis of their sexual behaviour.

Notes

Introduction

1 Joan Sangster, *Regulating Girls and Women: Sexuality, Family and the Law in Ontario, 1920–1960* (Toronto: Oxford University Press, 2001), 9.

2 Charlotte Whitton, 'Children's Rights and the Tax,' *Saturday Night*, 29 May 1943, 20.

3 *An Act Respecting the Legitimation of Children by the Subsequent Intermarriage of Their Parents*, S.O. 1921, c. 53.

4 *An Act Respecting the Adoption of Children*, S.O. 1921, c. 55.

5 *An Act for the Protection of the Children of Unmarried Parents*, S.O. 1921, c. 54.

6 Even in James Struthers' otherwise excellent study of welfare in Ontario, the acts merit a mere footnote as 'ineffective in extracting financial care for illegitimate children from putative fathers.' James Struthers, *The Limits of Affluence: Welfare in Ontario, 1920–1970* (Toronto: University of Toronto Press, 1994), 308n45.

7 There are two major exceptions to this, but both deal with the United States and not Canada: Regina Kunzel, *Fallen Women, Problem Girls: Unmarried Mothers and the Professionalization of Social Work, 1890–1945* (New Haven, CT: Yale University Press, 1993); and Rickie Solinger, *Wake Up Little Susie: Single Pregnancy and Race before Roe v. Wade* (New York: Routledge, 1992).

8 For the history of motherhood in Canada, see Katherine Arnup, *Education for Motherhood: Advice for Mothers in Twentieth-Century Canada* (Toronto: University of Toronto Press, 1994); Katherine Arnup, Andrée Lévesque,

and Ruth Roach Pierson, eds., *Delivering Motherhood: Maternal Ideologies and Practices in the Nineteenth and Twentieth Centuries* (London: Routledge, 1990); Andrée Lévesque, *Making and Breaking the Rules: Women in Quebec, 1919–1939*, trans. Yvonne M. Klein (Toronto: McClelland and Stewart, 1994); and Meg Luxton, *More Than a Labour of Love: Three Generations of Women's Work in the Home* (Toronto: Women's Press, 1980). For an insightful treatment of the impact of racism on ideas of motherhood, see Katrina Irving, *Immigrant Mothers: Narratives of Race and Maternity* (Urbana: University of Illinois Press, 2000).

 9 For the treatment of single mothers, within which there is little information on unwed mothers, see Linda Gordon, *Pitied But Not Entitled: Single Mothers and the History of Welfare, 1890–1935* (New York: Free Press, 1994); Nancy Dowd, 'Stigmatizing Single Parents,' *Harvard Women's Law Review* 18 (1995); Kathleen Kiernan, Hilary Land, and Jane Lewis, *Lone Motherhood in Twentieth-Century Britain: From Footnote to Front Page* (Oxford: Clarendon, 1998); Margaret Jane Hillyard Little, *No Car, No Radio, No Liquor Permit: The Moral Regulation of Single Mothers in Ontario, 1920–1997* (Toronto: Oxford University Press, 1998); and James Snell, *In the Shadow of the Law: Divorce in Canada, 1900–1939* (Toronto: University of Toronto Press, 1991).

10 Joel Braslow, *Mental Ills and Bodily Cures: Psychiatric Treatment in the First Half of the Twentieth Century* (Berkeley: University of California Press, 1997), 9. Case files, as Karen Tice asserts in her exploration of the textual politics of case file construction, played an important role in establishing the legitimacy of social work as a profession. See Karen Tice, *Tales of Wayward Girls and Immoral Women: Case Records and the Professionalization of Social Work* (Urbana: University of Illinois Press, 1998).

11 Little, *No Car, No Radio, No Liquor Permit*, xxii.

12 For an excellent defense of the use of such sources, despite their limitations, see Linda Gordon, 'Review of *Gender and the Politics of History*,' and Linda Gordon, 'Response to Joan Wallach Scott.' The limitations of such sources are detailed in Joan Wallach Scott, 'Review of *Heroes of their Own Lives*,' and Joan Wallach Scott, 'Response to Linda Gordon.' All of these reviews are to be found in *Signs* 15(4) (Summer 1990). See also Kathleen Canning, 'Feminist History after the Linguistic Turn: Historicizing Discourse and Experience,' *Signs* 19(2) (1992), 368–404.

13 Sangster, *Regulating Girls and Women*, 14.

14 Franca Iacovetta and Wendy Mitchinson, eds., *On the Case: Explorations in Social History* (Toronto: University of Toronto Press, 1998), 9.

15 Simple direct social control cannot be read from these files. Women contested expert definitions of themselves in a context in which they were dis-

empowered. For a discussion of critical (revisionist) social control theory,
see Stanley Cohen, 'The Critical Discourse on "Social Control": Notes on
the Concept as a Hammer,' *International Journal of the Sociology of Law* 17
(1989), 347–57; Dorothy Chunn and Shelly Gavigan, 'Social Control: Analytical Tool or Analytical Quagmire?' *Contemporary Crises* 12 (1988), 107–24;
and Dawn Currie, 'Feminist Encounters with Postmodernism: Exploring
the Impasse of Debates on Patriarchy and Law,' *Canadian Journal of Women
and the Law* 5 (1992), 63–86.

16 Regina Kunzel, 'White Neurosis, Black Pathology: Constructing Out-of-
Wedlock Pregnancy in the Wartime and Postwar United States,' in Joanne
Meyerowitz, ed., *Not June Cleaver: Women and Gender in Postwar America,
1945–1960* (Philadelphia: Temple University Press, 1994), 322.

17 Karen Dubinsky, 'Afterword: Telling Stories About Dead People,' in Iacovetta and Mitchinson, eds., *On the Case*, 364.

18 It should be noted that parallel fears existed in Quebec, but are not the subject of this study.

19 Women did have access to the birth control pill through family physicians
before this time, but such access was discretionary and uneven: Angus
McLaren, 'Birth Control and Abortion in Canada, 1870–1920,' *Canadian Historical Review* 59 (1978), 319–40.

20 *Child Welfare Act*, S.O. 1965, c. 14, s. 12. For further discussion of the funding
provided to the CAS, see N. Trocme, 'Child Welfare Services,' in R. Barnhorst and L. Johnson, eds., *The State of the Child in Ontario* (Toronto: Oxford
University Press, 1991).

21 *Re Mugford*, [1970] 1 O.R. 601–611 at 601.

22 Diana Dzwiekowski, 'Casenotes: Findings of Paternity in Ontario, *Sayer v.
Rollin*,' *Canadian Journal of Family Law* 3 (1980), 318–26. Instead, fathers can
now sign voluntary declarations of paternity, or mothers can require blood
tests of them.

23 *Family Law Reform Act*, R.S.O. 1980, c. 152, s. 1(a).

24 Veronica Strong-Boag, 'Wages for Housework: Mothers' Allowance and
the Beginnings of Social Security in Canada,' *Journal of Canadian Studies*
14(1) (Spring 1979), 25.

25 Similar findings apply in the context of the United States. As Linda Gordon
asserts, two groups of women bore children out of wedlock, 'never-married
women, often girls, who had become pregnant and had neither an abortion
nor a marriage ... [and] older women, often married and separated, who
often had some legitimate children.' See Gordon, *Pitied But Not Entitled*, 22.

26 Leontine Young, *Out of Wedlock: A Study of the Unmarried Mother and Her
Child* (New York: McGraw-Hill, 1954), 160.

27 Ibid., 147.
28 AO, Wentworth, Box 66-3-3-14, Case 233, 1955.

1: 'Such a Program of Legislation'

1 Karen Balcom, 'Scandal and Social Policy: The Ideal Maternity Home and the Evolution of Social Policy in Nova Scotia, 1940–1951,' *Acadiensis* 31(2) (Spring 2002), 6.
2 William Blackstone, *Commentaries on the Laws of England*, vol. 2 (London: Kerr, 1857), 485.
3 Jenny Teichman, *The Meaning of Illegitimacy* (Cambridge, UK: Englehardt, 1978), 83.
4 Roxanne Mykitiuk, 'Beyond Conception: Legal Determinations of Filiation in the Context of Assisted Reproductive Technologies,' *Osgoode Hall Law Journal* 39 (2001), 782.
5 The husband/father had exclusive right to custody, guardianship, discipline, and control over education and religion. The married woman had no legal rights whatsoever to her child. Blackstone, *Commentaries on the Laws of England*, vol. 2. It was also presumed that any child born to the wife of a married man was legitimate unless evidence showed that he had not had access to his wife throughout the period relevant to conception. *The King v. Luffe*, 103 English Reports, 316 (King's Bench, 1807). Mary Louise Fellows argues that the law's failure to consider any alternatives to the legitimate/illegitimate dichotomy is explained by the fact that such alternatives would constitute a public acknowledgement that a husband had lost sexual control of his wife. See Mary Louise Fellows, 'The Law of Legitimacy: An Instrument of Procreative Power,' *Columbia Journal of Gender and the Law* 3(2) (1993), 508.
6 *An Act for Setting the Poor on Work*, 1576, 18 Elizabeth, c. 3.
7 Alan MacFarlane, 'Illegitimacy and Illegitimates in English History,' in Peter Laslett, Karla Osterveen, and Richard Smith, eds., *Bastardy and Its Comparative History* (London: Edward Arnold Publishers, 1980), 75; Harry D. Krause, *Illegitimacy: Law and Social Policy* (New York: The Bobbs-Merrill Company, 1971).
8 Martha Bailey, 'Servant Girls and Masters: The Tort of Seduction and the Support of Bastards,' *Canadian Journal of Family Law* 10 (1991), 150–1.
9 Ibid., 151.
10 Ibid., 152.
11 Robert Thomas Malthus, *An Essay on the Principles of Population* (1798), edited by Geoffrey Gilbert (Oxford: Oxford University Press, 1993). For a

detailed discussion of Malthus's arguments, see Mitchell Dean, *The Consti-tution of Poverty: Towards a Genealogy of Liberal Governance* (London: Rout-ledge, 1991); and Mary Jacobus, 'Malthus, Matricide and the Marquis de Sade,' in *First Things: The Maternal Imaginary in Literature, Art and Psycho-analysis* (New York: Routledge, 1995).

12 See Russell Smandych, 'Colonial Welfare Law and Practices: Coping With-out and English Poor Law in Upper Canada, 1792–1837,' in Louis Knafla and Susan Binnie, eds., *Law, Society, and the State: Essays in Modern Legal History* (Toronto: University of Toronto Press, 1995), 214–46.

13 Perhaps because women had so few options, rates of infanticide in the col-ony were believed to be high. Despite official condemnation, the response of jurors to women charged with infanticide was surprisingly lenient, sug-gesting that the lack of options for unwed mothers aroused some sympa-thy. See Constance Backhouse, *Petticoats and Prejudice: Women and Law in Nineteenth Century Canada* (Toronto: Women's Press, 1991); and Constance Backhouse, 'Desperate Women and Compassionate Courts: Nineteenth-Century Infanticide in Canada,' *University of Toronto Law Journal* 34 (1984), 447–78.

14 Constance Backhouse, 'The Tort of Seduction: Fathers and Daughters in Nineteenth-Century Canada,' *Dalhousie Law Journal* 10 (1986), 45–80.

15 Dean P. Ramsay, 'The Development of Child Legislation in Ontario' (MA thesis, Toronto School of Social Work, 1949). Religiously run homes for unwed mothers also existed in Toronto during this period, but not in the smaller communities around the province, making their services inaccessi-ble for many young women. Moreover, such institutions charged for their services. Not only were residents subjected to religious indoctrination but also they owed their labour to the rescue home. Religiously run homes had the right to exclude those they did not think would be amenable to salvation.

16 For a full discussion of this issue in the American context, see Viviana Zelizer, *Pricing the Priceless Child: The Changing Social Value of Children* (New York: Basic Books, 1985), 173.

17 *Statutes of Upper Canada*, 1834, 7 William IV, c. 8. The mother had to swear an affidavit as to the child's paternity within six months of its birth. See Peter Ward, 'Unwed Mothers in Nineteenth-Century English Canada,' *Canadian Historical Association Historical Papers* (1981), 41.

18 The first part of the act amended the common law by making it possible for a father to sue his daughter's employer for the daughter's seduction. Previ-ously, only an employer had been able to sue someone who had seduced, and rendered unproductive through pregnancy, a woman in his employ. In

1877, the two parts of the original statute were severed. The civil remedy remained and a new criminal offence of seduction was created. Seduction legislation was controversial with commentators arguing that it provided women with unprecedented opportunity to blackmail men. This remedy was available only to a woman of previously chaste character. Ontario's *Seduction Act* was repealed in 1978. See Bailey, 'Servant Girls and Masters,' 154; Backhouse, 'The Tort of Seduction'; and Patrick Brode, *Courted and Abandoned: Seduction in Canadian Law* (Toronto: University of Toronto Press/The Osgoode Society for Canadian Legal History, 2002).

19 For further information on the child welfare movement, see Andrew Jones and Leonard Rutman, *In the Children's Aid: J.J. Kelso and Child Welfare in Ontario* (Toronto: University of Toronto Press, 1987); Joy Parr, *Labouring Children: British Immigrant Apprentices to Canada, 1869–1924* (Montreal: McGill-Queen's University Press, 1980); Joy Parr, ed., *Childhood and Family in Canadian History* (Toronto: McClelland and Stewart, 1982); Neil Sutherland, *Children in English-Canadian Society: Framing the Twentieth-Century Consensus* (Toronto: University of Toronto Press, 1976); and Neil Sutherland, *Growing Up: Childhood in English Canada from the Great War to the Age of Television* (Toronto: University of Toronto Press, 1997).

20 C.S. Walters, Mayor of Hamilton, 'The Duty of the City to the Child,' *Public Health Journal* 6 (1915), 540. One Canadian estimate declared that only 36 per cent of those examined for service were found to be physically fit, with 31 per cent unsound and 10 per cent 'absolutely no good.' Editorial, 'Social Hygiene,' *Social Welfare* 7 (1924), 48. During the period of the *Military Services Act*, 68 per cent of the men called up were rejected for overseas service as they were deemed unfit. H.E. Spencer, 'For a Healthy Canada,' *Chatelaine*, March 1930, 50.

21 Anna Davin, 'Imperialism and Motherhood,' *History Workshop Journal* 5 (Spring 1978), 12. Fears of race suicide and heightening controls on the dissemination of birth control also provided incentive for the improvement of the economic and health status of infants. Images of babies and soldiers were interwoven in the public health discourse of the war and immediate post-war periods. See Cynthia Abelle, 'The Infant Soldier: The Great War and the Medical Campaign for Child Welfare,' *Canadian Bulletin of Medical History* 5(2) (1988), 99–119. The price of public health advancements, for women, was compulsory marital motherhood. For information on birth control and abortion see Constance Backhouse, 'Involuntary Motherhood: Abortion, Birth Control and the Law in Nineteenth-Century Canada,' *Windsor Yearbook of Access to Justice* 3 (1983), 61–130; Linda Gordon, *Woman's Body, Woman's Right: A History of Birth Control in America* (New

York: Penguin, 1976); Angus McLaren, *Birth Control in Nineteenth-Century England* (London: Holmes and Meier, 1978); and Angus McLaren and Arlene Tigar McLaren, *The Bedroom and the State: Changing Practices and Politics of Contraception and Abortion in Canada 1880–1980* (Toronto: McClelland and Stewart, 1986).

22 Ethel M. Chapman, 'Could You Adopt a Baby?' *Maclean's*, December 1919, 116.

23 For further information, see John Bullen, 'J.J. Kelso and the "New" Child-Savers: The Genesis of the Children's Aid Society Movement in Ontario,' *Ontario History* 82(2) (June 1990), 107–28.

24 AO, Helen MacMurchy, *Infant Mortality* (1910), 30. MacMurchy served as Ontario's inspector of the feeble-minded (1906–18); assistant inspector of hospitals, prisons, and public charities (1913–20); investigator of infant mortality (1910–12); and inspector of auxiliary classes for the Ontario Department of Education (1915–20). In 1920 she was appointed chief of the Child Welfare Division of the federal Department of Health, a position she held until her retirement in 1934 at age seventy-two. She was also very active in the volunteer community, including the Toronto Local Council of Women, and was extremely important in promoting public health measures for the benefit of babies. Her views were, in many ways, conservative. For example, she opposed women with children working outside the home. She also, despite her concerns about infant mortality and the declining marital birth rate, endorsed eugenic sterilization of the 'unfit.' For a detailed discussion of the contradictions in MacMurchy's thought and an assessment of her achievements and influence, see Katherine Arnup, *Education for Motherhood: Advice for Mothers in Twentieth-Century Canada* (Toronto: University of Toronto Press, 1994); Cynthia Comacchio, *Nations Are Built of Babies: Saving Ontario's Mothers and Children, 1900–1940* (Montreal: McGill-Queen's University Press, 1993); Dianne Dodd, 'Helen MacMurchy, MD: Gender and Professional Conflict in the Medical Inspection of Toronto Schools, 1910–1911,' *Ontario History* 93(2) (Autumn 2001), 127–49; Diane Dodd, 'Advice to Parents: The Blue Books, Helen MacMurchy MD, and the Federal Department of Health, 1920–1934,' *Canadian Bulletin of Medical History* 8 (1991), 203–30; Kathleen McConnachie, 'Methodology in the Study of Women in History: A Case History of Helen MacMurchy, MD,' *Ontario History* 75 (March 1983), 61–87; Angus McLaren, *Our Own Master Race: Eugenics in Canada, 1885–1945* (Toronto: McClelland and Stewart, 1990); and Mariana Valverde, 'When the Mother of the Race Is Free,' in Franca Iacovetta and Mariana Valverde, eds., *Gender Conflicts: New Essays in Women's History* (Toronto: University of Toronto Press, 1992), 3–26.

25 Alan Brown, 'Infant and Child Welfare Work,' *Public Health Journal* 9 (April 1918), 145.
26 For detailed discussions of health and housing conditions in the early twentieth century, see Paul A. Bator, 'Saving Lives on [the] Wholesale Plan: Public Health Reform in the City of Toronto, 1900–1930' (PhD diss., University of Toronto, 1979); Paul A. Bator, 'The Struggle to Raise the Lower Classes: Public Health Reform and the Problem of Poverty in Toronto, 1910–1921,' *Journal of Canadian Studies* 14(1) (Spring 1979), 43–9; Terry Copp, *The Anatomy of Poverty* (Toronto: McClelland and Stewart, 1973); and Michael Piva, *The Condition of the Working Class in Toronto, 1900–1921* (Ottawa: University of Ottawa Press, 1979). For discussions of the public health movement, and its focus on children, see Catherine Lesley Biggs, 'The Response to Maternal Mortality in Ontario, 1920–1940' (MSc thesis, University of Toronto, 1983); Terry Crowley, 'Madonnas before Magdalenes: Adelaide Hoodless and the Making of the Canadian Gibson Girl,' *Canadian Historical Review* 67 (1986), 520–47; Janice Dickins McGinnis, 'From Health to Welfare: The Development of Federal Government Policy Regarding Standards for Public Health for Canadians, 1919–1945' (PhD diss., University of Alberta, 1980).
27 Richard Allen, *The Social Passion: Religion and Social Reform in Canada, 1914–1928* (Toronto: University of Toronto Press, 1971); Nancy Christie and Michael Gauvreau, *A Full-Orbed Christianity: The Protestant Churches and Social Welfare in Canada, 1900–1940* (Montreal: McGill-Queen's University Press, 1996); and Ramsay Cook, *The Regenerators: Social Criticism in Late-Victorian English Canada* (Toronto: University of Toronto Press, 1985).
28 The racism of many early Christian-inspired feminists and social reformers is well articulated by Mariana Valverde, 'When the Mother of the Race is Free,' 3–26.
29 Editorial, 'These Little Ones,' *Social Welfare* 1 (1918), 53. This echoed American 'scientific' strategies towards reducing infant deaths, see Richard Meckel, *Save the Babies: American Public Health Reform and the Prevention of Infant Mortality, 1850–1929* (Baltimore: Johns Hopkins University Press, 1990), 100.
30 Editorial, 'Infant Mortality,' *Public Health Journal* 6 (1915), 510.
31 See Nancy Christie, *Engendering the State: Family, Work and Welfare in Canada* (Toronto: University of Toronto Press, 2000).
32 AO, RG 7, 'Mothers' Allowance Investigation, Ontario, 1920,' 16.
33 On the rise of mandatory schooling, see Alison Prentice and Susan Houston, eds., *Family, School and Society in Nineteenth-Century Canada* (Toronto: Oxford University Press, 1975).

34 Helen MacMurchy, for example, went so far as to assert that 'institutions for infants are not the best solution to the problem of infant mortality among the poor, deserted and unfortunate. They have been established by the best and kindest people, and with the best intentions; but when they take the baby away from the mother, they sign the baby's death warrant.' MacMurchy, *Infant Mortality* (1910), 15–16. However, she did not advocate leaving vulnerable children with mothers who would not raise them well and by definition unwed mothers fit this category. Babies should be nourished with their mothers' milk for the first six to nine months of life and then they should be, in her estimation, released for adoption. The biological mother was only necessary in this equation because 'mother's milk is the only really safe food for baby.' Ibid., 5.

35 Peter Bryce, 'Mothers' Allowances,' *Social Welfare* 1(6) (1925), 131. See also Bator, 'Saving Lives on [the] Wholesale Plan'; Peter Bryce, 'Saving Canadians from the Degeneracy Due to Industrialism in Cities of Older Civilizations,' *Public Health Journal* 3(12) (December 1912), 686–92; and Heather MacDougall, 'Enlightening the Public: The Views and Values of the Association of Public Health Officers of Ontario 1886–1903,' in Charles Roland, ed., *Health, Disease and Medicine: Essays in Canadian History* (Toronto: Clarke Irwin and the Hannah Institute for the History of Medicine, 1984), 436–64.

36 James Struthers argues that 'the anomaly of orphanages providing care principally to children with living parents who, but for financial necessity, wished to keep their families intact, was a growing mockery of the sanctity of motherhood, home and family life,' in *The Limits of Affluence: Welfare in Ontario, 1920–1970* (Toronto: University of Toronto Press, 1994), 23.

37 In this context, support grew for a system of boarding out, or fostering, of children. See Toronto Children's Aid Society, 'History of the Children's Aid Society of Metropolitan Toronto' (23 January 1975).

38 AO, RG 7, report by Dr Bruce Smith, 'Memo on Mothers' Pensions,' 13 April 1917.

39 Desmond Morton, *Fight or Pay: Soldiers' Families in the Great War* (Vancouver: UBC Press, 2004), 38.

40 As cited in Margaret McCallum, 'Assistance to Veterans and Their Dependents: Steps on the Way to the Administrative State, 1914–1929,' in W. Wesley Pue and Barry Wright, eds., *Canadian Perspectives on Law and Society: Issues in Legal History* (Ottawa: Carleton University Press, 1988), 160. See also, Theda Skocpol, *Protecting Soldiers and Mothers: The Political Origins of Social Policy in the United States* (Cambridge, MA: Harvard University Press, 1992).

41 Interestingly, however, married women without children were denied support and had to go out and seek employment in order to replace the male wage. For a further discussion of these issues, see Christie, *Engendering the State*.

42 Susan Pedersen, 'Gender, Welfare and Citizenship in Britain during the Great War,' *American Historical Review* 95 (October 1990), 1004.

43 For a detailed discussion of these policies, see McCallum, 'Assistance to Veterans and Their Dependents,' 157–77; and Morton, *Fight or Pay*, 31–7.

44 Morton, *Fight or Pay*, 39. Such liberalism, however, had limitations. Where there were two claims against a man, one from a legitimate wife and the other from a relationship of cohabitation, the fund always gave precedent to the legal wife. Ibid., 99–100.

45 McCallum, 'Assistance to Veterans and Their Dependents,' 165.

46 Canada, House of Commons *Debates* at 4284–4285 (28 June 1919) as quoted in McCallum, 'Assistance to Veterans and Their Dependents,' 165.

47 PC 2615, NAC, RG 24, Box 1252, HQ 593-1-82, 112, as quoted in Morton, *Fight or Pay*, 39.

48 McLaren, *Birth Control in Nineteenth-Century England;* and McLaren and Tigar McLaren, *The Bedroom and the State*.

49 On the eugenics movement in Canada, see Ian Dowbiggin, *Keeping America Sane: Psychiatry and Eugenics in the United States and Canada* (Ithaca, NY: Cornell University Press, 1997); Kathleen McConnachie, 'Science and Ideology: The Mental Hygiene and Eugenics Movements in the Inter-War Years, 1919–1939' (PhD diss., University of Toronto, 1987); McLaren, *Our Own Master Race*; and Peter Ward, *White Canada Forever: Popular Attitudes and Public Policy Towards Orientals in British Columbia* (Montreal: McGill-Queen's University Press, 1990).

50 On the need for training for motherhood and the racist and classist implications of such rhetoric, see Arnup, *Education for Motherhood;* Commachio, *Nations Are Built of Babies;* and Cynthia Comacchio, *The Infinite Bonds of Family: Domesticity in Canada, 1850–1940* (Toronto: University of Toronto Press, 1999).

51 J.J. Kelso, *Ontario Educational Association Yearbook 1900*, 353.

52 For an extended discussion of an education for Italian-Canadian mothers in the post-war period which addresses these issues, see Franca Iacovetta, 'Making "New Canadians": Social Workers, Women and the Reshaping of Immigrant Families,' in Iacovetta and Valverde, eds., *Gender Conflicts*, 261–303.

53 U.S. Children's Bureau, *Illegitimacy as a Child Welfare Problem* (Washington DC: n.p., 1920), 35.

54 Wayne Carp, 'Professional Social Workers, Adoption and the Problem of Illegitimacy, 1915–1945,' *Journal of Policy History* 6(3) (1994), 166.

55 Ernst Freund, 'The Present Law Concerning Children Born Out of Wedlock and Possible Changes in Legislation,' in U.S. Children's Bureau, *Standards of Legal Protection for Children Born Out of Wedlock: A Report of Regional Conferences Held under the Auspices of the U.S. Children's Bureau* (Washington DC: n.p., 1921), 33.

56 Bryce, 'Mothers' Allowances,' 131.

57 It is clear that during both the First and Second World Wars rates of illegitimacy rose throughout Canada, the United States, and Britain. What is less clear, however, is whether or not such births reflected an increase in premarital sexual activity. With the separations imposed by war, the percentage of conceptions legitimated by marriage decreased. This may also have been a factor in the passage of the *Legitimation Act*. At least in Great Britain, after the war, rates of premarital conception rose as illegitimacy rates fell. See Kathleen Kiernan, Hiliar Land, and Jane Lewis, *Lone Motherhood in Twentieth-Century Britain: From Footnote to Front Page* (Oxford: Clarendon, 1998), 27. The extent of concern about illegitimacy, sexuality, and social ills is revealed in the fact that a government commission was conducted to examine the links between illegitimacy, venereal disease, and feeble-mindedness: AO, RG 18–65, Box 1, Justice Frank E. Hodgins, 'Report of the Royal Commission: Care of the Feeble-minded and Mentally Defective and the Prevalence of Venereal Disease' (18 October 1919). On venereal disease and its treatment in Canada, see Suzann Buckley and Janice Dickin McGinnis, 'Venereal Disease and Public Health Reform in Canada,' *Canadian Historical Review* 63(3) (September 1982), 337–54; Mary Louise Adams, 'In Sickness and in Health: State Formation, Moral Regulation and Early VD Initiatives in Ontario,' *Journal of Canadian Studies* 28 (Winter 1993–4), 117–30; and Jay Cassell, *The Secret Plague: Venereal Disease in Canada* (Toronto: University of Toronto Press, 1987).

58 Bryce, 'Mothers' Allowances,' 131.

59 On the social purity movement in Canada, see John McLaren, 'Chasing the Social Evil: Moral Fervour and the Evolution of Canada's Prostitution Laws, 1867–1917,' *Canadian Journal of Law and Society* 1 (1986), 125–65; John McLaren, 'White Slavers: The Reform of Canada's Prostitution Laws and Patterns of Enforcement, 1900–1920,' *Criminal Justice History* (1988), 53–119; Graham Parker, 'The Legal Regulation of Sexual Activities and the Protection of Females,' *Osgoode Hall Law Journal* 21(2) (1983), 187–244; Diana Pedersen, 'Keeping Our Good Girls Good: The YWCA and the Girl Problem,' *Canadian Woman's Studies* 7(4) (1986), 20–4; James Snell, 'The White Life for

Two: The Defence of Marriage and Sexual Morality in Canada, 1890–1914,' *Histoire sociale/Social History* 16(31) (May 1983), 111–28; Carolyn Strange, *Toronto's Girl Problem: The Perils and Pleasures of the City, 1880–1930* (Toronto: University of Toronto Press, 1995); and Mariana Valverde, *The Age of Light, Soap and Water: Moral Reform in English Canada, 1885–1925* (Toronto: McClelland and Stewart, 1991).

60 Vida Francis, 'The Delinquent Girl,' in *Proceedings of the National Conference of Charities and Corrections* (n.p.: Fred Herr Press, 1906), 145.

61 J.G. Adami, 'The Policy of the Ostrich,' *Canadian Medical Association Journal* 9(4) (April 1918), 289–301; and Cassel, *The Secret Plague*, 122.

62 Such attitudes dovetailed with eugenic arguments for sterilization of the unfit. See Molly Ladd-Taylor, 'Saving Babies and Sterilizing Mothers: Eugenics and Welfare Politics in the Interwar United States,' *Social Politics* 4 (Spring 1997), 138.

63 R.H. Patterson, 'Some Social Aspects of the Venereal Disease Problem,' *Canadian Public Health Journal* 11(12) (December 1920), 570.

64 M.T. Connelly, *The Response to Prostitution in the Progressive Era* (Chapel Hill: University of North Carolina Press, 1980), 6.

65 See Sherene Razack, 'Race, Space and Prostitution: The Making of a Bourgeois Subject,' *Canadian Journal of Women and the Law* 10 (1998), 1–39; and Strange, *Toronto's Girl Problem*. In direct contrast to prostitution, marriage was constructed as the proper forum for sexual expression. See Snell, 'The White Life for Two,' 112.

66 *An Act Respecting Industrial Refuges for Females (The Female Refuges Act)*, R.S.O. 1919, c. 84, s. 15.

67 Joan Sangster, 'Incarcerating Bad Girls: The Regulation of Sexuality through the *Female Refuges Act* in Ontario, Canada, 1920–19,' *Journal of the History of Sexuality*, 7(2) (1996), 246. Sangster found that almost half of the women incarcerated under this legislation 'either had an illegitimate child or were pregnant with one when they entered the reformatory' (248). For further details on how this legislation affected women's lives, see Viola Demerson, *Incorrigible* (Waterloo, ON: Wilfrid Laurier University Press, 2004).

68 United Nations, Department of Economic and Social Affairs, *Study on Traffic in Persons and Prostitution (Suppression of the Traffic in Persons and of the Exploitation of the Prostitution of Others)* (New York: United Nations, 1959), 21.

69 Regina Kunzel, 'Pulp Fictions and Problem Girls: Reading and Rewriting Single Pregnancy in the Postwar United States,' *American Historical Review* 100 (December 1995), 1473. See also Strange, *Toronto's Girl Problem*.

70 Charlotte Whitton, 'Unmarried Parenthood and the Social Order,' Parts I and II, *Social Welfare* (April–May, 1920), 184–7 and 222–3.

71 Although Drury's United Farmers of Ontario government needed the support of the labour members of parliament to survive – and even with such support had only a single-seat majority over the combined power of the Liberals and the Tories – the farmers could not support the central demands of labour for an eight-hour day and a minimum wage. They were afraid that such measures would increase the flood of young farming sons to the cities and, because of the long hours required in farm work, resented the demand for leisure time. For more information on the Drury government, see E.C. Drury, *Farmer Premier: Memoirs of the Honourable E.C. Drury* (Toronto: McClelland and Stewart, 1966); and Charles Johnston, *E.C. Drury: Agrarian Idealist* (Toronto: University of Toronto Press, 1986).

72 Other family-centred reforms that received assent included the minimum wage for women, allowances for impoverished widows, an expanded *Deserted Wives and Children's Maintenance Act*, and legislation that obligated grown children to support their indigent parents.

73 Drury, *Farmer Premier*, 108.

74 In 1918, Whitton, a recent graduate of Queen's, was hand-picked as the assistant secretary of the Social Service Council of Canada. She provided the liaison between the SSCC and Toronto's welfare agencies and was assistant editor of the newly founded *Social Welfare*, one of Canada's earliest and most influential social work journals. For more on Whitton's career and influence on Canadian social welfare, see Patricia Rooke and R.L. Schnell, *No Bleeding Heart: Charlotte Whitton, A Feminist on the Right* (Vancouver: UBC Press, 1988); Patricia Rooke and R.L. Schnell, 'Making the Way More Comfortable: Charlotte Whitton's Child Welfare Career,' *Journal of Canadian Studies* 17(4) (Winter 1983), 33–45; and James Struthers, 'A Profession in Crisis: Charlotte Whitton and Canadian Social Work in the 1930s,' *Canadian Historical Review* 62(2) (June 1981), 169–85.

75 Struthers, *The Limits of Affluence*, 19.

76 Once the Hearst government decided to go ahead with mothers' allowances, public hearings were scheduled in Ontario's four largest cities to test public opinion on the issue. Ninety-three witnesses spoke in favour of the allowances, but who would be deserving of relief was a more contentious issue. The act was passed by Drury's coalition government, but reflected the details of the legislation already worked out in the Riddell Report based on his 1919 investigations. See, Struthers, *The Limits of Affluence*, chapter 1. The petition and reports of the broadly middle-classed, Toronto-based lobby group, the Committee on Mother's Allowance, created a political cli-

mate in which government had to act: see Margaret Jane Hillyard Little, *No Car, No Radio, No Liquor Permit: The Moral Regulation of Single Mothers in Ontario, 1920–1997* (Toronto: University of Toronto Press, 1998), 166.

77 National Council of Women Collection, vol. 68, File 3, 'Letter from Vancouver Local Council to Mrs. Cummings, National Council of Women, Explaining the Vancouver position, November 5, 1914,' as cited in Little, *No Car, No Radio, No Liquor Permit*, 15.

78 AO, RG 7, 'Mothers' Allowances Investigation, Ontario, 1920,' 26–7.

79 AO, RG 7, Series II–I, 'Mothers' Pension Allowance: Hamilton Enquiry,' 20 February 1919, testimony of Mrs Hawkings.

80 AO, RG 7, Series II–I, Box 2, 'Mothers' Pension Allowance: Hamilton Enquiry,' Tom Moore, TLC, 18 February 1919.

81 Ibid., Mr Rollo, TLC, 18–19 February 1919.

82 *Mothers' Allowance Act*, S.O. 1920. In 1921, the eligibility criteria were amended to include wives of men who were inmates of insane asylums and the required period of desertion was reduced from seven to five years. It is not surprising that the vast majority of recipients were Anglo-Saxon, despite the fact that race was not mentioned anywhere in the enabling legislation. Not only did citizenship regulations reduce the right of 'undesirables' to apply, but application did not guarantee support, as the act was mediated through child welfare workers with considerable discretion in determining who was, and was not, a worthy mother. As Margaret Little notes, this placed non-white and non-Anglo-Saxon women at a distinct disadvantage (*No Car, No Radio, No Liquor Permit*, 67). In 1934 children were made eligible for support until the age of eighteen. In 1935 mothers with one child were included in the scheme and the required period of desertion was reduced from five years to three: *Mothers' Allowance Act*, S.O. 1934 and 1935. Only in 1956 was the act amended to enable unwed mothers to collect the allowance. They had to have cared for the child for a period of two years following the birth (which of course excluded many mothers who had to place their children with the CAS during this time because they couldn't afford to care for them). In 1958 the two year waiting period was abolished, but at the same time, unwed mothers with more than one child were no longer eligible for assistance. In 1959, the act was amended such that unwed mothers had to be eighteen years of age to be eligible for support and a six-month waiting period for unwed mothers was reinstated. In 1964 this waiting period was reduced to three months. This waiting period was not eliminated until 1991 under the *Family Benefits Act*, S.O. 1991.

83 Little, *No Car, No Radio, No Liquor Permit*, 17. See also Lisa Brush, 'Worthy

Widows, Welfare Cheats: Proper Womanhood in Expert Needs Talk About Single Mothers in the United States, 1900 to 1988,' *Gender and Society* 11(6) (December 1997), 720–45; Margaret Jane Hillyard Little, 'A Fit and Proper Person: The Moral Regulation of Single Mothers in Ontario, 1920–1940,' in Kathryn McPherson, Cecilia Morgan, and Nancy Forestell, eds., *Gendered Pasts: Essays in Femininity and Masculinity in Canada* (Toronto: Oxford University Press, 1999), 123–38.

84 AO, RG 7, Series II–I, Box 2, 'Memo on Mothers' Pensions Prepared by the Superintendent of Trades and Labour,' 1917, 2.

85 Province of Ontario, Mothers' Allowance Commission, *Annual Report* 1921, 27.

86 *Mothers' Allowance Act*, S.O. 1920.

87 Province of Ontario, Mothers' Allowance Commission, *Third Annual Report*, 1922–1923, 17.

88 Similar restrictions were imposed under American legislation. See Gordon, *Pitied But Not Entitled*, 298.

89 Only in 1965 did the provincial government commit itself fully to paying for child welfare services for unmarried mothers provided through the CAS through the *Child Welfare Act*, S.O. 1965, c. 14, s. 12. For further discussion of the funding provided to the CAS, see N. Trocme, 'Child Welfare Services,' in R. Barnhorst and L. Johnson, eds., *The State of the Child in Ontario* (Toronto: Oxford University Press, 1991).

90 For a further discussion of the CAS, see Bullen, 'J.J. Kelso and the "New" Childsavers,' 107–28; Jones and Rutman, *In the Children's Aid*; and R.L. Schnell, 'Female Separatism and Institution-Building: Continuities and Discontinuities in Canadian Child Welfare, 1913–1935,' *International Review of History and Political Science* 25(2) (May 1988), 14–46.

91 *An Act Respecting the Legitimation of Children by the Subsequent Intermarriage of Their Parents*, S.O. 1921, c. 53.

92 Snell, 'The White Life for Two,' 111–28.

93 Blackstone, *Commentaries on the Laws of England*, vol. 1, 454.

94 This lead has been followed throughout the Western world, but Ontario's statute came comparatively early. The majority of American states passed such legislation only in the 1950s and 1960s. See Krause, *Illegitimacy: Law and Social Policy*, 14.

95 *An Act Respecting the Adoption of Children*, S.O. 1921, c. 55. Despite the fact that adoption was not recognized in law, it has a long informal history: G.F. Lemby, *Family Law* (Toronto: International Self-Counsel Press, 1971), 157. Informal adoption, however, had no legal standing. For example, in 1909, foster parents who had cared for a female child for over a year, without

being paid for the child's upkeep, attempted to keep the child when the parents sought to reclaim her. Although the parents had signed an agreement with the fostering couple to release the child for adoption, the court asserted that 'the law of England knows nothing of adoption' and that 'parents cannot enter into an agreement legally binding to deprive themselves of the custody and control of their children; and, if they elect to do so, can at any moment resume their control over them.' *Re Davis*, [1909] O.L.R., 384 at 386.

96 Jamil Zainaldin, 'The Emergence of Modern American Family Law: Child Custody, Adoption and the Courts, 1796–1851,' *Northwestern University Law Review* 73(6) (1979), 1042.

97 Of course, in a manner that parallels the situation with regard to legislative divorce, this ensured that poorer families, while they might well have a non-kin child within the household, were denied the opportunity to bestow familial status upon such a child. For information on legislative divorce in Canada, see James Snell, *In the Shadow of the Law: Divorce in Canada, 1900–1939* (Toronto: University of Toronto Press, 1991). On informal adoption among the poor in early-twentieth-century Great Britain, see Ellen Ross, *Love and Toil: Motherhood in Outcast London, 1870–1918* (New York: Oxford University Press, 1993).

98 AO, RG 4-32, 1921, 1679, Memo of the Social Service Council of Ontario to AG W.E. Raney, re: Adoption bill.

99 This also had clear parallels in the residential school program imposed upon Aboriginal children. For further information, see Kim Anderson and Bonita Lawrence, eds., *Strong Women Stories: Native Vision and Community Survival* (Toronto: Sumach Press, 2003).

100 In 1924 the last baby left the Toronto Infants' Home. Children were now to be placed through a boarding system, but no formal provisions for the regulation of fostering were established: AO, Children's Aid Society, 'Infants' Home and Infirmary, Toronto,' MTA, Box 46592–1, Series 100, File 352, 'Child Care – Private Organizations: Children's Aid Society, 1931–1946,' 2. Foster parents were, and are, paid to board the children under their care. When such families formally adopt their charges, however, all state support ceases.

101 As quoted in Jones and Rutman, *In the Children's Aid*, 156. In the American context, there is considerable debate about the attitude of social workers towards illegitimate children and their mothers. Regina Kunzel argues that by the early 1920s, social workers uniformly advocated the separation of the unwed mother from her child and the child's relinquishment for adoption. This, she asserts, represented a departure from the nineteenth-

century practice of insisting that the unwed mother accept responsibility
and punishment for her sins by keeping her child. Wayne Carp, however,
argues that 'there were few, if any professional social workers who recommended separating unwed mothers from their children as a first resort.'
He believes that social workers came to support adoption only gradually
and largely after the 1930s. See Regina Kunzel, 'The Professionalization of
Benevolence: Evangelicals and Social Workers in the Florence Crittenton
Homes, 1915–1945,' *Journal of Social History* 22 (1988), 21–43; Kunzel, *Fallen
Women, Problem Girls;* Wayne Carp, 'Professional Social Workers, Adoption and the Problem of Illegitimacy, 1915–1945,' *Journal of Policy History*
6(3) (1994), 162.

102 The term 'sixties scoop' was coined by Patrick Johnson in *Native Children
and the Child Welfare System* (Toronto: James Lorimer, 1983). See also Canada, *Report of the Royal Commission on Aboriginal Peoples,* vol. 3 (Ottawa:
Ministry of Supply and Services, 1996).

103 S.O. 1921, c. 54. This codified and formalized what had already been the
practice of the Children's Aid Society. Under the combined effect of the
Juvenile Delinquent's Act, 7 & 8 Edw. VII, c. 40 (Dom.), and the *Children's
Protection Act,* R.S.O. 1914, c. 23, an illegitimate child whose mother was
unable to maintain it could be declared to be a neglected child under the
meaning of the statute. For further details, see *S (Re),* [1919] O.J. No. 103.
The *prima facie* right of the mother to the custody of her illegitimate
child was only firmly established by the Supreme Court of Canada in
1950 in *Re: Baby Duffell, Martin et al. v. Duffell,* [1950] S.C.R., 737; [1950] 4
D.L.R. 1.

104 *An Act for the Protection of the Children of Unmarried Parents,* S.O. 1921, c. 54,
s. 10.

105 *An Act for the Prevention of Cruelty to, and the Better Protection of Children,*
S.O. 1893. As Dorothy Chunn illustrates, the statutes passed at the end of
the nineteenth century sanctioned 'unprecedented intervention into deviant or potentially deviant families.' See Dorothy Chunn, *From Punishment
to Doing Good: Family Courts and Socialized Justice in Ontario, 1880–1940*
(Toronto: University of Toronto Press, 1992), 44. Before this time, state
programs with regard to children's welfare had been limited to children in
state institutions and those who had committed criminal offences.

106 This provision was not overturned until 1970 when an impoverished
mother, whose child had been seized by the Children's Aid Society under
the provisions of the act and placed for adoption without her consent, suc-
ceeded in having the child delivered to her as the evidence 'did not even
remotely suggest [she was] unfit to enjoy her parental right to custody.' *Re*

Mugford [1970] 1 O.R. 601–11. This order was affirmed by the Supreme
Court of Canada.

107 This paragraph summarizes the *Children of Unmarried Parents Act*, S.O.
1921, c. 54, ss. 18, 13, and 25.

108 AO, Wentworth, Box 66-3-3-14, Case 89, 1942.

109 This paragraph summarizes the *Children of Unmarried Parents Act*, S.O.
1921, c. 54, ss. 18 and 11.

110 AO, Wentworth, Box 24-2-3-2, Case 585, 1962.

111 It was only in the 1970s that the rights of putative fathers with regard to
their children began to be discussed by the courts. See Diana
Dzwiekowski, 'Casenotes, Commentaries: Findings of Paternity in
Ontario,' *Canadian Journal of Family Law* 3 (1980), 318–26; Debra Ratterman,
'Adoption and the Rights of Putative Fathers,' *Children's Legal Rights Jour-
nal* 11(1) (Spring 1990), 13–21; and Ontario Law Reform Commission,
Report on Family Law, Part III, *Children* (Toronto: Ministry of the Attorney
General, 1973), 10.

112 Patronymy 'encompasses three closely linked practices: the practice of
passing on a father's name to children; the practice of a woman taking her
husband's name; and to the use of the father's name as the family name.'
The practice of women taking their husbands' names has been critiqued
but little discussion of the impact of patronymy on children has occurred.
Patronymy makes women seem unimportant in the family, but also it
ensures that children without fathers, and without the father's name, are
stigmatized. See Emily Carasco, 'What's in a Name?' *University of British
Columbia Law Review* 37 (2004), 263.

113 AO, York, Box 411-1-4-1, Case 477, 1953.

114 Similar themes have been noted in the United States. See Rickie Solinger,
*Beggars and Choosers: How the Politics of Choice Shapes Abortion, Adoption and
Welfare in the United States* (New York: Hill and Wang, 2001), 213.

2: 'Doubtful of Her Veracity'

1 Robert Viet Sherwin, 'The Law and Sex Relationships,' *Journal of Social
Issues* 22(2) (April 1966), 109.

2 In *Grawburger and Moyer (Re)*, [1929] O.J. No 96, it was confirmed that the
court has jurisdiction to hear cases even when the mother had not conceived in the municipality in which the case was to be heard. In *Hilton v.
Tassman*, [1944] O.J. No. 337, the court confirmed that an appeal by a putative father against an order made by the court could only be initiated
within the time frame detailed under legislation. In *Duckworth v. Skinkle*

(Re), [1924] O.J. No. 18, the court determined that marriage of the mother, before the birth of the child, did not preclude proceedings if the husband admitted non-access before the time of the marriage.

3 *Re Yeo and Benner*, [1926] O.J. No 339.

4 *Carleton v. MacLean*, [1953] O.J. No. 275.

5 *Leskey v. VanHorne*, [1954] O.J. No. 346.

6 *M.G. (Re)*. [1943] O.J. No. 270.

7 *Kirkpatrick and Moroughan (Re)*, [1927] O.J. No. 58.

8 *Power (Re)*, [1952] O.J. No. 336 and *Adrian and McGuire (Re)* [1925] O.J. No. 449.

9 *Walker v. Foster*, [1923] O.J. No. 23.

10 *Wicks v. Armstrong*, [1928] O.J. No. 160.

11 *C.S. v. M.R.*, [1954] O.J. No. 281.

12 *Brown and Argue (Re)*, [1925] O.J. No. 50.

13 *Re Eisenmenger and Doherty*, [1924] O.J. No. 558.

14 *Gwyllt (Re)*, [1944] O.J. No. 85.

15 *Re Nunn v. Featherstone*, [1927] O.J. No. 173.

16 Confirmation that the civil, not the criminal, burden of proof applied in affiliation cases was achieved in Ontario only in 1976. *Panaccione v. McNab*, [1976] 28 R.F.L., 182–9. In a 1987 case, the Saskatchewan Unified Family Court asserted that the *Unmarried Parents Act* of that province (very similar in its provisions to that of Ontario) violated the Charter by discriminating against 'single women as a class. The section is based on the assumption that single women seeking affiliation orders are likely to lie under oath, unlike women in other civil suits who are required to prove their cases on a preponderance of probabilities.' *Bomboir v. Harlow*, [1987] 5 W.W.R., 55.

17 *Hunt v. Lindensmith (Re)*, [1921] O.J. No. 50.

18 *Gabel v. Bolander*, [1943] O.J. No. 162.

19 *Middleton v. Bryce*, [1931] O.J. No. 234.

20 *Children of Unmarried Parents Act*, S.O. 1921, c. 54, s. 7.

21 An interesting question that cannot be answered from evidence from these case files is how women knew to seek aid through the auspices of the CAS. In twenty-one cases evidence from the files suggests that women were referred to the CAS by their physicians, but other sources of information about child welfare services must have existed.

22 *An Act Respecting Houses of Refuge for Females*, R.S.O., 1987, c. 311; *An Act Respecting Industrial Refuges for Females (The Female Refuges Act)*, R.S.O., 1927, c. 347, secs. 15, 16, 17; Ontario, Legislative Assembly Debates (March 1958), 742.

23 Joan Sangster, 'Incarcerating Bad Girls: The Regulation of Sexuality through the Female Refugees Act in Ontario, 1920–1945,' *Journal of the History of Sexuality* 7(2) (1996): 239–75.

24 Harry D. Krause, *Illegitimacy: Law and Social Policy* (New York: Bobbs-Merrill, 1971), 28; *Children of Unmarried Parents Act*, S.O. 1921, c. 54, s. 11. The *prima facie* right of the mother to the custody of her illegitimate child was only firmly established by the Supreme Court of Canada in 1950. *Re: Baby Duffell, Martin et al. v. Duffell*, [1950] S.C.R., 737; [1950] 4 D.L.R. 1.

25 Michel Foucault, *The History of Sexuality: An Introduction*, Vol. 1, trans. Robert Hurley (New York: Random House, 1978), 45.

26 Joan Sangster, *Regulating Girls and Women: Sexuality, Family and Law in Ontario, 1920–1960* (Toronto: Oxford University Press, 2001), 123.

27 Ibid.

28 On the rhetorical construction of Black women, and their exclusion from legal protection, see Elizabeth Spelman, 'Theories of Race and Gender: The Erasure of Black Women,' *Quest: A Feminist Quarterly* 4 (1982), 36–62; Dorothy Roberts, 'Racism and Patriarchy in the Meaning of Motherhood,' in Martha Albertson Fineman and Isabel Karpin, eds., *Mothers in Law: Feminist Theory and the Legal Regulation of Motherhood* (New York: Columbia University Press, 1995), 224–49; Patricia Hill Collins, *Black Feminist Thought: Knowledge, Consciousness and the Politics of Empowerment* (Boston: Unwin Hyman, 1990); and Jacqueline Jones, *Labor of Love, Labor of Sorrow: Black Women, Work and the Family from Slavery to the Present* (New York: Basic Books, 1985).

29 On the abysmal treatment of Aboriginal mothers and their children in Canada, see Marlee Kline, 'Complicating the Ideology of Motherhood: Child Welfare Law and First Nations Women,' in Fineman and Karpin, eds., *Mothers in Law*, 118–41; Verna Kirkness, 'Emerging Native Women,' *Canadian Journal of Women and the Law* 2 (1987–88), 408–15.

30 The questionnaire was used in all jurisdictions for which cases are extant.

31 For comparison with the use of such evidence in the courts of Montreal, see Tamara Myers, 'The Voluntary Delinquent: Parents, Daughters and the Montreal Juvenile Delinquents' Court in 1918,' *Canadian Historical Review* 80(2) (1999), 256.

32 Jean Pochin, *Without a Wedding Ring: Casework with Unmarried Parents* (London: Constable, 1969), 135.

33 Linda Gordon, *Heroes of Their Own Lives: The Politics and History of Family Violence, Boston, 1880–1960* (New York: Penguin, 1988), 195.

34 *Children of Unmarried Parents Act*, S.O. 1921, c. 54, s. 25.

35 AO, Wentworth, Box 24-2-3-4, Case 221, 1958.

36 H. Clark, 'The Burden of Proof in a Paternity Action,' *Journal of Family Law* 25 (1986–87), 357.
37 *An Act for the Protection of the Children of Unmarried Parents*, R.S.O. 1921, c. 54, s. 24.
38 AO, Wentworth, Box 24-2-3-3, Case 15, 1966.
39 As will become evident in later chapters of this book, however, admission of paternity did not often translate into full payment of child support: *Children of Unmarried Parents Act*, S.O. 1921, c. 54, s. 18 (2).
40 In 124 cases the outcome of the case is unclear; in 56 cases couples were married and proceedings therefore were halted; and in 203 cases men signed limited agreements for costs pending adoption, but without formally admitting paternity.
41 *Massingham-Pearce v. Konkolus*, [1995] 7 W.W.R., 196.
42 Renee Monson, 'State-ing Sex and Gender: Collecting Information from Mothers and Fathers in Paternity Cases,' *Gender and Society* 11 (1997), 285.
43 AO, Wentworth, Box 66-3-3-14, Case 104, 1953.
44 AO, Wentworth, Box 66-3-3-14, Case 110, 1956.
45 AO, Wentworth, Box 24-2-3-2, Case 538, 1960.
46 Sidney Katz, 'The Forgotten Fathers,' *Maclean's*, 1 May 1949, 73.
47 AO, Middlesex, Box 27-9-1-1, Case 303, 1953. In this case the mother, after finding the CAS to be unreceptive to her claims, had hired a lawyer for herself, and Bury's letter was in response to queries by the lawyer regarding court procedure. This letter provides confirmation of the practical problems created for lawyers by the paucity of reported cases regarding the application and interpretation of the *Children of Unmarried Parents Act*.
48 Only in 1965 did the provincial government commit itself fully to paying for child welfare services for unmarried mothers provided through the CAS. *Child Welfare Act*, S.O. 1965, c. 14, s. 12. For further discussion of the funding provided to the CAS, see N. Trocme, 'Child Welfare Services,' in R. Barnhorst and L. Johnson, eds., *The State of the Child in Ontario* (Toronto: Oxford University Press, 1991).
49 AO, York, Box 11-26-4-17, Case 2362, 1963.
50 Social Planning Council of Metropolitan Toronto, *A Report on Maternity Homes in Metropolitan Toronto* (Toronto, 1960), 51.
51 Marianna Valverde, 'Building Anti-Delinquent Communities: Morality, Gender, and Generation in the City,' in Joy Parr, ed., *A Diversity of Women* (Toronto: University of Toronto Press, 1995), 33. Pamela Cox, in her examination of the treatment of 'bad girls' in Britain, argues that the protective

impulse defined women's 'freedoms in narrow and often highly illiberal terms.' Pamela Cox, *Gender, Justice and Welfare: Bad Girls in Britain, 1900–1950* (Basingstoke: Palgrave, 2003), 15.

52 T.D. Williams, 'Desertion and Non-Support: The Importance of the Problem,' *Proceedings of the First Annual Meeting of the Canadian Conference on Social Work* (Ottawa, 1928), 49.

53 Dorothy Chunn, 'Regulating the Poor in Ontario: From Police Courts to Family Courts,' *Canadian Journal of Family Law* 6 (1987), 88.

54 Ibid., 90.

55 Sara Edlin, *The Unmarried Mother in Our Society* (New York: Farrar, Straus and Young, 1954), 169.

56 AO, York, Box 411-1-4-1, Case 433, 1959.

57 AO, Wentworth, Box 66-4-4-6, Case 190, 1947.

58 AO, Algoma, Box 512-2-3-4, Case 1025, 1927.

59 Family members and friends testified that he had been jealous and possessive and that they supported the woman's decision to refuse the offer of marriage.

60 AO, Algoma, Box 512-2-3-4, Case 1025, 1927.

61 Social Planning Council of Metropolitan Toronto, *A Report on Maternity Homes in Metropolitan Toronto*, 51.

62 AO, York, Box 411-1-3-10, Case 369, 1951.

63 No payments were received under this order and the CAS did not pursue the man for support. The mother's parents, who were helping to care for the child, continued to negotiate informally with the man and eventually settled for a lump sum of $600. The grandmother of the child wrote to the CAS asking for help in collecting this sum. 'Please make him come across with the money. If his credit is any good at all he could borrow it and erase this debt that hangs over his head. We could put the money in the bank and use it to educate this little girl who is entitled to just as good an education as the 2 children he has home with him.' The lump sum, however, was never paid and it does not appear that the CAS agreed that this illegitimate mulatto girl was 'entitled to just as good an education,' or as prosperous and comfortable a life, as the white children the man had fathered since his marriage: AO, York, Box 411-1-3-15, Case 917, 1958.

64 AO, Wentworth, Box 66-4-4-6, Case 155, 1956.

65 Viola Demerson, *Incorrigible* (Waterloo, ON: Wilfrid Laurier University Press, 2004), 44.

66 Until the 1980s, even cohabiting fathers had no explicit legal right to participate in this decision. The only exception occurred when biological parents subsequently married. If such a child had been released for adoption by the

sole mother, her husband's consent was now also required to validate the adoption. *Re G., G. et ux v. C. et ux*, [1951] 3 D.L.R., 138.

67 AO, York, Box 411-1-3-11, Case 501, 1947.

68 AO, York, Box 411-1-3-9, Case 397, 1955.

69 AO, Wentworth, Box 24-2-3-4, Case 291, 1954.

70 AO, York, Box 411-1-3-12, Case 2050, 1950.

71 Sherwin, 'The Law and Sexual Relationships,' 113–14.

72 Sanford Katz, 'Legal Protections for the Unmarried Mother and Her Child,' *Children* 10(2) (March–April, 1963), 56.

73 For further information on the nature of rape trials, see Carolyn Strange, 'Patriarchy Modified: The Criminal Prosecution of Rape in York County, 1880–1930,' in Jim Phillips, Tina Loo, and Susan Lewthwaite, eds., *Essays in the History of Canadian Law: Volume V – Crime and Criminal Justice* (Toronto: The Osgoode Society, 1994), 207–51; Constance Backhouse, 'Nineteenth-Century Rape Law, 1800–1892,' in David H. Flaherty, ed., *Essays in the History of Canadian Law: Volume II* (Toronto: The Osgoode Society, 1983), 200–47; and T. Brettel Dawson, 'Sexual Assault Law and Past Sexual Conduct of the Primary Witness: The Construction of Relevance,' *Canadian Journal of Women and the Law* 2 (1987–88), 310–34.

74 AO, York, Box 411-1-4-2, Case 703, 1954.

75 AO, York, Box 411-1-4-6, Case 2295, 1964.

76 AO, York, Box 11-26-4-17, Case 2366, 1963.

77 AO, Wentworth, Box 66-3-3-14, Case 89, 1942.

78 *Panaccione v. McNab*, [1976] 28 R.F.L., 184.

79 AO, Wentworth, Box 24-2-3-2, Case 599, 1952.

80 AO, Algoma, Box 512-2-3-4, Case 1039, 1935.

81 AO, Algoma, Box 512-2-3-4, Case 1037, 1932.

82 AO, York, Box 411-1-4-6, Case 2420, 1961.

83 AO, York, Box 11-26-4-20, Case 2553, 1966.

84 AO, York, Box 411-1-4-6, Case 2484, 1966.

85 AO, York, Box 411-1-2-9, Case 985, 1957.

86 Krause, *Illegitimacy: Law and Social Policy*, 106.

87 The cruelty of these proceedings has now been recognized at law. Statutes that distinguish between children based on the marital status of the mother are 'based on biased and stereotypical ideas about the moral character of unmarried women with children. It also denied children of unmarried women financial support from the children's fathers, support that children of married women could receive. That discrimination violated the *Charter* and could not be justified under s. 1.' *M. (R.H.) v. H.(S.S.)*, [1994] 2 R.F.L. (4th), 207.

88 Sherwin, 'The Law and Sex Relationships,' 118.

3: 'I Did Not Bring This Child'

1 Constance Nathanson, *Dangerous Passage: The Social Control of Sexuality in Women's Adolescence* (Philadelphia: Temple University Press, 1991), 4.
2 Kathy Piess, 'Charity Girls and City Pleasures: Historical Notes on Working-Class Sexuality, 1880–1920,' in Kathy Piess and Christina Simmons, eds., *Passion and Power: Sexuality in History* (Philadelphia: Temple University Press, 1989), 57. See also, Kathy Piess, *Cheap Amusements: Working Women and Leisure in Turn-of-the-Century New York* (Philadelphia: Temple University Press, 1986).
3 Mary Richmond, *Social Diagnosis* (New York: Russell Sage Foundation, 1917), 357. This text was foundational within social work education and practice. For a description of its extraordinary influence, see Roy Lubove, *The Professional Altruist: The Emergence of Social Work as a Career, 1880–1930* (Cambridge, MA: Harvard University Press, 1965); and Karen Tice, *Tales of Wayward Girls and Immoral Women: Case Records and the Professionalization of Social Work* (Urbana: University of Illinois Press, 1998). See also, Ada Elliot Sheffield, *The Social Case History: Its Construction and Content* (New York: Russell Sage Foundation, 1920).
4 Nancy Fraser, *Unruly Practices: Power, Discourse and Gender in Contemporary Social Theory* (Minneapolis: University of Minnesota Press, 1989), 155. See also Ellie Pozatek, 'The Problem of Certainty: Clinical Social Work in the Post Modern Era,' *Social Work* 39(4) (1994), 394–404; Thomas Holland, 'Narrative, Knowledge and Professional Practice,' *Social Thought* 17(1) (1991), 32–40; and Tice, *Tales of Wayward Girls*.
5 Charlotte Whitton, 'Unmarried Parenthood and the Social Order,' Parts I and II, *Social Welfare* (April–May, 1920), 184–7 and 222–3.
6 Henry Schumacher, 'The Unmarried Mother: A Socio-Psychiatric Viewpoint,' *Mental Hygiene* 11 (October 1927), 775.
7 For definitions of delinquency, see Ruth Alexander, *The 'Girl Problem': Female Sexual Delinquency in New York, 1900–1930* (Ithaca: Cornell University Press, 1995); Meda Chesney-Lind, *Girls, Delinquency and Juvenile Justice* (Belmont: Brooks Cole, 1992); Linda Mahood, *Policing Gender, Class and Family: Britain 1850–1940* (London: UCL Press, 1995); Joanne Meyerowitz, *Women Adrift: Independent Wage Earners in Chicago, 1880–1930* (Chicago: University of Chicago Press, 1988); Tamara Myers, 'Qui t'a debauchée?' in Lori Chambers and Edgar-Andre Montigny, eds., *Family Matters: Papers in Post-Confederation Canadian Family History* (Tor-

onto: Canadian Scholars' Press, 1998); Mary Odem, *Delinquent Daughters: Protecting and Policing Adolescent Female Sexuality in the United States, 1885–1920* (Chapel Hill: University of North Carolina University Press, 1995); Joan Sangster, *Girl Trouble: Female Delinquency in English Canada* (Toronto: Between the Lines, 2002); Carolyn Strange, *Toronto's Girl Problem: The Perils and Pleasures of the City, 1880–1930* (Toronto: University of Toronto Press, 1995); and Marianna Valverde, 'Building Anti-Delinquent Communities: Morality, Gender and Generation in the City,' in Joy Parr, ed., *A Diversity of Women* (Toronto: University of Toronto Press, 1995).

8 Meda Chesney-Lind, 'Judicial Enforcement of the Female Sex Role: The Family Court and the Female Delinquent,' *Issues in Criminology* 8(2) (Fall 1973), 54.

9 Dale Harris, 'Delinquency in Adolescent Girls,' *Mental Hygiene* 28 (October 1944), 597.

10 Lucy Brooking, 'A Study of the Delinquent Girl,' *Social Welfare* (April 1921). See also, Charlotte Lowe, 'The Intelligence and Social Background of the Unmarried Mother,' *Mental Hygiene* 4 (October 1927), 783–94. Few articles on female delinquency were published in *Social Welfare*, the most prominent social work journal in Canada, between 1920 and 1960 and, as Joan Sangster asserts, 'Canadians relied heavily on influential U.S. studies of girl delinquents. Many of these studies started from the premise that girls' delinquency involved rejection of their gender roles relating to sexuality, domesticity and motherhood.' Sangster, *Girl Trouble*, 33.

11 Virginia Wimperis, *The Unmarried Mother and Her Child* (London: George Allen and Unwin, 1960), 55.

12 See Elizabeth Lunbeck, *The Psychiatric Persuasion: Knowledge, Gender and Power in Modern America* (Princeton: Princeton University Press, 1994); and Theresa Richardson, *The Century of the Child: The Mental Hygiene Movement and Social Policy in the United States and Canada* (Albany: State University of New York Press, 1989).

13 Lunbeck, *The Psychiatric Persuasion*, 63.

14 For a detailed description of the importance of Freudian ideas in Canadian psychological thinking, see Mona Gleason, *Normalizing the Ideal: Psychology, Schooling and the Family in Postwar Canada* (Toronto: University of Toronto Press, 1999).

15 Betty Isserman, 'The Casework Relationship with Unmarried Mothers,' *The Social Worker* 17(1) (1948), 12–17.

16 Helene Deutsch, *The Psychology of Women: A Psychoanalytic Interpretation*, vol. 2, *Motherhood* (New York: Grune and Stratton, 1945), 377.

17 Leontine Young, *Out of Wedlock: A Study of the Unmarried Mother and Her Child* (New York: McGraw-Hill, 1954), 37.

18 Philip Solomon, M.D., and Morris Ward Kilgore, M.D., 'The Psychiatric Case Conference in a Maternity Home Setting,' American Protestant Hospital Association Conference, Salvation Army Session Papers, 1965, Accession No. 82–1, Salvation Army Archives, as quoted in Rickie Solinger, *Beggars and Choosers: How the Politics of Choice Shapes Abortion, Adoption and Welfare in the United States* (New York: Hill and Wang, 2001), 158. See also, James P. Cattell, 'Psychodynamic and Clinical Observations in a Group of Unmarried Mothers,' *American Journal of Psychiatry* 3 (November 1954), 337–42; Edmund Pollock, 'An Investigation into Certain Personality Characteristics of Unmarried Mothers' (PhD diss., New York University, 1957); and Stephen Fleck, 'Pregnancy as a Symptom of Adolescent Maladjustment,' *International Journal of Social Psychiatry* 2 (Autumn 1956), 120–1.

19 Canadian Youth Commission, *Youth, Marriage and Family* (Toronto: Ryerson Press, 1948), 214–19.

20 For further information on the power of popular psychology in the postwar period, see Gleason, *Normalizing the Idea;* and Mary Louise Adams, *The Trouble with Normal: Postwar Youth and the Making of Heterosexuality* (Toronto: University of Toronto Press, 1997).

21 L. Hoffman, 'Constructing Realities: An Art of Lens,' *Family Process* 29 (1989), 1–12.

22 It is important to note that many of these cases overlapped.

23 Wimperis, *The Unmarried Mother and Her Child*, 55.

24 These stereotypes continue to be powerful, but 'a historical perspective on the problem of adolescent pregnancy offers a somewhat different and more complex picture than the one supplied by the news media and policymakers. ... the overall rate of teenage pregnancy has not increased dramatically. In fact, the overall rate of teenage fertility has declined during the past twenty-five years. The rate of teenage childbearing increased sharply after WWII and reached a peak of 97.3 births per 1,000 women aged 15 to 19 in 1957. After 1957 the rate of teenage fertility declined to 52.8 births per 1,000 women aged 15 to 19 in 1977. Phillips Cutright, 'The Teenage Sexual Revolution and Myth of the Abstinent Past,' *Family Planning Perspectives* 4 (1972), 26.

25 It should be noted that these averages include only never-married women, not those who were cohabiting with the fathers of their children, who were often considerably older.

26 Vanier Centre, *Profiling Canada: Families* (Montreal: Vanier Institute of the Family, 1994), 39.

27 Joan Sangster, *Regulating Girls and Women: Sexuality, Family and the Law in Ontario, 1920–1960* (Toronto: Oxford University Press, 2001), 123.

28 Ibid.

29 Harris, 'Delinquency in Adolescent Girls,' 598.

30 Veronica Strong-Boag, *The New Day Recalled: Lives of Girls and Women in English Canada, 1919–1939* (Toronto: Copp Clark Pitman, 1988), 53.

31 AO, York, Box 411-1-3-9, Case 402, 1945.

32 D. Gough, 'Work with Unmarried Mothers,' *Almoner* 12 (13 March 1961), 491.

33 AO, Hamilton, Box 24-2-3-3, Case 17, 1954.

34 Regina Kunzel, 'Pulp Fictions and Problem Girls: Reading and Rewriting Single Pregnancy in the Postwar United States,' *American Historical Review* 100 (December 1995), 1465.

35 AO, York, Box 411-1-3-9, Case 413, 1938. Emphasis in original.

36 AO, York, Box 411-1-3-9, Case 397, 1927.

37 AO, York, Box 411-1-3-9, Case 395, 1948.

38 Ruth Chaskel, 'The Unmarried Mother: Is She Different?' *Child Welfare* 45 (February 1967), 66.

39 AO, York, Box 411-1-4-1, Case 473, 1952.

40 AO, Hamilton, Box 24-2-3-3, Case 13, 1953.

41 Strong-Boag, *The New Day Recalled*, 90–1.

42 Beth Bailey, *Sex in the Heartland* (Cambridge, MA: Harvard University Press, 1999), 3. See also Ellen Rothman, *Hands and Hearts: A History of Courtship in America* (Cambridge, MA: Harvard University Press, 1984).

43 Bailey, *Sex in the Heartland*, 11.

44 John D'Emilio and Estelle Freedman, *Intimate Matters: A History of Sexuality in America* (New York: Harper and Row, 1988), 256.

45 Alfred Kinsey, Wardell Pomeroy, and Clyde Martin, *Sexual Behavior in the Human Female* (Philadelphia: Saunders, 1953).

46 Cutright, 'The Teenage Sexual Reviolution and the Myth of the Abstinence Past,' 30. It has been speculated, in fact, that the aberration is the Victorian period, during which sexual taboos were extremely rigid.

47 James Snell, *In the Shadow of the Law: Divorce in Canada, 1900–1939* (Toronto: University of Toronto Press, 1991), 138.

48 H. Philips Hepworth, *Foster Care and Adoption in Canada* (Ottawa: Canadian Council on Social Development, 1980), 21; Cutright, 'The Teenage Sexual Revolution and the Myth of the Abstinent Past,' 25. 'For youth this new convention had many appealing features. Young marriage allowed them to sidestep some of the problems of the contemporary code of sexual morality,' writes Beth Bailey in *From Front Porch to Back Seat: Courtship in*

Twentieth-Century America (Baltimore: Johns Hopkins University Press, 1988), 47.

49 Denise Baillargeon, *Making Do: Women, Family and Home in Montreal During the Great Depression*, trans. Yvonne Klein (Waterloo, ON: Wilfrid Laurier University Press, 1999), 48.

50 Svanhuit Josie, 'The American Caricature of the Unmarried Mother,' *Canadian Welfare* 29(12) (December 1955), 247.

51 Patricia Garland, 'The Community's Part in Preventing Illegitimacy,' *Children* 10(2) (March–April 1963), 71.

52 Kunzel, 'Pulp Fictions and Problem Girls,' 1476.

53 See Cynthia Comacchio, 'Dancing to Perdition: Adolescence and Leisure in Interwar English Canada,' *Journal of Canadian Studies* 32 (Autumn 1997), 5–35.

54 Bailey, *From Front Porch to Back Seat*, 80.

55 Cynthia Comacchio, 'The Rising Generation: Laying Claim to the Health of Adolescents in English Canada, 1920–1970,' *Canadian Bulletin of Medical History* 19 (2002), 139–78.

56 Ethel MacLachlan, 'The Delinquent Girl,' *Social Welfare* (December 1921), 54.

57 Bailey, *From Front Porch to Back Seat*, 20.

58 Dulan Barber, *Unmarried Fathers* (London: Hutchinson, 1975), 19.

59 AO, York, Box 411-1-4-1, Case 477, 1957.

60 Roy Ernest Dickerson, *So Youth May Know: New Viewpoints on Sex and Love* (1930; rev. ed., New York: Association Press, 1948), as quoted in Patricia J. Campbell, *Sex Education Books for Young Adults, 1892–1979* (New York: Bowker, 1979), 69–70.

61 Dickerson, *So Youth May Know*, as quoted in Campbell, *Sex Education Books for Young Adults*, 70.

62 Sidney Furie, 'Birth Control and the Lower-Class Unmarried Mother,' *Social Work* 11(1) (January 1966), 43.

63 AO, York, Box 11-26-4-22, Case 2667, 1968. Emphasis in original.

64 AO, York, Box 411-1-3-9, Case 413, 1938. Emphasis in original.

65 AO, Hamilton, Box 24-2-3-3, Case 11, 1963. Emphasis in original.

66 AO, York, Box 411-1-3-10, Case 369, 1951.

67 AO, Hamilton, Box 24-2-3-4, Case 217, 1962.

68 AO, York, Box 411-1-3-12, Case 2037, 1953.

69 Such privacy could, however, be disrupted. For example, one woman was successful in her claim against the putative father because the date of conception coincided with a police report: 'Intercourse took place in November 1953, when they were parked in his car on Longwood Road, Hamilton in

the vicinity of the bay. This was quite late at night and 2 city policemen in uniform opened the car doors and questioned them for some time. They took their names and addresses.' AO, Wentworth, Box 24-2-3-3, Case 9, 1953.

70 AO, York, Box 411-1-3-13, Case 323, 1934.

71 AO, York, Box 411-1-3-10, Case 366, 1955.

72 AO, Algoma, Box 512-2-3-4, Case 1031, 1951.

73 AO, Hamilton, Box 66-4-4-6, Case 152, 1960.

74 AO, York, Box 411-1-4-6, Case 2347, 1964.

75 AO, York, Box 411-1-4-1, Case 463, 1960. It is, of course, ironic, that the court would accept this evidence in the paternity suit, but that the police had deemed it inadequate to justify criminal charges. Such discrepancies, however, are consistent with the findings of Clark and Lewis in their classic study of rape accusations and prosecutions in Toronto. They assert that the rape victim was often victimized a second time by a disbelieving legal system. For greater detail see Lorene Clark and Debra Lewis, *Rape: The Price of Coercive Sexuality* (Toronto: Women's Press, 1977).

76 AO, York, Box 411-1-3-12, Case 2039, 1952.

77 AO, York, Box 411-1-2-9, Case 989, 1959.

78 AO, York, Box 411-1-4-6, Case 2298, 1964.

79 Ibid.

80 Helen MacMurchy, *Sterilization? Birth Control? A Book for Family Welfare and Safety* (Toronto: The Macmillan Company of Canada, 1934), 148–51. For information regarding opposition to sexual education in the schools, see Christabelle Sethna, 'The Cold War and the Sexual Chill: Freezing Girls out of Sexual Education,' *Canadian Woman Studies/les cahiers de la femme* 17(4) (Spring 1998), 57–61. For a general history regarding the inaccessibility of birth control, see Angus McLaren, 'Birth Control and Abortion in Canada, 1870–1920,' *Canadian Historical Review* 59 (1978), 319–40, and Angus McLaren and Arlene T. McLaren, *The Bedroom and the State* (Toronto: McClelland and Stewart, 1986).

81 Deutsch, *The Psychology of Women*, 128.

82 Barber, *Unmarried Fathers*, 158.

83 AO, York, Box 411-1-3-13, Case 337, 1950.

84 AO, York, Box 411-1-4-2, Case 703, 1964.

85 AO, Hamilton, Box 24-2-3-3, Case 7, 1958.

86 AO, York, Box 411-1-3-15, Case 922, 1958.

87 AO, Middlesex, Box 27-9-1-2, Case 661, 1961.

88 Furie, 'Birth Control and the Lower-Class Unmarried Mother,' 48. See also Francis Fila, 'Sex Education and the Prevention of Illegitimacy,' in

Unmarried Parenthood: Clues to Agency and Community Action (New York: National Council on Illegitimacy, 1967), 90–101. Reformers also called for improved access to abortion, believing that this too would reduce rates of illegitimacy. Evidence suggests that they were correct. In the first year after the partial legalization of abortion in 1969, there were 5,657 therapeutic abortions in Ontario. Numbers rose steadily to approximately 30,000 a year by 1980, and have since remained stable. See Statistics Canada, *Therapeutic Abortions, 1982*, Catalogue No. 82–211 Annual, 1984 (Ottawa: Statistics Canada, 1984).

89 AO, Hamilton, Box 24-2-3-2, Case 596, 1963. This girl had particular reason to seek an abortion. Although her relationship with the putative father remained stable, her father was prosecuting the boy, who was only nineteen years old. The girl had admitted to her boyfriend that her father had molested her repeatedly and that while they would have gladly had a child together, she feared that this baby might have been the product of incest and rape. Three years later, the address of both the girl and the putative father were unknown, and it is tempting to speculate that they had fled the abusive father together.

90 AO, York, Box 411-1-4-2, Case 704, 1961.

91 AO, York, Box 411-1-3-11, Case 498, 1947.

92 AO, York, Box 411-1-3-8, Case 413, 1938.

93 Dickerson, *So Youth May Know*, as quoted in Campbell, *Sex Education Books for Young Adults*, 70.

94 AO, York, Box 411-1-3-11, Case 501, 1947.

95 AO, York, Box 411-1-2-9, Case 1013, 1959.

96 AO, York, Box 411-1-3-14, Case 1083, 1962.

97 AO, York, Box 411-1-3-8, Case 425, 1953.

98 AO, Hamilton, Box 24-2-3-3, Case 43, 1961.

99 AO, Algoma, Box 512-2-3-4, Case 1038, 1932. Not surprisingly, this putative father fled the jurisdiction of the court.

100 AO, York, Box 411-1-3-11, Case 508, 1950.

101 AO, Hamilton, Box 66-4-4-6, Case 157, 1950.

102 AO, Middlesex, Box 27-9-1-1, Case 305, 1944.

103 Ibid.

104 AO, York, Box 411-1-3-13, Case 335, 1954.

105 AO, York, Box 411-1-3-8, Case 415, 1953.

106 AO, Hamilton, Box 66-4-4-6, Case 191, 1947.

107 AO, Wentworth, Box 66-4-4-6, Case 200, 1952.

108 AO, Wentworth, Box 24-2-3-2, Case 585, 1962.

109 AO, Hamilton, Box 24-2-3-4, Case 286, 1962.
110 Chaskel, 'The Unmarried Mother,' 67.

4: 'Best for Our Babies'

1 Elizabeth Herzog, 'Who Are the Unmarried Mothers?' *Children* 9(4) (July–August 1962), 159.
2 John L. Brown, 'Rootedness,' *Involvement* 6(5) (May–June 1974), 8.
3 Veronica Strong-Boag, *Finding Families, Finding Ourselves: English Canada Encounters Adoption from the Nineteenth Century to the 1990s* (Don Mills, ON: Oxford University Press, 2006), 31. See also Rickie Solinger, *Beggars and Choosers: How the Politics of Choice Shapes Adoption, Abortion and Welfare in the United States* (New York: Hill and Wang, 2001), 67.
4 Leontine Young, *Out of Wedlock: A Study of the Unmarried Mother and Her Child* (New York: McGraw-Hill, 1954), 74.
5 In Ontario, before 1921, adoptions could be formalized only through private acts of the provincial legislature. The cost of such procedures was prohibitive. Moreover, the status of these children remained anomalous. For example, in 1909, foster parents who had cared for a child for over a year, without being paid for the child's upkeep, attempted to keep the child when the parents sought to reclaim her. Although the parents had signed an agreement with the fostering couple to release the child for adoption, the court asserted that 'the law of England knows nothing of adoption' and that 'parents cannot enter into an agreement legally binding to deprive themselves of the custody and control of their children; and, if they elect to do so, can at any moment resume their control over them.' *Re Davis*, [1909] O.L.R., 384 at 386.
6 *An Act Respecting the Adoption of Children*, S.O. 1921, c. 55, s. 2(a). (Hereafter *Adoption Act*.)
7 *Adoption Act*, 1921 c. 55, s. 4(1)(e). It was expressly provided, however, for the protection of the child from social censure, that the fact of illegitimacy would not be recorded on the adoption order. *Adoption Act*, 1921, c. 55, s. 4(2)(b). In 1929, this provision was amended such that the consent of a father was required if the child resided with, and was maintained by, the father at the time of the application. *The Statute Law Amendment Act*, S.O. 1929, c. 23, s. 11.
8 *Adoption Act*, 1921, c. 55, s. 5.
9 *Children of Unmarried Parents Act*, S.O. 1921, c. 54, s. 11. This codified and formalized what had already been the practice of the Children's Aid Society. Under the combined effect of the *Juvenile Delinquent's Act*, 7 & 8 Edw.

VII. c. 40 (Dom.), and the *Children's Protection Act*, R.S.O. 1914, c. 23, an illegitimate child whose mother was unable to maintain it could be declared to be a neglected child under the meaning of the statute. For further details, see *S (Re)*, [1919] O.J. No. 103.

10 This paragraph summarizes the provisions of the *Adoption Act*, 1921, c. 55, s. 10(1)(a), (b), (c), and 11(2).

11 *Adoption Act*, 1921, c. 55, s. 11(1) and 11(2). Until 1970, however, the child had no legal status with regard to wider kin. By the *Child Welfare Act, 1970*, this was amended and adopted children were made equal with natural born children unless a contrary intention was expressed in the will of wider kin. This was confirmed in *Re Barthelmes*, [1971] 1 O.R., 752.

12 Courts have consistently held that secrecy is essential to the security of the adoption: 'The sense of security of the child in his new home ought not to be disturbed. He must continue to know that this is indeed his home; that he is entitled to demand the loyalty of his new parents and that he is obliged to give them his loyalty in return. That sense of security and loyalty would be diminished if the adopting parents felt that a natural parent could interfere with the affection of the child or with their authority over him.' *S. v. Minister of Social Services*, [1982] 3 W.W.R., 358 at 366.

13 Katrysha Bracco, 'Patriarchy and the Law of Adoption: Beneath the Best Interests of the Child,' *Alberta Law Review* 35(4) (1997), 1041.

14 This paragraph summarizes the provisions of the *Adoption Act*, 1921, c. 55, s. 8 and s. 9(1)(a).

15 *Re: Baby Duffell*, [1950] S.C.R., 737; *Martin v. Duffell*, [1950] S.C.R., 737. For an extensive discussion of consent in Canadian adoption laws, see Strong-Boag, *Finding Families, Finding Ourselves*, chap. 2.

16 *Adoption Amendment Act*, S.O. 1951, c. 2.

17 Obviously, this gave considerably more power over adoption to adopting parents than to those relinquishing their children for adoption. For this reason, the confirmation of the right of the unwed mother, in particular, to reclaim her child before an adoption was finalized, while raising fears for adoptive couples, was considered just by progressive social workers engaged with unwed mothers: 'Those interested in social problems of unmarried mothers and their children should welcome the Supreme Court's decision. There has never been any question of the legal responsibility of the unmarried mother to maintain her child. But the rights of the natural mother have been getting less and less attention. They have been almost forgotten by many who have been all for helping childless couples satisfy their desire for children ... It has been argued in some quarters that the mother should lose all her rights when she signs the preliminary agree-

ment to hand over the child to strangers who plan to adopt it. This in spite of the fact that the law does not permit her to sign away her liability to maintain the child. Those who would take it away from here are free to hand it back to her at any time before the court makes an adoption order.' Svanhuit Josie, 'The Unwed Mother – Her Right to Her Child,' *Saturday Night*, 15 August 1950, 26.

18 *Adoption Act*, 1921, c. 55, s. 14.

19 Until 1930 adoption legislation was administered in Ontario by the CAS, which acted in concert with the Neglected and Dependent Children's Branch of the Department of the Provincial Secretary. In 1930, Ontario established the Department of Public Welfare, within which the Department of Children's Aid Branch was created to supervise the activities of the CAS across the province, specifically the administration of both the adoption provisions and the *Children of Unmarried Parents Act*. For more details, see Harry Cassidy, *Public Health and Welfare Organization in Canada* (Toronto: The Ryerson Press, 1945). Very little supervision of various CAS offices seems to have been carried out.

20 June Callwood, 'Adoption: Not All Hearts and Flowers,' *Chatelaine*, April 1976, 41.

21 As quoted in Andrew Jones and Leonard Rutman, *In the Children's Aid: J.J. Kelso and Child Welfare in Ontario* (Toronto: University of Toronto Press, 1986), 156. With regard to American history, there is considerable debate about the attitude of social workers to illegitimate children and their mothers. Regina Kunzel argues that by the early 1920s, social workers uniformly advocated the separation of the unwed mother from her child and the child's relinquishment for adoption. This, she asserts, represented a departure from the nineteenth-century practice of insisting that the unwed mother accept responsibility and punishment for her sins by keeping her child. Wayne Carp, however, argues that 'there were few, if any professional social workers who recommended separating unwed mothers from their children as a first resort.' He believes that social workers came to support adoption only gradually and largely after the 1930s. See Regina Kunzel, 'The Professionalization of Benevolence: Evangelicals and Social Workers in the Florence Crittenton Homes, 1915–1945,' *Journal of Social History* 22 (1988), 21–43; Regina Kunzel, *Fallen Women, Problem Girls: Unmarried Mothers and the Professionalization of Social Work, 1890–1945* (New Haven: Yale University Press, 1993); and Wayne Carp, 'Professional Social Workers, Adoption and the Problem of Illegitimacy, 1915–1945,' *Journal of Policy History* 6(3) (1994), 162.

22 Ada Elliot Sheffield, 'Program of the Committee on Illegitimacy – Commit-

tee Report,' in *Proceedings of the National Conference of Social Work*, (Chicago: University of Chicago Press, 1921), 78. See also Harley Dickinson, 'Scientific Parenthood: The Mental Hygiene Movement and the Reform of Canadian Families, 1925–1950,' *Journal of Comparative Family Studies* 24 (Autumn 1993), 387–402.

23 Charlotte Whitton, 'Unmarried Parents and the Social Order,' Parts I and II, *Social Welfare* (April–May 1920), 187.

24 The Stanford revision of the Binet-Simon intelligence test was particularly popular. See Sophie van Senden Theis, *How Foster Children Turn Out* (New York: State Charities Association, 1924); and James W. Trent, *Inventing the Feeble-Minded: A History of Mental Retardation in the United States* (Berkeley: University of California Press, 1994).

25 Helen D. Sargent, 'Is It Safe to Adopt a Child?' *Parents' Magazine*, October 1935, 26.

26 Elizabeth Frazier, 'The Baby Market,' *Saturday Evening Post*, 1 February 1930, 25.

27 Julie Berebitsky, *Like Our Very Own: Adoption and the Changing Culture of Motherhood, 1851–1950* (Lawrence: University of Kansas Press, 2000), 34.

28 G.F. Lemby, *Family Law* (Toronto: International Self-Counsel Press, 1971), 158.

29 Jones and Rutman, *In the Children's Aid*, 163.

30 Wayne Carp, *Family Matters: Secrecy and Disclosure in the History of Adoption* (Cambridge, MA: Harvard University Press, 1998), 29. See also Elaine Tyler May, *Homeward Bound: American Families in the Cold War Era* (New York: Basic Books, 1988); and Elaine Tyler May, *Barren in the Promised Land: Childless Americans and the Pursuit of Happiness* (New York: Basic Books, 1995).

31 Carp, *Family Matters*, 29.

32 Katherine Bain and Martha Eliot, 'Adoption as a National Problem,' *Pediatrics* 20 (1957), 367.

33 Winston Ehrmann, 'Illegitimacy in Florida II: Social and Psychological Aspects of Illegitimacy,' *Eugenics Quarterly* 3 (December 1956), 227.

34 John Bowlby, *Maternal Care and Mental Health*, World Health Organization Monograph Series, No. 2 (Geneva: World Health Organization, 1951), 101, 103.

35 Florence G. Brown, 'What Do We Seek in Adoptive Parents?' *Social Casework* 1 (April 1951), 155.

36 Ruth Pierce, *Single and Pregnant* (Boston: Beacon Press, 1970), 133.

37 AO, York, Box 411-1-3-9, Case 407, 1951. For information on the racial specificity of adoption in the United States, see Rickie Solinger, 'Race and Value:

Black and White Illegitimate Babies in the U.S.A., 1945–1965,' *Gender and History* 4 (1992), 343–63.

38 See Rickie Solinger, *Wake Up Little Susie: Single Pregnancy and Race before Roe v. Wade* (New York: Routledge, 1992). For a disturbing account of the illegal seizure and sale of the babies of unwed mothers in Nova Scotia during this period, see Bette Cahill, *Butterbox Babies* (Toronto: Seal Books, 1992).

39 Margaret Thornhill, 'Unprotected Adoptions,' *Children* 2(5) (September–October 1955), 179.

40 Ibid., 183.

41 Certainly, baby selling from maternity homes happened in other provinces. For a detailed description of the corruption in one Nova Scotia home, see Cahill, *Butterbox Babies*.

42 AO, Middlesex, Box 27-9-1-1, Case 295, 1945.

43 Lemby, *Family Law*, 158.

44 Brown, 'Rootedness,' 8.

45 *Child Welfare* Act, S.O. 1965, c. 14, s. 12. See also H. Philips Hepworth, *Foster Care and Adoption in Canada* (Ottawa: Canadian Council on Social Development, 1980); and N. Trocme, 'Child Welfare Services,' in R. Barnhorst and L. Johnson, eds., *The State of the Child in Ontario* (Toronto: Oxford University Press, 1991), 63–91.

46 AO, N. Emily Mohr, *A Study of Illegitimacy in Ontario* (Toronto: Social Service Council, 1921), 23, RG 4-32, 1871–1947, Central Registry, No. 2023.

47 Florence Clothier, 'Problems of Illegitimacy as They Concern the Worker in the Field of Adoption,' *Mental Hygiene* 25 (October 1941), 579.

48 Ibid.

49 AO, Wentworth, Box 24-2-3-3, Case 43, 1944. There is little doubt that the adoption market favoured parents who were wealthy.

50 Ruth Honderich Spielberg, 'Dollars and Adoption,' *Maclean's*, 29 November 1952, 48.

51 This was ironic and hypocritical since when money was owed to mothers, the policy of the court was to allow large arrears to accrue before court action would be taken; in fact, no action would be taken until arrears reached at least $100.

52 Ironically, they enforced collection against men even when women would have preferred that they not do so. One mother, who had released her child for adoption and subsequently married someone else, asserted that she and the putative father were finally no longer bitter with one another and that she did not want his new marriage disrupted by collection of an old debt. Nonetheless, collection proceeded against him, although the mother took

the step of informing the father that she had requested that this not be done: AO, Wentworth, Box 24-2-3-3, Case 58, 1958.

53 AO, Wentworth, Box 24-2-3-2, Case 528, 1963.

54 Svanhuit Josie, 'The American Caricature of the Unmarried Mother,' *Canadian Welfare* 29(12) (December 1955), 247.

55 The majority of this evidence is drawn from American sources, as very limited discussion of adoption appeared in Canadian journals.

56 Mary Speers, 'Case Work and Adoption,' *The Social Worker* 16(3) (February 1948), 18

57 Esther Levitt, 'Repeated Out-of-Wedlock Pregnancies: Services to the Unwed Mother,' *Child Welfare* 38 (1959), 9.

58 Clothier, 'Problems of Illegitimacy,' 584.

59 Editorial, 'Get the Babies to Those Who Want Them,' *Maclean's*, 5 February 1966, 4.

60 Josie, 'The American Caricature of the Unmarried Mother,' 249. The most prominent American critic of the adoption mandate was Clark Vincent. See Clark Vincent, 'The Adoption Market and the Unwed Mother's Baby,' *Marriage and Family Living* 18 (May 1956), 124–7; Clark Vincent, 'Unmarried Mothers: Society's Dilemma,' *Sexology* 28 (1962), 451–5; and Clark Vincent, 'Illegitimacy in the Next Decade: Trends and Implications,' *Child Welfare* 43 (December 1964), 513–20.

61 Josie, 'The American Caricature of the Unmarried Mother,' 248.

62 Kathleen Sutherton, 'Another View,' *Canadian Welfare* 31(5) (December 1955), 249–52. See also Francis Coffino, 'Helping a Mother Surrender Her Child for Adoption,' *Child Welfare* 39 (February 1960), 25–8.

63 AO, York, Box 411-1-3-11, Case 498, 1947.

64 AO, York, Box 411-1-4-5, Case 2316, 1960.

65 Anne Petrie, *Gone to an Aunt's: Remembering Canada's Homes for Unwed Mothers* (Toronto: McClelland and Stewart, 1998), 147.

66 AO, York, Box 411-1-3-11, Case 488, 1946

67 Petrie, *Gone to an Aunt's*, 147.

68 This mother was not alone in refusing to relinquish a second illegitimate child for adoption. Statistics indicate that women in a second or subsequent illicit pregnancy are less likely to release those babies than are first time mothers. In a New York study completed in 1963, for example, the rates were 38 per cent and 12 per cent respectively. See William Rashbaum, Janice Paneth, Helen Rehr, and Martin Greenberg, 'Use of Social Services by Unmarried Mothers,' *Children* 10(1) (January–February 1963), 15.

69 AO, York, Box 411-1-2-9, Case 976, 1959. This court procedure must have been unbearably painful for the young woman in question. She had been

seventeen years of age when her first illegitimate child was born; she had fled her hometown, given birth and released the child in Toronto. Her parents had not known about this pregnancy. When she decided to keep her second child, however, not only did she have to reveal the facts of this pregnancy to her family but also court proceedings forced her to admit her earlier pregnancy to family members.

70 Note that 9 of 2,031 (0.4 per cent) cohabiting mothers released their babies for adoption.

71 It should be noted that these averages include only never-married women, not those who were cohabiting with the putative fathers, who were often considerably older.

72 They were, however, very vulnerable to having their children seized on the basis that they were declared to be unfit mothers; all nine Aboriginal women ultimately lost custody of their children.

73 AO, York, Box 411-1-3-9, Case 397, 1955.

74 AO, Wentworth, Box 66-3-3-14, Case 111, 1957.

75 Young, *Out of Wedlock*, 74.

76 This is consistent with the findings of other authors who have investigated the reasons for relinquishment of children born out of wedlock. See Kate Inglis, *Living Mistakes: Mothers Who Consented to Adoption* (London: George Allen and Unwin, 1984), 191; and E.K. Rynearson, 'Relinquishment and Its Maternal Complications: A Preliminary Study,' *American Journal of Psychiatry* 123 (March 1982), 338–40.

77 This paragraph summarizes *Re Mugford*, [1970] 1 O.R. 601–611 at 601, 603, 606, and 605.

78 *Re Mugford*, [1970] 1 O.R. 601–611 at 605.

79 Josie, 'The American Caricature of the Unmarried Mother,' 248.

80 Young, *Out of Wedlock*, 160.

81 Social Planning Council of Metropolitan Toronto, *A Report on Maternity Homes in Metropolitan Toronto* (Toronto, 1960), vii.

82 Petrie, *Gone to an Aunt's*, 148.

83 Inglis, *Living Mistakes*, 294.

84 Adam Pertman, *Adoption Nation: How the Adoption Revolution Is Transforming America* (New York: Basic Books, 2000), 12.

85 AO, York, Box 411-1-2-9, Case 976, 1959.

86 AO, York, Box 411-1-3-12, Case 2033, 1954.

87 AO, York, Box 411-1-3-12, Case 2066, 1952.

88 *Tyler v. District Court of Ontario*, [1986] 1 R.F.L. (3d), 139. In this case the mother asserted that she was submitted to social pressures to release her child for adoption and 'complains of lack of counseling as to how she could

keep her baby and thrive on her own, lack of congratulatory messages on her pregnancy out of wedlock, and lack of offers for financial support; she links her emotional breakdowns in 1975 and 1985 to her guilt at having offered her child for adoption.'

89 Max Braithwaite, 'Born Out of Wedlock,' *Maclean's*, 15 November 1947, 65.

90 Honore Willsie, 'When Is a Child Adoptable?' *Delineator* 95 (1919), 35.

91 Solinger, *Wake Up Little Susie*, 155.

92 R.L. Jenkins, 'Adoption Practices and the Physician,' *Journal of the American Medical Association* 103(6) (1934), 403.

93 Solinger, *Wake Up Little Susie*, 155.

94 Clothier, 'Placing the Child for Adoption,' 564–5.

95 Joseph McNicholas, 'Adoptions: Happiness or Tragedy?' *Hospital Progress* 39 (April 1958), 66.

96 Alice Kunz Ray, 'A Good Adoption Program: Can Standards Be Maintained without Sacrificing Flexibility?' in *Proceedings of the National Conference of Social Work* (New York: Columbia University Press, 1945), 299.

97 Strong-Boag, *Finding Families, Finding Ourselves*, 72.

98 Ibid., 52.

99 AO, Algoma, Box 512-2-3-4, Case 1018, 1923.

100 Rita Loadman, 'What's New in Adoption?' *Canadian Welfare* 30(3) (March 1956), 336.

101 Social Planning Council of Metropolitan Toronto, *A Report on Maternity Homes in Metropolitan Toronto*, xviii.

102 'Adopted Mother by Herself,' *Scribner's Magazine*, January 1935, 57.

103 Dorothy Thompson, 'Fit for Adoption,' *Ladies' Home Journal*, May 1939, 4.

104 Lillian Gatlin, 'Adopting a Baby: The Stork Gives Blindly, but Only the Fittest Qualify as Parents by Proxy,' *Sunset, the Pacific Monthly*, February 1921, 85; and 'Chosen Children,' *Time Magazine*, 15 May 1939.

105 AO, York, Box 411-1-4-1, Case 455, 1960.

106 Callwood, 'Adoption,' 108.

107 Debra Poulin, 'The Open Adoption Records Movement: Constitutional Cases and Legislative Compromise,' *Journal of Family Law* 26 (1987–1988), 396. It was only in 1978, 'after long and heated debate,' that the Ontario legislature, by a 37–36 vote, established a three-party disclosure registry. H. David Kirk, *Adoptive Kinship: A Modern Institution in Need of Reform* (Toronto: Butterworths, 1981), 136.

108 Berebitsky, *Like Our Very Own*, 3.

109 The biological definition of what constitutes a family is much more challenged by open adoption. Interracial adoption, international adoption, adoption by single persons, and, most recently, gay and lesbian adoption

have resulted in the creation of families that represent a radical and potentially transformative alternative to the biological norm. Berebitsky, *Like Our Very Own*, 168. For a discussion of the changing meaning and possibilities of adoption, see Elizabeth Bartholet, *Family Bonds: Adoption and the Politics of Parenting* (Boston: Houghton Mifflin, 1993).

110 Berebitsky, *Like Our Very Own*, 3.
111 David Howe, Phillida Sawbridge, and Diana Hinings, *Half a Million Women: Mothers Who Lose Their Children by Adoption* (London: Penguin, 1992), 18.

5: 'Haunted by Bills'

1 Today, this description applies equally well not only to children born outside of traditional two-parent families but also to the children of divorced parents who overwhelmingly remain in the care of mothers. According to *Transitions*, the Report of the Social Assistance Review Committee of Ontario (Toronto: Ontario Ministry of Community and Social Services, 1988), 'female-headed families remain four times more likely to be living in poverty than are male-headed families' (63).
2 Marianne Takas, 'Assisting Young Mothers with Paternity and Child Support Services,' *Children's Legal Rights Journal* 13(1) (Winter 1992), 2.
3 The mother in this case spiritedly defended her virtue. She and the putative father had planned to marry and she felt no shame about her behaviour. She asserted that she would survive, with her child, because her mother, whom she described as a 'pretty terrific person,' was standing by her, providing her with a home and financial aid. She resented her lover's abandonment of their child and the attitudes of a society that condemned her to outcast status. She resented the fact that he was not also judged. AO, York, Box 411-1-3-15, Case 917, 1958.
4 Svanhuit Josie, 'The Unwed Mother – Her Right to Her Child,' *Saturday Night*, 15 August 1950, 27.
5 For details regarding the ongoing disadvantage of women in the Canadian workforce, see Pat Armstrong and Hugh Armstrong, *The Double Ghetto: Canadian Women and Their Segregated Work*, 3rd ed. (Toronto: McClelland and Stewart, 1994).
6 For more information on attitudes towards working mothers, see Joan Sangster, 'Doing Two Jobs: The Wage Earning Mother, 1945–1970,' in Joy Parr, ed., *A Diversity of Women, Ontario, 1945–1980* (Toronto: University of Toronto Press, 1995), 98–134.
7 For information on public day care in Canada, see Patricia Schulz, 'Day

Care in Canada, 1850–1962,' in Kathleen Gallagher Ross, ed., *Good Day Care* (Toronto: Women's Press, 1978); and Susan Prentice, 'Workers, Mothers, Reds: Toronto's Post-War Day Care Fight,' *Studies in Political Economy* 30 (Autumn 1989), 115–41.

8 *Children of Unmarried Parents Act,* S.O. 1921, c. 54, s. 11.

9 York, AO, Box 411-1-3-9, Case 404, 1952.

10 Cathryne Schmitz, 'Reframing the Dialogue on Female-Headed Single-Parent Families,' *Affilia* 10(4) (Winter 1995), 429.

11 AO, York, Box 411-1-3-9, Case 401, 1933.

12 AO, York, Box 27-9-1-3, Case 613, 1956.

13 Mignon Sauber and Elaine Rubinstein, *Experiences of the Unwed Mother as a Parent: A Longitudinal Study of Unmarried Mothers Who Keep Their First-Born* (New York: Community Council of Greater New York, 1965), 35.

14 Marian Radke Yarrow, 'Maternal Employment and Child Rearing,' *Children* 8(6) (November–December 1961), 223.

15 Eleanor Maccoby, 'Children and Working Mothers,' *Children* 5(3) (May–June, 1958), 83.

16 Sheldon Glueck and Eleanor Glueck, 'Working Mothers and Delinquency,' *Mental Hygiene* 41 (July 1957), 327.

17 *Fortune* 54 (July 1956), 172.

18 AO, Algoma, Box 512-2-3-4, Case 1032, 1930.

19 Glueck and Glueck, 'Working Mothers and Delinquency,' 327.

20 Rose Bernstein, *Helping Unmarried Mothers* (New York: Association Press, 1971), 99.

21 Dennis Marsden, *Mothers Alone: Poverty and the Fatherless Family* (London: Penguin, 1969), 173.

22 AO, York, Box 411-1-2-9, Case 989, 1959.

23 Colin Lindsay, *Lone-Parent Families in Canada: Target Groups Project* (Ottawa: Minister of Industry, Science and Technology, 1992), 22.

24 *Children of Unmarried Parents Act,* 1921, s.19.

25 This should not be surprising; once women realized that the CAS was not going to provide help in obtaining support from putative fathers, they had little incentive to encourage an investigation into their lives.

26 Sauber and Rubinstein, *Experiences of the Unwed Mother as a Parent,* 41.

27 AO, York, Box 411-1-3-11, Case 508, 1950.

28 Immigrant women, and women who were living in the city away from family and friends, were of course least likely to be able to rely on such resources for aid. Also, it is interesting to note that while some parents refused to allow underage daughters to marry or to take on economic responsibility for the illegitimate child, thereby making relinquishment for

adoption more likely, most parents did at least continue to provide a home for the mother herself. Only in two cases were daughters 'kicked out' of the parental home as a result of pregnancy. In one of these two cases, the daughter went to live with an aunt and uncle and it is unclear to what degree her contact with her family was severed. AO, Wentworth, Box 66-3-3-14, Case 79, 1945. In the other case the girl was clearly not from a working-class background. She and the putative father of her child had met while undergraduates at Queen's University. When her father, a prominent Toronto businessman, learned of her pregnancy, she was disowned and she cohabited, temporarily, with another student from Queen's. She stated from the outset that she would keep her child, whatever the consequences, and this may have been what precipitated her break with her parents. It is possible that had she been willing to quietly disappear, and to make use of the services of a home for unwed mothers and discreetly release her child for adoption, her relationship with her parents might have survived. Poorer women, however, did not have the same options with regard to maternity homes that charged significant fees for services. Ultimately, however, this woman's education aided her in supporting her child. Despite non-payment under her support order, she was able to pay a sitter to keep her child during the day while she found work as an accounting assistant. AO, York, Box 411-1-4-1, Case 433, 1959.

29 AO, York, Box 411-1-3-13, Case 344, 1945.
30 AO, York, Box 411-1-4-6, Case 2457, 1965.
31 AO, Middlesex, Box 27-9-1-1, Case 305, 1944.
32 Virginia Wimperis, *The Unmarried Mother and Her Child* (London: George Allen and Unwin, 1960), 262.
33 AO, Wentworth, Box 66-3-3-14, Case 128, 1958.
34 AO, Wentworth, Box 24-2-3-4, Case 228, 1948.
35 AO, Wentworth, Box 66-3-3-14, Case 81, 1946.
36 AO, Middlesex, Box 27-9-1-1, Case 315, 1947. Eventually, however, she married and her new husband adopted the child, relieving her of the stress of collection.
37 Dulan Barber, *Unmarried Fathers* (London: Hutchinson, 1975), 131.
38 Leontine Young, *Out of Wedlock: A Study of the Unmarried Mother and Her Child* (New York: McGraw-Hill, 1954), 131.
39 Barber, *Unmarried Fathers*, 131.
40 *Children of Unmarried Parents Act*, S.O. 1921, c. 54, s. 18(2).
41 Ibid., c. 54, s. 11.
42 Andrew Jones and Leonard Rutman, *In the Children's Aid: J.J. Kelso and Child Welfare in Ontario* (Toronto: University of Toronto Press, 1981), 160.

43 *Children of Unmarried Parents Act*, S.O. 1921, s. 18(2).

44 AO, Middlesex, Box 27-9-1-2, Case 633, 1956.

45 The father continued to resist payment, and when he died in 1963, the case was greatly in arrears (for which his wife was not held responsible). AO, Middlesex, Box 27-9-1-1, Case 301, 1952.

46 Ibid.

47 AO, York, Box 411-1-1-13, Case 329, 1953.

48 Only one child in this sample of 4,023 cases seems to have received financial support, while living with a single mother, that exceeded a minimal level required for subsistence. It is significant that this is also the only case in which the mother was involved with a putative father outside her own social class. She was a saleslady, but the putative father of her child was the president of a large factory and owned an expensive home. Although she had not known he was married at the time of their affair, he was a married man with five legitimate children. When she threatened him with public humiliation through affiliation proceedings, he hired a lawyer and granted her a generous private allowance for the child. While court orders and agreements with the CAS were rarely more than $10 a week, this father paid the mother's exceptionally high hospital expenses in full and $40 a week in support. He also paid the child's school fees when she attended Havergal College preschool. The baby was born blind and the father supported her, not only until the age of sixteen as required under legislation, but until she completed high school at the Brantford School for the Blind. Because of his social position, and the fact that he did not want his wife to learn of his sexual indiscretion, this man could not, like so many other fathers, simply flee the jurisdiction. Instead, the threat of court proceedings was a valuable weapon for this mother. AO, York, Box 411-1-3-9, Case 410, 1952.

49 AO, Wentworth, Box 66-3-3-14, Case 101, 1957.

50 AO, York, Box 411-1-3-13, Case 336, 1943.

51 Sidney Katz, 'The Forgotten Fathers,' *Maclean's*, 1 May 1949, 73.

52 AO, Middlesex, Box 27-9-1-1, Case 301, 1952.

53 In 1950, when her illegitimate daughter was five years old, the woman married another man who happily took the child into the marital home, but he refused to release the putative father from his financial obligation. AO, Wentworth, Box 24-2-3-3, Case 69, 1956.

54 AO, Middlesex, Box 27-9-1-2, Case 649, 1959.

55 AO, Middlesex, Box 27-9-1-2, Case 637, 1957.

56 AO, Wentworth, Box 24-2-3-2, Case 608, 1958.

57 AO, Middlesex, Box 27-9-1-2, Case 625, 1955.

58 AO, York, Box 411-1-4-1, Case 468, 1959. Emphasis in original.

59 AO, Middlesex, Box 27-9-1-1, Case 296, 1941.

60 Ibid.

61 AO, Wentworth, Box 66-4-4-6, Case 168, 1953.

62 AO, Middlesex, Box 27-9-1-1, Case 310, 1955.

63 AO, York, Box 411-1-4-2, Case 699, 1961.

64 AO, York, Box 11-26-4-16, Case 2162, 1961.

65 AO, York, Box 11-26-4-21, Case 3141, 1969.

66 AO, Middlesex, Box 27-9-1-1, Case 305, 1953.

67 Wimperis, *The Unmarried Mother and Her Child*, 122. The ineffectiveness of affiliation proceedings plagues other jurisdictions as well. In a study of British unwed mothers it was found that 'somewhat more than a third of the women in this study did not receive any financial assistance from the putative fathers.' Sauber and Rubinstein, *Experiences of the Unwed Mother as a Parent*, 90.

68 AO, York, Box 411-1-3-11, Case 463, 1963.

69 AO, York, Box 411-1-3-8, Case 417, 1949.

70 AO, York, Box 411-1-3-11, Case 498, 1947. Emphasis in original.

71 AO, Wentworth, Box 411-1-3-10, Case 356, 1939. Emphasis in original.

72 AO, York, Box 411-1-3-10, Case 359, 1956.

73 AO, York, Box 411-1-4-1, Case 452, 1959.

74 AO, York, Box 411-1-3-12, Case 2052, 1955.

75 Unmarried Parenthood Committee of the Welfare Council of Toronto and District, *A Study of the Adjustment of Teen-age Children Born Out of Wedlock Who Remained in the Custody of Their Mothers or Relatives* (Toronto, 1943).

76 AO, Wentworth, Box 24-2-3-3, Case 44, 1959.

77 AO, York, Box 411-1-3-15, Case 923, 1954.

78 AO, York, Box 11-26-4-19, Case 2472, 1966. Inadequate housing was a common problem faced by unmarried mothers. One study, conducted in 1960–3, found that 'problems with housing were widespread ... 43% of the unmarried mothers mentioned that problems of shabby, deteriorated conditions, rats, roaches and inadequate facilities existed in their housing.' Sauber and Rubinstein, *The Experiences of the Unwed Mother as a Parent*, 79.

79 AO, Wentworth, Box 24-2-3-2, Case 608, 1954.

80 AO, Wentworth, Box 24-2-3-4, Case 278, 1962.

81 Roger Levesque, 'The Role of Unwed Fathers in Welfare Law: Failing Legislative Initiatives and Surrendering Judicial Responsibility,' *Law and Inequality: A Journal of Theory and Practice* 12 (1993), 105.

82 AO, Middlesex, Box 27-9-1-1, Case 294, 1945.

83 'Annual Report of the Ontario Department of Public Welfare, 1955–56,' 43, as cited in Margaret Jane Hillyard Little, *No Car, No Radio, No Liquor Permit: The Moral Regulation of Single Mothers in Ontario, 1920–1977* (Toronto: University of Toronto Press, 1998), 135.

84 James Struthers, *The Limits of Affluence: Welfare in Ontario, 1920–1970* (Toronto: University of Toronto Press, 1994), 162. By 1959, unwed mothers made up 8 per cent of the provincial mothers' allowance caseload; however, evidence from these case files suggests that the unwed mothers in such cases were likely to have been deserted informal wives.

85 Metropolitan Toronto Records and Archives (MTRA), RG 5.1, Box 43, File 47, 'Mothers' Allowances and Dependent Fathers, 1931–1961'; letter from the chairman of the Toronto Welfare Council to Harold Kirby, 31 March, 1943, as quoted in Struthers, *The Limits of Affluence*, 120.

86 AO, RG 29, Series 74, Box 3, File 3.5 – 1959, 'Never Fared So Well as On Welfare,' *The Glengarry News*, 28 October 1959, as cited in Little, *No Car, No Radio, No Liquor Permit*, 135–6.

87 K.J. Rea, *The Prosperous Years: The Economic History of Ontario, 1939–1975* (Toronto: University of Toronto Press, 1985), 7.

88 Michael Katz, *In the Shadow of the Poorhouse: A Social History of Welfare in America* (New York: Basic Books, 1986), 290.

89 Struthers, *The Limits of Affluence*, 261.

90 Ibid., 262.

91 AO, Wentworth, Box 24-2-3-4, Case 247, 1963.

92 AO, York, Box 411-1-4-2, Case 707, 1961.

93 AO, York, Box 411-1-3-12, Case 2033, 1953.

94 MTRA, RG 46.17.3 'GWA – District Work, Minutes of Meetings, Jan 58–Nov/65,' Box 98, File 5, minutes of meeting, 20 November 1958, as quoted in Struthers, *The Limits of Affluence*, 155.

95 MTRA, RG 46.17.3, Box 98, File 3, 'General Welfare Assistance – District Work – Minutes of Meetings Nov 49-May 53, meeting on "Support from Putative Fathers," 11 May 1950,' as quoted in Struthers, *The Limits of Affluence*, 155.

96 Ontario *Hansard*, 18 March 1965, 1775.

97 Struthers, *The Limits of Affluence*, 211.

98 Ontario *Hansard* 18 March 1964, 1757. For further details, see Struthers, *The Limits of Affluence*.

99 Struthers, *The Limits of Affluence*, 219. See also George Bain, 'The State of Welfare,' *Globe and Mail*, 16 April 1965.

100 Struthers, *The Limits of Affluence*, 231.

101 Ibid., 234.

102 These authors assert that 'despite the hopes of feminists that women will become economically independent of men, marriage remains a major source of economic security for women with children, especially if they have few job skills. Hence, encouraging such unions ought to be as important an issue in welfare reform as job training and work.' Douglas Besharov and Timothy Sullivan, 'Welfare Reform and Marriage,' *The Public Interest* 125 (Fall 1996), 81. Such initiatives must be resisted because women cannot be free when they are only economically secure when attached to, and dependent upon, an individual man.

103 AO, Wentworth, Box 66-3-3-14, Case 79, 1945.

104 Charles Bowerman, Donald Irish, and Hallowell Pope, *Unwed Motherhood: Personal and Social Consequences* (Chapel Hill: Institute for Research in Social Science, University of North Carolina, 1966), 165.

105 Dickerson, *So Youth May Know*, as quoted in Patricia J. Campbell, *Sex Education Books for Young Adults, 1892–1979* (New York: Bowker, 1979), 70.

106 AO, Wentworth, Box 66-3-3-14, Case 61, 1951.

107 For a description of a similar pattern in the temporary use of orphanages by desperate women in nineteenth-century Montreal, see Bettina Bradbury, 'The Fragmented Family: Family Strategies in the Face of Death, Illness and Poverty, Montreal, 1860–1885,' in Joy Parr, ed., *Childhood and Family in Canadian History* (Toronto: McClelland and Stewart, 1982).

108 AO, York, Box 411-1-4-2, Case 703, 1957.

109 AO, Wentworth, Box 66-4-4-6, Case 165, 1960.

110 AO, York, Box 411-1-3-15, Case 872, 1957.

111 Bernstein, *Helping Unmarried Mothers*, 80. See also Rose Bernstein, 'Gaps in Services to Unwed Mothers,' *Children* 10(2) (1963), 49–54.

112 Sophinisba Breckinridge, *The Family and the State: Select Documents* (Chicago: University of Chicago Press, 1934), 370.

113 AO, York, Box 411-1-3-11, Case 509, 1940. It was explicitly stated in this case file that the probability of adoption was very low, since the child was chronically ill with bronchial infections.

114 AO, Wentworth, Box 66-3-3-14, Case 112, 1954. As Joan Sangster has also noted, assessments 'denoting "low intelligence" often came immediately after a statement describing the woman as Native, a psychological slip of consequence.' Joan Sangster, 'Criminalizing the Colonized: Ontario Native Women Confront the Criminal Justice System, 1920–1960,' *Canadian Historical Review* 80(1) (1999), 50.

115 Bernstein, *Helping Unmarried Mothers*, 105.

116 Sylvie Pierce, 'Single Mothers and the Concept of Female Dependency in

the Development of the Welfare State in Britain,' *Journal of Comparative Family Studies* 11(1) (1980), 57.

117 Margrit Eichler, 'The Limits of Family Law Reform or the Privatization of Female and Child Poverty,' *Canadian Family Law Quarterly* 17 (1996), 82.

6: 'Known as MRS S'

1 McKenzie Porter, 'The Unmarried Wives,' *Maclean's*, 27 January 1962, 18.
2 Kathleen Kiernan, Hilary Land, and Jane Lewis, *Lone Motherhood in Twentieth-Century Britain: From Footnote to Front Page* (Oxford: Clarendon, 1998), 41.
3 Wentworth, AO, Box 24-2-3-4, Case 242, 1964.
4 Henry Schumacher, 'The Unmarried Mother: A Socio-Psychiatric Viewpoint,' *Mental Hygiene* 11 (October 1927), 775.
5 By contrast, for never-married women, ages fluctuated by decade with a mean of 22 in the 1920s, 23 in the 1930s, 26 in the 1940s, 23 in the 1950s, and 21 in the 1960s.
6 Vanier Centre, *Profiling Canada: Families* (Montreal: Vanier Institute of the Family, 1994), 39.
7 Wentworth, AO, Box 24-2-3-2, Case 597, 1947.
8 For further information on divorce, see James Snell, *In the Shadow of the Law: Divorce in Canada, 1900–1939* (Toronto: University of Toronto Press, 1991).
9 Ibid., 214. Snell asserts that the average cost for a judicial divorce in Ontario in the 1930s, for example, was $241.90 (215).
10 Winter, 'Common Law Wife,' *Chatelaine*, January 1952, 17.
11 AO, York, Box 411-1-3-14, Case 1084, 1950.
12 AO, York, Box 411-1-3-8, Case 411, 1945. Emphasis in original letter to the CAS.
13 AO, York, Box 411-1-2-9, Case 1015, 1946.
14 AO, York, Box 411-1-3-8, Case 415, 1948.
15 It was only in the 1970s that the rights of putative fathers with regard to their children began to be discussed by the courts. See Diana Dzwiekowski, 'Casenotes: Findings of Paternity in Ontario, *Sayer v. Rollin*,' *Canadian Journal of Family Law* 3 (1980), 318–26; and Debra Ratterman, 'Adoption and the Rights of Putative Fathers,' *Children's Legal Rights Journal* 11(1) (Spring 1990), 13–21. As the Ontario Law Reform Commission asserted in 1973, the affiliation order did 'not serve as a judicial finding of paternity for any other purpose but holding the father responsible for the monetary payments mentioned in section 59 (1) of *The Child Welfare Act*.' Ontario Law

Reform Commission, *Report on Family Law*, Part III, *Children* (Toronto: Ministry of the Attorney General, 1973), 10.

16 Joan Sangster, 'Creating Social and Moral Citizens: Defining and Treating Delinquent Boys and Girls in Canada, 1920–1965,' in Robert Adamoski, Dorothy Chunn, and Robert Menzies, eds., *Contesting Canadian Citizenship: Historical Readings* (Peterborough, ON: Broadview, 2002), 354.

17 J. Kasanin and S. Handschin, 'Psychodynamic Factors in Illegitimacy,' *American Journal of Orthopsychiatry* 11 (January 1941), 70.

18 Florence Clothier, 'The Unmarried Mother of School Age as Seen by a Psychiatrist,' *Mental Hygiene* 39 (October 1955), 640.

19 Virginia Wimperis, *The Unmarried Mother and Her Child* (London: George Allen and Unwin, 1960), 68.

20 Ibid., 252.

21 Esther Levitt, 'Repeated Out-of-Wedlock Pregnancies: Services to the Unmarried Mother,' *Child Welfare* 38 (1959), 8.

22 For details regarding the ongoing disadvantage of women in the Canadian workforce, see Pat Armstrong and Hugh Armstrong, *The Double Ghetto: Canadian Women and Their Segregated Work*, 3rd ed. (Toronto: McClelland and Stewart, 1994).

23 For more information on attitudes towards working mothers, see Joan Sangster, 'Doing Two Jobs: The Wage Earning Mother, 1945–1970,' in Joy Parr, ed., *A Diversity of Women, Ontario, 1945–1980* (Toronto: University of Toronto Press, 1995), 98–134.

24 AO, York, Box 411-1-3-12, Case 2033, 1952.

25 AO, York, Box 26-11-26-4-16, Case 2449, 1959.

26 AO, York, Box 411-1-4-1, Case 491, 1958.

27 AO, York, Box 411-1-4-1, Case 487, 1952.

28 AO, York, Box 411-1-2-9, Case 974, 1955.

29 AO, York, Box 411-1-3-7, Case 1054, 1962.

30 AO, York, Box 411-1-3-12, Case 2056, 1950.

31 In eleven cases informal discussions with the CAS contributed to the decision of couples to resume cohabitation for the sake of their children, but, not surprisingly, none of the couples in these cases were convinced to enter into legal marriage, as they were unlikely to be free to do so.

32 *Children of Unmarried Parents Act*, S.O. 1921, c. 54, s. 18(2).

33 AO, Middlesex, Box 27-9-1-1, Case 310, 1955.

34 *Children of Unmarried Parents Act*, (1921) s.18 (2).

35 AO, Hamilton, Box 24-2-3-4, Case 241, 1946.

36 AO, Middlesex, Box 27-9-1-1, Case 310, 1955.

37 AO, York, Box 411-1-3-7, Case 371, 1953. Grammatical errors in the original.

38 AO, York, Box 411-1-4-1, Case 494, 1959.
39 AO, York, Box 411-1-4-1, Case 454, 1960.
40 AO, York, Box 411-1-4-1, Case 464, 1960.
41 AO, Middlesex, Box 27-9-1-1, Case 301, 1952.
42 AO, York, Box 411-1-3-12, Case 2034, 1952.
43 AO, Middlesex, Box 27-9-1-2, Case 653, 1955.
44 AO, Hamilton, Box 24-2-3-3, Case 22, 1962.
45 AO, York, Box 411-1-4-1, Case 434, 1955.
46 AO, York, Box 411-1-3-15, Case 970, 1958.
47 AO, Wentworth, Box 24-2-3-4, Case 282, 1961.
48 AO, Wentworth, Box 24-2-3-3, Case 56, 1959.
49 AO, York, Box 411-1-4-6, Case 2452, 1966. Emphasis in original.
50 AO, Wentworth, Box 66-4-4-6, Case 197, 1960.
51 AO, Wentworth, Box 24-2-3-4, Case 211, 1960.
52 AO, York, Box 411-1-3-15, Case 930, 1960.
53 AO, York, Box 411-1-3-8, Case 414, 1944.
54 AO, York, Box 411-1-4-6, Case 2289, 1960.
55 Winter, 'Common Law Wife,' 17.
56 Margaret Jane Hillyard Little, *No Car, No Radio, No Liquor Permit: The Moral Regulation of Single Mothers in Ontario, 1920–1997* (Toronto: Oxford University Press, 1998), 122.
57 'Unmarried Mother Victim of Legalism,' *Globe and Mail*, 13 February 1943; 'Help is Refused to Unwed Mother,' *Globe and Mail*, 26 January 1943.
58 'Annual Report of the Ontario Department of Public Welfare, 1955–56,' 43, as cited in Little, *No Car, No Radio, No Liquor Permit*, 135.
59 James Struthers, *The Limits of Affluence: Welfare in Ontario, 1920–1970* (Toronto: University of Toronto Press, 1994), 162. By 1959, unwed mothers made up 8 per cent of the provincial mothers' allowance caseload.
60 *Mothers' Allowance Act*, S.O. 1958.
61 Metropolitan Toronto Records and Archives (MTRA), RG 5.1, Box 43, File 47, 'Mothers' Allowances and Dependent Fathers, 1931–1961'; letter from the chairman of the Toronto Welfare Council to Harold Kirby, 31 March, 1943, as quoted in Struthers, *The Limits of Affluence*, 120.
62 AO, York, Box 411-1-3-12, Case 2033, 1953.
63 AO, York, Box 411-1-3-9, Case 406, 1946.
64 AO, Hamilton, Box 24-2-3-3, Case 8, 1962.
65 AO, York, Box 411-1-3-9, Case 459, 1949.
66 Dzwiekowski, 'Casenotes,' 325.
67 Winter, 'Common Law Wife,' 62.
68 Ibid., 62.

69 Ibid.
70 Phyllis Haslam, 'The Damaged Girl in a Distorted Society,' *Canadian Welfare* (15 March 1961), 84.
71 Margaret Thornhill, 'Problems of Repeated Out-of-Wedlock Pregnancies,' *Child Welfare* 38 (1959), 1.
72 Stephen Cretney, 'The Law Relating to Unmarried Partners from the Perspective of a Law Reform Agency,' in John Eekelaar and Sanford Katz, eds., *Marriage and Cohabitation in Contemporary Societies* (Toronto: Butterworths, 1980), 357.

Conclusions

1 Ontario Law Reform Commission, *Report on Family Law*, Part III, *Children* (Ontario: Ministry of the Attorney General, 1973), 1.
2 Diana Dzwiekowski, 'Casenotes: Findings of Paternity in Ontario, *Sayer v. Rollin*,' *Canadian Journal of Family Law* 3 (1980), 318–26.
3 *Family Law Reform Act*, R.S.O. 1980, c. 152, s. 1(a).
4 Lynn Fels, *Living Together: Unmarried Couples in Canada* (Toronto: Personal Library, 1981), 155.
5 Doing away with the word 'illegitimate' does not solve the problem of child poverty. Indeed, it may simply render these problems less visible. The inadequacy of simple changes in nomenclature was recognized by early advocates of changes in the law of illegitimacy: 'Indeed, over-concern with nomenclature carries with it the danger that a legislature, having outlawed an unpleasant word, may come to think it has solved an unpleasant problem.' Harry D. Krause, *Illegitimacy: Law and Social Policy* (New York: Bobbs-Merrill, 1971), 21.
6 Sharon Hays, *Flat Broke with Children: Women in the Age of Welfare Reform* (New York: Oxford University Press, 2003), 18.

Bibliography

PRIMARY SOURCES

Archival Materials

Archives of Ontario (AO). Unprocessed case files, *Children of Unmarried Parents Act*, bankers' boxes by county: Algoma, Bruce, Frontenac, Grey, Hamilton, Huron, Kent, Middlesex, Norfolk, Waterloo, Wentworth, York.

Children's Aid Society. 'Infants' Home and Infirmary, Toronto.' MTA, Box 46592–1, Series 100, File 352, Child Care-Private Organizations: The Children's Aid Society, 1931–1946.

– 'History of the Children's Aid Society of Metropolitan Toronto.' 23 January 1975.

Justice Frank E. Hodgins. 'Report of the Royal Commission: Care of the Feeble-minded and Mentally Defective and the Prevalence of Venereal Disease.' 18 October 1919. RG 18–65, Box 1.

Kelso, J.J. *Ontario Educational Association Yearbook 1900.*

MacMurchy, Helen. *Second Special Report on Infant Mortality.* 1911. Pamphlet No. 93.

– *Infant Mortality.* 1910.

'Memo of the Social Service Council of Ontario to AG W.E. Raney, re: Adoption bill,' 1921. RG 4–32, 1921, 1679.

'Memo on Mothers' Pensions Prepared by the Superintendent of Trades and Labour,' 1917. RG 7, Series II–I, Box 2.

Mohr, N. Emily. *A Study of Illegitimacy in Ontario*. Toronto: Social Service
   Council, 1921). RG 4–32, 1871–1947, Central Registry, 1921, No. 2023.
'Mothers' Allowance Investigation, Ontario, 1920.' RG 7.
'Mothers' Pension Allowance: Hamilton Enquiry.' 20 February, 1919. RG 7,
   series II–I.
Report by Dr Bruce Smith. 'Memo on Mothers' Pensions.' 13 April 1917. RG7.

Cases

Adrian and McGuire (Re), [1925] O.J. No. 449.
B.S. v. G.J.W., [1988] 18 R.F.L. (3d), 138–142.
Bodnar v. Popovich, [1973] 15 R.F.L. 392–8.
Bomboir v. Harlow, [1987] 5 W.W.R., 55–70.
Brown and Argue (Re), [1925] O.J. No. 50.
C. v. K., [1959] 22 D.L.R. (2d), 81–91.
C.S. v M.R., [1954] O.J. No. 281.
Carleton v. MacLean, [1953] O.J. No. 275.
Duckworth v. Skinkle (Re), [1924] O.J. No. 18.
E.A.S. v. K.M.B., [1989] 24 R.F.L. (3d), 220–5.
Ferguson v. Director of Child Welfare, Ministry of Community and Social Services,
   [1983] 36 R.F.L. (2d), 405–8.
Fillion v. Payment, [1957] 21 W.W.R., 591–4.
Gabel v. Bolander, [1943] O.J. No. 162.
Gerk v. Ventress et ux, [1964] 48 W.W.R., 245–50.
Grawburger and Moyer (Re), [1929] O.J. No. 96.
Griffioen v. Bickley, [1993] 1 R.F.L. (4th), 233–46.
Gwyllt (Re), [1944] O.J. No. 85.
Hilton v. Tassman, [1944] O.J. No. 337.
Hunt v. Lindensmith (Re), [1921] O.J. No. 50.
H.J.L. v. L.A. and R.D.A, [1986] 1 R.F.L. (3d), 395–400.
In re Adoption of Medley, [1951] 4 W.W.R., 524–6.
In re Clement, Gardner et al v. Gardner et al, [1962] S.C.R., 235–41.
Kirkpatrick and Moroughan (Re), [1927] O.J. No. 58.
Leskey v. VanHorne, [1954] O.J. No. 346.
Lord v. Fudge, [1956] 4 D.L.R. (2d), 100–9.
M. v. F., [1978] 3 R.F.L. (2d), 132–139.
M.G. (Re), [1943] O.J. No. 270.
M.(R.H.) v. H.(S.S.), [1994] 2 R.F.L. (4th), 207–18.
Martin v. Duffell, [1950] S.C.R.
Massingham-Pearce v. Konkolus, [1995] 7 W.W.R., 183–204.
Middleton v. Bryce, [1931] O.J. No. 234.

Ontario (A.G.) v. Nevins Prov. J., [1988] 64 O.R. (2d), 475.

Panaccione v. McNab, [1976] 28 R.F.L., 182–9.

Pearce v. Hubic Estate, [1992] 95 D.L.R. (4th), 140–228.

Power (Re), [1952] O.J. No. 336.

Re A., [1944] 4 D.L.R., 496.

Re A.H., C.E.S., and J.M.S.; Attorney General of Ontario v. Nevins Prov. J. et al, [1988] 13 R.F.L. (3d), 113–22.

Re Agar, McNeilly et al v. Agar, [1957] S.C.R., 53–6.

Re Baby Duffell, [1950] S.C.R., 727–48.

Re Barthelmes, [1971] 1 O.R., 752–4.

Re Blackwell, [1959] O.R., 377–405.

Re British Columbia Birth Registration No. 77–09–004–368, [1988] 18 R.F.L. (3d), 222–4.

Re Brown v. Argue, [1925] O.L.R., 297–300.

Re Child Welfare Act; Brysh v. Davidson, [1963] 44 W.W.R., 654–60.

Re Clarke, [1916] O.L.R., 498–502.

Re Davis, [1909] O.L.R., 384–7.

Re Eisenmenger and Doherty, [1924] O.J. No. 558.

Re F and F and D, [1965] 51 D.L.R. (2d), 36–54.

Re Fulford and Townsend, [1971] 3 O.R., 142–7.

Re G., G. et ux v. C. et ux, [1951] 3 D.L.R., 138–51.

Re H. and A., [1990] 74 D.L.R. (4th), 437–45.

Re J., [1979] 9 R.F.L. (2d), 281–94.

Re Kras and Sardo, [1979] 26 O.R. (2d), 785–7.

Re Lesieur, [1952] 1 D.L.R., 93–7.

Re Logue and Burrell, [1970] 15 D.L.R. (3d), 129–35.

Re M.L.A. and three other applications, [1979] 25 O.R. (2d), 779–800.

Re Mugford, [1970] 1 O.R., 601–11.

Re Nichols, [1974] 18 R.F.L., 127–38.

Re Nunn v. Featherstone, [1927] O.J. No. 173.

Re T. and Children's Aid Society and Family Services of Colchester County, [1992] 91 D.L.R. (4th), 230–55.

Re Wade et al and Director of Child Welfare et al, [1981] 127 D.L.R. (3d), 508–11.

Rex v. Vahey, [1932] O.R. 211.

Re X, [1957] 12 D.L.R. (2d), 367–9.

Re Yeo and Benner, [1926] O.J. No. 339.

S (Re), [1919] O.J. No. 103.

S. v. Minister of Social Services, [1982] 3 W.W.R., 358.

The King v. Luffe. 103 English Reports, 316 (King's Bench, 1807).

Thomas v. Jones, [1921] 1 K.B. (Great Britain) 22.
Thomas v. Ryan, [1937] 4 D.L.R., 729–31.
Tyler v. District Court of Ontario, [1986] 1 R.F.L. (3d), 139–41.
Walker v. Foster. [1923] O.J. No. 23.
Wicks v. Armstrong. [1928] O.J. No. 160.

Legislation

An Act for Further Introduction of the Criminal Law of England into the Province and for the More Effectual Punishment of Certain Offenders, 1800, 40 George III, c. I., s. 1.
An Act for Setting the Poor on Work, 1576, 18 Elizabeth, c. 3.
An Act for the Prevention of Cruelty to, and the Better Protection of Children, S.O. 1893.
An Act for the Protection of the Children of Unmarried Parents, S.O. 1921, c. 54.
An Act Respecting Industrial Refuges for Females, R.S.O. 1919, c. 84, s. 15.
An Act Respecting Offenses against the Person, 1869, 32–33 Vict., c. 20, s. 26.
An Act Respecting the Adoption of Children, S.O. 1921, c. 55.
An Act Respecting the Legitimation of Children by the Subsequent Intermarriage of Their Parents, S.O. 1921, c. 53.
Adoption Amendment Act, S.O. 1951, c. 2.
Child Welfare Act, S.O. 1954, 1965, and 1970.
Children's Protection Act, R.S.O. 1914, c. 23.
Family Benefits Act, S.O. 1991.
Family Law Reform Act, S.O. 1978; 1980, c. 152, s. 1(a).
Juvenile Delinquent's Act, 7 & 8 Edw. VII, c. 40 (Dom.).
Mothers' Allowance Act, S.O. 1920; S.O. 1958.
Seduction Act, 1837, 7 William IV, c. 8.
Statutes of Upper Canada, 1834, 7 William IV, c. 8.

Books

Bernstein, Rose. *Helping Unmarried Mothers*. New York: Association Press, 1971.
Blackstone, William. *Commentaries on the Laws of England*. Vol. 2. London: Kerr, 1857.
Bowerman, Charles, Donald Irish, and Hallowell Pope. *Unwed Motherhood: Personal and Social Consequences*. Chapel Hill: Institute for Research in Social Science, University of North Carolina, 1966.
Bowlby, John. *Maternal Care and Mental Health*. World Health Organization Monongraph Series, No. 2. Geneva: World Health Organization, 1951.

Breckenridge, Sophonisba. *The Family and the State*. Chicago: University of Chicago Press, 1934.

Cassidy, Harry. *Public Health and Welfare Organization in Canada*. Toronto: The Ryerson Press, 1945.

Deutsch, Helene. *The Psychology of Women: A Psychoanalytic Interpretation*. Vol. 2, *Motherhood*. New York: Grune and Stratton, 1945.

Edlin, Sara. *The Unmarried Mother in Our Society*. New York: Farrar, Straus and Young, 1954.

Kinsey, Alfred, Wardell Pomeroy, and Clyde Martin. *Sexual Behavior in the Human Female*. Philadelphia: Saunders, 1953.

Lemby, G.F. *Family Law*. Toronto: International Self-Counsel Press, 1971.

Lubove, Roy. *The Professional Altruist: The Emergence of Social Work as a Career, 1880–1930*. Cambridge, MA: Harvard University Press, 1965.

MacMurchy, Helen. *Sterilization? Birth Control? A Book for Family Welfare and Safety*. Toronto: The Macmillan Company of Canada, 1934.

Malthus, Robert Thomas. *An Essay on the Principles of Population*. 1798. Reprint, edited by Geoffrey Gilbert, Oxford: Oxford University Press, 1993.

Marsden, Dennis. *Mothers Alone: Poverty and the Fatherless Family*. London: Penguin Press, 1969.

McWhinnie, A.M. *Adopted Children: How They Grow Up*. London: Routledge and Kegan Paul, 1967.

Pierce, Ruth. *Single and Pregnant*. Boston: Beacon, 1970.

Pochin, Jean. *Without a Wedding Ring: Casework with Unmarried Parents*. London: Constable, 1969.

Richmond, Mary. *Social Diagnosis*. New York: Russell Sage Foundation, 1917.

Sauber, Mignon, and Elaine Rubinstein. *Experiences of the Unwed Mother as a Parent: A Longitudinal Study of Unmarried Mothers Who Keep Their First-Born*. New York: Community Council of Greater New York, 1965.

Sheffield, Ada Elliot. *The Social Case History: Its Construction and Content*. New York: Russell Sage Foundation, 1920.

Theis, Sophie van Senden. *How Foster Children Turn Out*. New York: State Charities Association, 1924.

Vanier Centre. *Profiling Canada: Families*. Montreal: Vanier Institute of the Family, 1994.

Wimperis, Virginia. *The Unmarried Mother and Her Child*. London: George Allen and Unwin, 1960.

Young, Leontine. *Out of Wedlock: A Study of the Unmarried Mother and Her Child*. New York: McGraw-Hill, 1954.

Articles

Adami, J.G. 'The Policy of the Ostrich.' *Canadian Medical Association Journal* 9(4) (April 1918): 289–301.

'Adopted Mother By Herself.' *Scribner's Magazine*, January 1935, 56.

Bain, Katherine, and Martha Eliot. 'Adoption as a National Problem.' *Pediatrics* 20 (1957): 366–86.

Bernstein, Rose. 'Are We Still Stereotyping Unmarried Mothers?' *Social Work* 5(3) (July 1960): 22–8.

– 'Gaps in Services to Unwed Mothers.' *Children* 10(2) (1963): 49–54.

– 'Perspectives on Services for Teenage Unwed Mothers.' *Child Welfare* 43 (January 1964): 5–13.

Braithwaite, Max. 'Born Out of Wedlock.' *Maclean's*, 15 November 1947, 16, 64–6.

Brooking, Lucy. 'A Study of the Delinquent Girl.' *Social Welfare* 4 (April 1921).

Brown, Alan. 'Infant and Child Welfare Work.' *Public Health Journal* 9 (April 1918): 145.

Brown, Florence. 'What Do We Seek in Adoptive Parents?' *Social Casework* 1 (April 1951): 155–61.

Brown, John. 'Rootedness.' *Involvement* 6(5) (May–June 1974): 3–9.

Bryce, Peter. 'Mothers' Allowance.' *Social Welfare* 8 (1925): 131–3.

– 'Saving Canadians from the Degeneracy Due to Industrialism in Cities of Older Civilizations.' *Public Health Journal* 3, no. 12 (December 1912): 686–692.

Callwood, June. 'Adoption: Not All Hearts and Flowers.' *Chatelaine*, April 1976, 41.

Cattell, James. 'Psychodynamic and Clinical Observations in a Group of Unmarried Mothers.' *American Journal of Psychiatry* 3 (November 1954): 337–42.

Chapman, Ethel M. 'Could You Adopt a Baby?' *Maclean's*, December 1919, 116.

Chaskel, Ruth. 'The Unmarried Mother: Is She Different?' *Child Welfare* (February 1967): 65–74; 99.

'Chosen Children.' *Time Magazine*, 15 May 1939, 39.

Clothier, Florence. 'Problems of Illegitimacy as They Concern the Worker in the Field of Adoption.' *Mental Hygiene* 25 (October 1941): 576–90.

– 'Placing the Child for Adoption.' *Mental Hygiene* 26 (April 1942): 257–74.

– 'The Unmarried Mother of School Age as Seen by a Psychiatrist.' *Mental Hygiene* 39 (October 1955): 631–46.

Coffino, Frances. 'Helping a Mother Surrender Her Child for Adoption.' *Child Welfare* 39 (February 1960): 25–8.

Editorial. 'Get the Babies to Those Who Want Them.' *Maclean's*, 5 February 1966, 4.

Editorial. 'Infant Mortality.' *Public Health Journal* 6 (1915): 510.

Editorial. 'Social Hygiene.' *Social Welfare* 7 (1924): 48.

Editorial. 'These Little Ones.' *Social Welfare* 1 (1918): 53.

Ehrmann, Winston. 'Illegitimacy in Florida II: Social and Psychological Aspects of Illegitimacy.' *Eugenics Quarterly* 3 (December 1956): 223–7.

Fils, Francis. 'Sex Education and the Prevention of Illegitimacy.' In *Unmarried Parenthood: Clues to Agency and Community Action*, 90–101. New York: National Council on Illegitimacy, 1967.

Fleck, Stephen. 'Pregnancy as a Symptom of Adolescent Maladjustment.' *International Journal of Social Psychiatry* 2 (Autumn 1956): 118–31.

Francis, Vida. 'The Delinquent Girl.' In *Proceedings of the National Conference of Charities and Corrections*. N.p.: Fred Herr Press, 1906.

Frazier, Elizabeth. 'The Baby Market.' *Saturday Evening Post*, 1 February 1930, 25.

Freund, Ernst. 'The Present Law Concerning Children Born Out of Wedlock and Possible Changes in Legislation.' In U.S. Children's Bureau, *Standards of Legal Protection for Children Born Out of Wedlock: A Report of Regional Conferences Held under the Auspices of the U.S. Children's Bureau*. Washington, DC: n.p., 1921.

Furie, Sidney. 'Birth Control and the Lower-Class Unmarried Mother.' *Social Work* 11(1) (January 1966): 42–9.

Garland, Patricia. 'The Community's Part in Preventing Illegitimacy.' *Children* 10(2) (March–April 1963): 71–5.

Gatlin, Lillian. 'Adopting a Baby: The Stork Gives Blindly, but Only the Fittest Qualify as Parents by Proxy.' *Sunset, the Pacific Monthly*, February 1921, 83–6.

Glueck, Sheldon, and Eleanor Glueck. 'Working Mothers and Delinquency.' *Mental Hygiene* 41 (July 1957): 327–50.

Gough, D. 'Work with Unmarried Mothers.' *Almoner* 12 (13 March 1961): 490–7.

Harris, Dale. 'Delinquency in Adolescent Girls.' *Mental Hygiene* 28 (October 1944): 596–601.

Haslam, Phyllis. 'The Damaged Girl in a Distorted Society.' *Canadian Welfare* (15 March 1961): 81–5.

Herzog, Elizabeth. 'Who Are the Unmarried Mothers?' *Children* 9(4) (July–August 1962): 157–9.

Hoffman, L. 'Constructing Realities: An Art of Lens.' *Family Process* 29 (1989): 1–12.

Isserman, Betty. 'The Casework Relationship with Unmarried Mothers.' *The Social Worker* 17(1) (October 1948): 12–17.

Jenkins, R.L. 'Adoption Practices and the Physician.' *Journal of the American Medical Association* 103(6) (August 1934): 403–8.

Josie, Svanhuit. 'The Unwed Mother – Her Right to Her Child.' *Saturday Night*, 15 August 1950, 26–7.

– 'The American Caricature of the Unmarried Mother.' *Canadian Welfare* 29(12) (December 1955): 246–9.

Kasanin, J., and S. Handschin. 'Psychodynamic Factors in Illegitimacy.' *American Journal of Orthopsychiatry* 11 (January 1941): 66–84.

Katz, Sidney. 'The Forgotten Fathers.' *Maclean's*, 1 May 1949, 9, 72–5.

Levitt, Esther. 'Repeated Out-of-Wedlock Pregnancies: Services to the Unmarried Mother.' *Child Welfare* 38 (1959): 5–9.

Loadman, Rita. 'What's New in Adoption?' *Canadian Welfare* 30(3) (March 1956): 335–6.

Lowe, Charlotte. 'The Intelligence and Social Background of the Unmarried Mother.' *Mental Hygiene* 4 (October 1927): 783–94.

Maccoby, Eleanor. 'Children and Working Mothers.' *Children* 5(3) (May–June, 1958): 83–9.

MacLachlan, Ethel. 'The Delinquent Girl.' *Social Welfare* (December 1921): n.p.

McNicholas, Joseph. 'Adoptions: Happiness or Tragedy?' *Hospital Progress* 39 (April 1958): 64–7.

Patterson, R.H. 'Some Social Aspects of the Venereal Disease Problem.' *Canadian Public Health Journal* 11(12) (December 1920): 570.

Porter, McKenzie. 'The Unmarried Wives.' *Maclean's*, 27 January 1962, 18, 32–3.

Rashbaum, William, Janice Paneth, Helen Rehr, and Martin Greenberg. 'Use of Social Services by Unmarried Mothers.' *Children* 10(1) (January–February 1963): 11–16.

Ray, Alice Kunz. 'A Good Adoption Program: Can Standards Be Mantained without Sacrificing Flexibility?' In *Proceedings of the National Conference of Social Work*. New York: Columbia University Press, 1945.

Schumacher, Henry. 'The Unmarried Mother: A Socio-Psychiatric Viewpoint.' *Mental Hygiene* 11 (1927): 775–82.

Sheffield, Ada Ellliot. 'Program of the Committee on Illegitimacy – Committee Report.' In *Proceedings of the National Conference of Social Work*. Chicago: University of Chicago Press, 1921.

Sherwin, Robert Viet. 'The Law and Sexual Relationships.' *Journal of Social Issues* 22(2) (1966): 109–22.

Speers, Mary. 'Case Work and Adoption.' *The Social Worker* 16(3) (February 1948): 18–21.

Spencer, H.E. 'For a Healthy Canada.' *Chatelaine*, March 1930, 50.

Sutherton, Kathleen. 'Another View.' *Canadian Welfare* 31(5) (December 1955): 249–52.

Thompson, Dorothy. 'Fit for Adoption.' *Ladies' Home Journal*, May 1939, 4.

Thornhill, Margaret. 'Unprotected Adoptions.' *Children* 2(5) (September–October, 1955): 179–84.

– 'Problems of Repeated Out-of-Wedlock Pregnancies.' *Child Welfare* 38 (1959): 1–5.

Vincent, Clark. 'The Adoption Market and the Unwed Mother's Baby.' *Marriage and Family Living* 18 (May 1956): 124–27.

– 'Unmarried Mothers: Society's Dilemma.' *Sexology* 28 (1962): 451–5.

– 'Illegitimacy in the Next Decade: Trends and Implications.' *Child Welfare* 43 (December 1964): 513–20.

Walters, C.S. 'The Duty of the City to the Child.' *Public Health Journal* 6 (1915): 540.

Whitton, Charlotte. 'Children's Rights and the Tax.' *Saturday Night*, 29 May 1943, 20.

– 'Unmarried Parenthood and the Social Order.' Parts I and II. *Social Welfare* (April–May 1920): 184–7, 222–3.

Williams, T.D. 'Desertion and Non-Support: The Importance of the Problem.' *Proceedings of the First Annual Meeting of the Canadian Conference on Social Work*. Ottawa, 1928.

Willsie, Honore. 'When is a Child Adoptable?' *Delineator* 95 (1919): 35.

Winter, 'Common Law Wife.' *Chatelaine*, January 1952, 16–17, 62.

Yarrow, Marian Radke. 'Maternal Employment and Child Rearing.' *Children* 8(6) (November–December 1961): 223–8.

Young, Leontine. 'Personality Patterns in Unmarried Mothers.' *Family* 26 (December 1945).

Government Publications

Canada. *Report of the Royal Commission on Aboriginal Peoples, vol. 3.* Ottawa: Ministry of Supply and Services, 1996.

Canadian Youth Commission. *Youth, Marriage and Family.* Toronto: The Ryerson Press, 1948.

Lindsay, Colin. *Lone-Parent Families in Canada: Target Groups Project.* Ottawa: Minister of Industry, Science and Technology, 1992.

Ontario Law Reform Commission. *Report on Family Law.* Part III, *Children.* Toronto: Ministry of the Attorney General, 1973.

Province of Ontario. Mothers' Allowance Commission. *Annual Report.* 1921.

Social Planning Council of Metropolitan Toronto. *A Report on Maternity Homes in Metropolitan Toronto.* Toronto, 1960.

Statistics Canada. 1984. *Therapeutic Abortions, 1952.* Catalogue No. 82–211 Annual, 1984. Ottawa: Statistics Canada.

United Nations, Department of Economic and Social Affairs. *Study on Traffic in Persons and Prostitution (Suppression of the Traffic in Persons and of the Exploitation of the Prostitution of Others).* New York: United Nations, 1959.

Unmarried Parenthood Committee of the Welfare Council of Toronto and District. *A Study of the Adjustment of Teen-age Children Born Out of Wedlock Who Remained in the Custody of their Mothers or Relatives.* Toronto, 1943.

U.S. Children's Bureau. *Illegitimacy as a Child Welfare Problem.* Washington, DC: n.p., 1920.

SECONDARY SOURCES

Books

Adams, Mary Louise. *The Problem with Normal: Postwar Youth and the Construction of Heterosexuality.* Toronto: University of Toronto Press, 1997.

Alexander, Ruth. *The 'Girl Problem': Female Sexual Delinquency in New York, 1900–1930.* Ithaca, NY: Cornell University Press, 1995.

Allen, Richard. *The Social Passion: Religion and Social Reform in Canada, 1914–1928.* Toronto: University of Toronto Press, 1971.

Anderson, Kim, and Bonita Lawrence, eds. *Strong Women Stories: Native Vision and Community Survival.* Toronto: Sumach, 2003.

Armstrong, Pat, and Hugh Armstrong. *The Double Ghetto: Canadian Women and Their Segregated Work.* 3rd ed. Toronto: McClelland and Stewart, 1994.

Arnup, Katherine. *Education for Motherhood: Advice for Mothers in Twentieth-Century Canada.* Toronto: University of Toronto Press, 1994.

Arnup, Katherine, Andrée Lévesque, and Ruth Roach Pierson, eds. *Delivering Motherhood: Material Ideologies and Practices in the Nineteenth and Twentieth Centuries.* London: Routledge, 1990.

Backhouse, Constance. *Petticoats and Prejudice: Women and Law in Nineteenth-Century Canada.* Toronto: Women's Press, 1991.

Bailey, Beth. *From Front Porch to Back Seat: Courtship in Twentieth-Century America.* Baltimore: Johns Hopkins University Press, 1988.

– *Sex in the Heartland.* Cambridge, MA: Harvard University Press, 1999.

Baillargeon, Denise. *Making Do: Women, Family and Home in Montreal during the*

Great Depression. Translated by Yvonne Klein. Waterloo, ON: Wilfrid Laurier University Press, 1999.

Barber, Dulan. *Unmarried Fathers*. London: Hutchinson, 1975.

Bartholet, Elizabeth. *Family Bonds: Adoption and the Politics of Parenting*. Boston: Houghton Mifflin, 1993.

Berebitsky, Julie. *Like Our Very Own: Adoption and the Changing Culture of Motherhood, 1851–1950*. Lawrence: University of Kansas Press, 2000.

Braslow, Joel. *Mental Ills and Bodily Cures: Psychiatric Treatment in the First Half of the Twentieth Century*. Berkeley: University of California Press, 1997.

Brode, Patrick. *Courted and Abandoned: Seduction in Canadian Law*. Toronto: University of Toronto Press/The Osgoode Society for Legal History, 2002.

Cahill, Bette. *Butterbox Babies*. Toronto: Seal Books, 1992.

Campbell, Patricia, J. *Sex Education Books for Young Adults, 1892–1979*. New York: Bowker, 1979.

Carp, Wayne. *Family Matters: Secrecy and Disclosure in the History of Adoption*. Cambridge, MA: Harvard University Press, 1998.

Cassell, Jay. *The Secret Plague: Venereal Disease in Canada*. Toronto: University of Toronto Press, 1987.

Chesney-Lind, Meda. *Girls, Delinquency and Juvenile Justice*. Belmont: Brooks Cole, 1992.

Christie, Nancy. *Engendering the State: Family, Work and Welfare in Canada*. Toronto: University of Toronto Press, 2000.

Christie, Nancy, and Michael Gauvreau. *A Full-Orbed Christianity: The Protestant Churches and Social Welfare in Canada, 1900–1940*. Montreal: McGill-Queen's University Press, 1996.

Chunn, Dorothy. *From Punishment to Doing Good: Family Courts and Socialized Justice in Ontario, 1880–1940*. Toronto: University of Toronto Press, 1992.

Clark, Lorene, and Debra Lewis. *Rape: The Price of Coercive Sexuality*. Toronto: Women's Press, 1977.

Collins, Patricia Hill. *Black Feminist Thought: Knowledge, Consciousness and the Politics of Empowerment*. Boston: Unwin Hyman, 1990.

Commachio, Cynthia. *The Infinite Bonds of Family: Domesticity in Canada, 1850–1940*. Toronto: University of Toronto Press, 1999.

– *Nations Are Built of Babies: Saving Ontario's Mothers and Children, 1900–1940*. Montreal: McGill-Queen's University Press, 1993.

Connelly, M.T. *The Response to Prostitution in the Progressive Era*. Chapel Hill: University of North Carolina Press, 1980.

Cook, Ramsay. *The Regenerators: Social Criticism in Late-Victorian English Canada*. Toronto: University of Toronto Press, 1985.

Copp, Terry. *The Anatomy of Poverty*. Toronto: McClelland and Stewart, 1973.

Cox, Pamela. *Gender, Justice and Welfare: Bad Girls in Britain, 1900–1950*. Basingstoke: Palgrave, 2003.

Dean, Mitchell. *The Constitution of Poverty: Towards a Genealogy of Liberal Governance*. London: Routledge, 1991.

Demerson, Viola. *Incorrigible*. Waterloo: Wilfrid Laurier University Press, 2004.

D'Emilio, John, and Estelle Freedman. *Intimate Matters: A History of Sexuality in America*. New York: Harper and Row, 1988.

Dowbiggin, Ian. *Keeping America Sane: Psychiatry and Eugenics in the United States and Canada*. Ithaca, NY: Cornell University Press, 1997.

Drury, E.C. *Farmer Premier: Memoirs of the Honourable E.C. Drury*. Toronto: McClelland and Stewart, 1966.

Fels, Lynn. *Living Together: Unmarried Couples in Canada*. Toronto: Personal Library, 1981.

Foucault, Michel. *The History of Sexuality: An Introduction*. Vol. 1. Translated by Robert Hurley. New York: Random House, 1978.

Fraser, Nancy. *Unruly Practices: Power, Discourse and Gender in Contemporary Social Theory*. Minneapolis: University of Minnesota Press, 1989.

Gleason, Mona. *Normalizing the Ideal: Psychology, Schooling and the Family in Postwar Canada*. Toronto: University of Toronto Press, 1999.

Gordon, Linda. *Heroes of Their Own Lives: The Politics and History of Family Violence, Boston, 1880–1960*. New York: Penguin, 1988.

– *Pitied But Not Entitled: Single Mothers and the History of Welfare, 1890–1935*. New York: Free Press, 1994.

– *Woman's Body, Woman's Right: Birth Control in America*. New York: Penguin, 1977.

Hays, Sharon. *Flat Broke with Children: Women in the Age of Welfare Reform*. New York: Oxford University Press, 2003.

Hepworth, H. Philps. *Foster Care and Adoption in Canada*. Ottawa: Canadian Council on Social Development, 1980.

Howe, David, Phillida Sawbridge, and Diana Hinings. *Half a Million Women: Mothers Who Lose Their Children by Adoption*. London: Penguin, 1992.

Iacovetta, Franca, and Wendy Mitchinson, eds. *On the Case: Explorations in Social History*. Toronto: University of Toronto Press, 1998.

Inglis, Kate. *Living Mistakes: Mothers Who Consented to Adoption*. London: George Allen and Unwin, 1984.

Irving, Katrina. *Immigrant Mothers: Narratives of Race and Maternity*. Urbana: University of Illinois Press, 2000.

Johnson, Patrick. *Native Children and the Child Welfare System*. Toronto: James Lorimer, 1983.

Johnston, Charles. *E.C. Drury: Agrarian Idealist*. Toronto: University of Toronto Press, 1986.

Jones, Andrew, and Leonard Rutman. *In the Children's Aid: J.J. Kelso and Child Welfare in Ontario*. Toronto: University of Toronto Press, 1981.

Jones, Jacqueline. *Labor of Love, Labor of Sorrow: Black Women, Work and the Family from Slavery to the Present*. New York: Basic Books, 1985.

Katz, Michael. *In The Shadow of the Poorhouse: A Social History of Welfare*. New York: Basic Books, 1986.

Kett, Joseph. *Rites of Passage: Adolescence in America*. New York: Basic Books, 1977.

Kiernan, Kathleen, Hilary Land, and Jane Lewis. *Lone Motherhood in Twentieth-Century Britain: From Footnote to Front Page*. Oxford: Clarendon, 1998.

Kirk, H. David. *Adoptive Kinship: A Modern Institution in Need of Reform*. Toronto: Butterworths, 1981.

Kline, Wendy. *Building a Better Race: Gender, Sexuality and Eugenics from the Turn of the Century to the Baby Boom*. Berkeley: University of California Press, 2001.

Krause, Harry D. *Illegitimacy: Law and Social Policy*. New York: Bobbs-Merrill, 1971.

Kunzel, Regina. *Fallen Women, Problem Girls: Unmarried Mothers and the Professionalization of Social Work, 1890–1945*. New Haven: Yale University Press, 1993.

Lévesque, Andrée. *Making and Breaking the Rules: Women in Quebec, 1919–1939*. Translated by Yvonne M. Klein. Toronto: McClelland and Stewart, 1994.

Little, Margaret Jane Hillyard. *No Car, No Radio, No Liquor Permit: The Moral Regulation of Single Mothers in Ontario, 1920–1997*. Toronto: University of Toronto Press, 1998.

Lunbeck, Elizabeth. *The Pyschiatric Persuasion: Knowledge, Gender and Power in Modern America*. Princeton: Princeton University Press, 1994.

Luxton, Meg. *More Than a Labour of Love: Three Generations of Women's Work in the Home*. Toronto: Women's Press, 1980.

Mahood, Linda. *Policing Gender, Class and Family: Britain, 1850–1940*. London: UCL Press, 1995.

May, Elaine Tyler. *Barren in the Promised Land: Childless Americans and the Pursuit of Happiness*. New York: Basic Books, 1995.

– *Homeward Bound: American Families in the Cold War Era*. New York: Basic Books, 1988.

McLaren, Angus. *Birth Control in Nineteenth-Century England*. London: Holmes and Meir, 1978.

– *Our Own Master Race: Eugenics in Canada, 1885–1945*. Toronto: McClelland and Stewart, 1990.

McLaren, Angus, and Arlene Tigar McLaren. *The Bedroom and the State: Changing Practices and Politics of Contraception and Abortion in Canada 1880–1980*. Toronto: McClelland and Stewart, 1986.

McLaren, John, Robert Menzies, and Dorothy Chunn, eds. *Regulating Lives: Historical Essays on the State, Society, the Individual and the Law*. Vancouver: UBC Press, 2002.

Meckel, Richard. *Save the Babies: American Public Health Reform and the Prevention of Infant Mortality, 1850–1929*. Baltimore: Johns Hopkins University Press, 1990.

Meyerowitz, Joanne. *Women Adrift: Independent Wage Earners in Chicago, 1880–1930*. Chicago: University of Chicago Press, 1988.

Morton, Desmond. *Fight or Pay: Soldiers' Families in the Great War*. Vancouver: UBC Press, 2004.

Nathanson, Constance. *Dangerous Passage: The Social Control of Sexuality in Women's Adolescence*. Philadelphia: Temple University Press, 1991.

Odem, Mary. *Delinquent Daughters: Protecting and Policing Adolescent Female Sexuality in the United States, 1885–1920*. Chapel Hill: University of North Carolina Press, 1995.

Parr, Joy, ed. *Childhood and Family in Canadian History*. Toronto: McClelland and Stewart, 1982.

– *Labouring Children: British Immigrant Apprentices to Canada, 1865–1924*. Montreal: McGill-Queen's University Press, 1980.

Pertman, Adam. *Adoption Nation: How the Adoption Revolution Is Transforming America*. New York: Basic Books, 2000.

Petrie, Anne. *Gone to an Aunt's: Remembering Canada's Homes for Unwed Mothers*. Toronto: McClelland and Stewart, 1998.

Piess, Kathy. *Cheap Amusements: Working Women and Leisure in Turn-of-the-Century New York*. Philadelphia: Temple University Press, 1986.

Piva, Michael. *The Condition of the Working Class in Toronto, 1900–1921*. Ottawa: University of Ottawa Press, 1979.

Prentice, Alison and Susan Houston, eds. *Family, School and Society in Nineteenth Century Canada*. Toronto: Oxford University Press, 1975.

Rea, K.J. *The Prosperouos Years: The Economic History of Ontario, 1939–1975*. Toronto: University of Toronto Press, 1985.

Richardson, Theresa. *The Century of the Child: The Mental Hygiene Movement and Social Policy in the United States and Canada*. Albany: State University of New York Press, 1989.

Rooke, Patricia, and R.L. Schnell. *No Bleeding Heart: Charlotte Whitton, A Feminist on the Right*. Vancouver: UBC Press, 1988.

Ross, Ellen. *Love and Toil: Motherhood in Outcast London, 1870–1918.* New York: Oxford University Press, 1993.

Rothman, Ellen. *Hands and Hearts: A History of Courtship in America.* Cambridge, MA: Harvard University Press, 1984.

Sachdev, Paul. *Unlocking the Adoption Files.* Toronto: Heath, 1989.

Sangster, Joan. *Girl Trouble: Female Delinquency in English Canada.* Toronto: Between the Lines, 2002.

– *Regulating Girls and Women: Sexuality, Family and Law in Ontario, 1920–1960.* Toronto: Oxford University Press, 2001.

Schull, Joseph. *Ontario Since 1867.* Toronto: McClelland and Stewart, 1978.

Skocpol, Theda. *Protecting Soldiers and Mothers: The Political Origins of Social Policy in the United States.* Cambridge, MA: Harvard University Press, 1992.

Snell, James. *In the Shadow of the Law: Divorce in Canada, 1900–1939.* Toronto: University of Toronto Press, 1991.

Solinger, Rickie. *Beggars and Choosers: How the Politics of Choice Shapes Abortion, Adoption and Welfare in the United States.* New York: Hill and Wang, 2001.

– *Wake Up Little Susie: Single Pregnancy and Race before Roe v. Wade.* New York: Routledge, 1992.

Sorosky, A.D., A. Baran, and R. Pannor. *The Adoption Triangle.* New York: Anchor, 1978.

Strange, Carolyn. *Toronto's Girl Problem: The Perils and Pleasures of the City, 1880–1930.* Toronto: University of Toronto Press, 1995.

Strong-Boag, Veronica. *Finding Families, Finding Ourselves: English Canada Encounters Adoption from the Nineteenth Century to the 1990s.* Don Mills, ON: Oxford University Press, 2006.

– *The New Day Recalled: Lives of Girls and Women in English Canada, 1919–1939.* Toronto: Copp Clark Pitman, 1988.

Struthers, James. *The Limits of Affluence: Welfare in Ontario, 1920–1970.* Toronto: University of Toronto Press, 1994.

Sutherland, Neil. *Children in English-Canadian Society: Framing the Twentieth Century Consensus.* Toronto: University of Toronto Press, 1976.

– *Growing Up: Childhood in English Canada from the Great War to the Age of Television.* Toronto: University of Toronto Press, 1997.

Teichman, Jenny. *Illegitimacy: An Examination of Bastardy.* Ithaca, NY: Cornell University Press, 1982.

Teichman, Jenny. *The Meaning of Illegitimacy.* Cambridge, UK: Englehardt, 1978.

Tice, Karen. *Tales of Wayward Girls and Immoral Women: Case Records and the Professionalization of Social Work.* Urbana: University of Illinois Press, 1998.

Trent, James W. *Inventing the Feeble-Minded: A History of Mental Retardation in the United States*. Berkeley: University of California Press, 1994.

Valverde, Mariana. *The Age of Light, Soap and Water: Moral Reform in English Canada, 1885–1925*. Toronto: McClelland and Stewart, 1991.

Ward, Peter. *White Canada Forever: Popular Attitudes and Public Policy Towards Orientals in British Columbia*. Montreal: McGill-Queen's University Press, 1990.

Zelizer, Viviana. *Pricing the Priceless Child: The Changing Social Value of Children*. New York: Basic Books, 1985.

Articles

Abelle, Cynthia. 'The Infant Soldier: The Great War and the Medical Campaign for Child Welfare.' *Canadian Bulletin of Medical History* 5(2) (Winter 1988): 99–119.

Adams, Mary Louise. 'In Sickness and in Health: State Formation, Moral Regulation and Early VD Initiatives in Ontario.' *Journal of Canadian Studies* 28 (Winter 1993–1994): 117–30.

Backhouse, Constance. 'Desperate Women and Compassionate Courts: Nineteenth-Century Infanticide in Canada.' *University of Toronto Law Journal* 34 (1984): 447–78.

– 'Involuntary Motherhood: Abortion, Birth Control and the Law in Nineteenth-Century Canada.' *Windsor Yearbook of Access to Justice* 3 (1983): 61–130.

– 'Nineteenth-Century Canadian Rape Law.' In David H. Flaherty, ed., *Essays in the History of Canadian Law*. Vol. 2, 200–47. Toronto: The Osgoode Society, 1983.

– 'Shifting Patterns in Nineteenth-Century Canadian Custody Law.' In David Flaherty, ed., *Essays in the History of Canadian Law*. Vol. 1, 212–48, Toronto: The Osgoode Society, 1981.

– 'The Tort of Seduction: Fathers and Daughters in Nineteenth-Century Canada.' *Dalhousie Law Journal* 10 (1986): 45–80.

Bailey, Martha. 'Servant Girls and Masters: The Tort of Seduction and the Support of Bastards.' *Canadian Journal of Family Law* 10 (1991): 137–62.

Balcom, Karen. 'Scandal and Social Policy: The Ideal Maternity Home and the Evolution of Social Policy in Nova Scotia, 1940–1951.' *Acadiensis* 31(2) (Spring 2002): 3–37.

Bartholet, Elizabeth. 'What's Wrong with Adoption Law?' *The International Journal of Children's Rights* 4 (1996): 263–72.

Bator, Paul A. 'The Struggle to Raise the Lower Classes: Public Health Reform and the Problem of Poverty in Toronto, 1910–1921.' *Journal of Canadian Studies* 14(1) (Spring 1979): 43–9.

Besharov, Douglas, and Timothy Sullivan. 'Welfare Reform and Marriage.' *The Public Interest* 125 (Fall 1996): 81–94.

Bracco, Katrysha. 'Patriarchy and the Law of Adoption: Beneath the Best Interests of the Child.' *Alberta Law Review* 35(4) (1997): 1035–50.

Bradbury, Bettina. 'The Fragmented Family: Family Strategies in the Face of Death, Illness and Poverty in Montreal, 1860–1885.' In Joy Parr, ed., *Childhood and Family in Canadian History*, 109–28. Toronto: McClelland and Stewart, 1982.

Brush, Lisa. 'Worthy Widows, Welfare Cheats: Proper Womanhood in Expert Needs Talk about Single Mothers in the United States, 1900 to 1988.' *Gender and Society* 1(6) (December 1997): 720–45.

Buckley, Suzanne, and Janice Dickin McGinnis. 'Venereal Disease and Public Health Reform in Canada.' *Canadian Historical Review* 63(3) (September 1982): 337–54.

Bullen, John. 'J.J. Kelso and the "New" Childsavers: The Genesis of the Children's Aid Movement in Ontario.' *Ontario History* 82(2) (June 1990): 107–28.

Canning, Kathleen. 'Feminist History after the Linguistic Turn: Historicizing Discourse and Experience.' *Signs* 19(2) (1992): 368–404.

Carasco, Emily. 'What's in a Name?' *University of British Columbia Law Review* 37 (2004): 259–70.

Carp, Wayne. 'Professional Social Workers, Adoption and the Problem of Illegitimacy, 1915–1945.' *Journal of Policy History* 6(3) (1994): 161–84.

Chesney-Lind, Meda. 'Judicial Enforcement of the Female Sex Role: The Family Court and the Female Delinquent.' *Issues in Criminology* 8(2) (Fall 1973): 51–69.

Chunn, Dorothy. 'Regulating the Poor in Ontario: From Police Courts to Family Courts.' *Canadian Journal of Family Law* 6 (1987): 85–102.

Chunn, Dorothy, and Shelley Gavigan. 'Social Control: Analytical Tool or Analytical Quagmire?' *Contemporary Crises* 12 (1988): 107–24.

Clark, H. 'The Burden of Proof in a Paternity Action.' *Journal of Family Law* 25 (1986–1987): 357–72.

Cohen, Stanley. 'The Critical Discourse on "Social Control": Notes on the Concept as a Hammer.' *International Journal of the Sociology of Law* 17 (1989): 347–57.

Comacchio, Cynthia. 'Dancing to Perdition: Adolescence and Leisure in Interwar English Canada.' *Journal of Canadian Studies* (Autumn 1997): 5–35.

– 'The Infant Soldier: The Great War and the Medical Campaign for Child Welfare.' *Canadian Bulletin of Medical History* 5(2) (Winter 1988): 99–119.

– 'The Rising Generation: Laying Claim to the Health of Adolescents in

English Canada, 1920–1970.' *Canadian Bulletin of Medical History* 19 (2002): 139–78.

Cretney, Stephen. 'The Law Relating to Unmarried Partners from the Perspective of a Law Reform Agency.' In John Eekelaar and Sanford Katz, eds., *Marriage and Cohabitation in Contemporary Societies*, 357–67. Toronto: Butterworths, 1980.

Crowley, Terry. 'Madonnas Before Madgalenes: Adelaide Hoodless and the Making of the Canadian Gibson Girl.' *Canadian Historical Review* 67 (1986): 520–47.

Currie, Dawn. 'Feminist Encounters with Postmodernism: Exploring the Impasse of Debates on Patriarchy and Law.' *Canadian Journal of Women and the Law* 5 (1992): 63–86.

Cutright, Phillips. 'The Teenage Sexual Revolution and the Myth of the Abstinent Past.' *Family Planning Perspectives* 4 (1972): 24–31.

Davin, Anna. 'Imperialism and Motherhood.' *History Workshop Journal* 5 (Spring 1978): 9–65.

Dawson, T. Brettel. ' Sexual Assault Law and Past Sexual Conduct of the Primary Witness: The Construction of Relevance.' *Canadian Journal of Women and the Law* 2 (1987–8): 310–34.

Dickinson, Harley. 'Scientific Parenthood: The Mental Hygiene Movement and the Reform of Canadian Families, 1925–1950.' *Journal of Comparative Family Studies* 24 (Autumn 1993): 387–402.

Dodd, Diane. 'Advice to Parents: The Blue Books, Helen MacMurchy, MD, and the Federal Department of Health, 1920–1934.' *Canadian Bulletin of Medical History* 8 (1991): 203–30.

– 'Helen MacMurchy, MD: Gender and Professional Conflict in the Medical Inspection of Toronto Schools, 1910–1911.' *Ontario History* 93(2) (Autumn 2001): 127–49.

Dowd, Nancy. 'Stigmatizing Single Parents.' *Harvard Women's Law Review* 18 (1995): 19–82.

Dubinsky, Karen. 'Afterword: Telling Stories about Dead People.' In Franca Iacovetta and Wendy Mitchinsin, eds., *On The Case: Explorations in Social History*, 359–66. Toronto: University of Toronto Press, 1999.

Dzwiekowski, Diana. 'Casenotes: Findings of Paternity in Ontario, *Sayer v. Rollin.' Canadian Journal of Family Law* 3 (1980): 318–26.

Eichler, Margrit. 'The Limits of Family Law Reform, or the Privatization of Female and Child Poverty.' *Canadian Family Law Quarterly* 17 (1996): 59–84.

Fellows, Mary Louise. 'The Law of Legitimacy: An Instrument of Procreative Power.' *Columbia Journal of Gender and Law* 3(2) (1993): 485–537.

Fineman, Martha Albertson. 'Images of Mothers in Poverty Discourses.' *Duke Law Journal* (1991): 274–95.

Gordon, Linda. 'Review of *Gender and the Politics of History.*' *Signs* 15(4) (Summer 1990): 852–3.

Holland, Thomas. 'Narrative, Knowledge and Professional Practice.' *Social Thought* 17(1) (1991): 32–40.

Iacovetta, Franca. 'Making "New Canadians": Social Workers, Women and the Reshaping of Immigrant Families.' In Franca Iacovetta and Mariana Valverde, eds., *Gender Conflicts: New Essays in Women's History*, 261–303. Toronto: University of Toronto Press, 1992.

Jacobus, Mary. 'Malthus, Matricide and the Marquis de Sade.' In *First Things: The Maternal Imaginary in Literature, Art and Psychoanalysis*. New York: Routledge, 1995.

Kirkness, Verna. 'Emerging Native Women.' *Canadian Journal of Women and the Law* 2 (1987–88): 408–15.

Kline, Marlee. 'Complicating the Ideology of Motherhood: Child Welfare Law and First Nation Women.' In Martha Albertson Fineman, and Isabel Karpin, eds., *Mothers in Law: Feminist Theory and the Legal Regulation of Motherhood*, 118–41. New York: Columbia University Press, 1995.

Kunzel, Regina. 'The Professionalization of Benevolence: Evangelicals and Social Workers in Florence Crittenton Homes, 1915–1945.' *Journal of Social History* 22 (Fall 1988): 21–43.

– 'Pulp Fictions and Problem Girls: Reading and Rewriting Single Pregnancy in the Postwar United States.' *American Historical Review* 100 (December 1995): 1465–87.

– 'White Neurosis, Black Pathology: Constructing Out-of-Wedlock Pregnancy in the Wartime and Postwar United States.' In Joanne Meyerowitz, ed., *Not June Cleaver: Women and Gender in Postwar America, 1945–1960*, 304–31. Philadelphia: Temple University Press, 1994.

Ladd-Taylor, Molly. 'Saving Babies and Sterilizing Mothers: Eugenics and Welfare Policies in the Interwar United States.' *Social Politics* 4 (Spring 1997): 136–53.

Lessard, Hester. 'The Empire of the Lone Mother: Parental Rights, Child Welfare and State Restructuring.' *Osgoode Hall Law Journal* 39 (2001): 717–70.

Levesque, Roger. 'The Role of Unwed Fathers in Welfare Law: Failing Legislative Intiatives and Surrendering Judicial Responsibility.' *Law and Inequality: A Journal of Theory and Practice* 12 (1993): 93–126.

Little, Margaret Jane Hillyard. 'A Fit and Proper Person: The Moral Regulation of Single Mothers in Ontario, 1920–1940.' In Kathryn McPherson, Cecilia

Morgan, and Nancy Forestell, eds., *Gendered Pasts: Essays in Femininity and Masculinity in Canada*, 123–38. Toronto: Oxford University Press, 1999.

MacDougall, Heather. 'Enlightening the Public: The Views and Values of the Association of Public Health Officers of Ontario, 1886–1903.' In Charles Roland, ed., *Health, Disease and Medicine: Essays in Canadian History*, 436–64. Toronto: Clarke Irwin and the Hannah Institute for the History of Medicine, 1984.

MacFarlane, Alan. 'Illegitimacy and Illegitimates in English History.' In Peter Laslett, Karla Oosterveen, and Richard Smith, eds., *Bastardy and Its Comparative History*, 71–85. London: Edward Arnold, 1980.

McCallum, Margaret. 'Assistance to Veterans and their Dependents: Steps on the Way to the Administrative State, 1914–1929.' In W. Wesley Pue and Barry Wright, eds., *Canadian Perspectives on Law and Society: Issues in Legal History*, 157–77. Ottawa: Carleton University Press, 1988.

McConnachie, Kathleen. 'Methodology in the Study of Women in History: A Case History of Helen MacMurchy, MD.' *Ontario History* 75 (March 1983): 61–87.

McLaren, Angus. 'Birth Control and Abortion in Canada, 1870–1920.' *Canadian Historical Review* 59 (1978): 319–40.

McLaren, John. 'Chasing the Social Evil: Moral Fervour and the Evolution of Canada's Prostitution Laws, 1867–1917.' *Canadian Journal of Law and Society* 1 (1986): 125–65.

Monson, Renee. 'State-ing Sex and Gender: Collecting Information From Mothers and Fathers in Paternity Cases.' *Gender and Society* 11 (1997): 279–96.

Myers, Tamara. 'Qui t'a debauchée? Female Adolescent Sexuality and the Juvenile Delinquents' Court in Early Twentieth-Century Montreal.' In Lori Chambers, and Edgar-Andre Montigny, eds., *Family Matters: Papers in Post-Confederation Canadian Family History*. Toronto: Canadian Scholars' Press, 1998.

– 'The Voluntary Delinquent: Parents, Daughters and the Montreal Juvenile Delinquents' Court in 1918.' *Canadian Historical Review* 80(2) (1999): 242–68.

Parker, Graham. 'The Legal Regulation of Sexual Activity and the Protection of Females.' *Osgoode Hall Law Journal* 21(2) (1983): 187–244.

Pedersen, Diana. 'Keeping Our Good Girls Good: The YWCA and the Girl Problem.' *Canadian Woman Studies* 7(4) (1986): 20–4.

Pedersen, Susan. 'Gender, Welfare and Citizenship in Britain During the Great War.' *American Historical Review* 95 (October 1990): 983–1006.

Pierce, Sylvie. 'Single Mothers and the Concept of Female Dependency in the

Development of the Welfare State in Britain.' *Journal of Comparative Family Studies* 11(1) (1980): 57–85.

Piess, Kathy. 'Charity Girls and City Pleasures: Historical Notes on Working-Class Sexuality, 1880–1920.' In Kathy Piess and Christina Simmons, eds., *Passion and Power: Sexuality in History*. Philadelphia: Temple University Press, 1989.

Pozatek, Ellie. 'The Problem of Certainty: Clinical Social Work in the Post Modern Era.' *Social Work* 39(4) (1994): 394–404.

Poulin, Debra. 'The Open Adoption Records Movement: Constitutional Cases and Legislative Compromise.' *Journal of Family Law* 26 (1987–1988): 395–418.

Prentice, Susan. 'Workers, Mothers, Reds: Toronto's Post-War Daycare Fight.' *Studies in Political Economy* 30 (Autumn 1989): 115–42.

Ratterman, Debra. 'Adoption and the Rights of Putative Fathers.' *Children's Legal Rights Journal* 11(1) (Spring 1990): 13–21.

Razack, Sherene. 'Race, Space and Prostitution: The Making of a Bourgeois Subject.' *Canadian Journal of Women and the Law* 10 (1998): 1–39.

Roberts, Dorothy. 'Racism and Patriarchy in the Meaning of Motherhood.' In Martha Albertson Fineman and Isabel Karpin, eds., *Mothers in Law: Feminist Theory and the Legal Regulation of Motherhood*, 224–49. New York: Columbia University Press, 1995.

Rooke, Patricia, and R.L. Schnell. 'Making the Way More Comfortable: Charlotte Whitton's Child Welfare Career.' *Journal of Canadian Studies* 17(4) (Winter 1983): 33–45.

Rynearson, Edward. 'Relinquishment and Its Maternal Complications: A Preliminary Study.' *American Journal of Psychiatry* 123 (March 1982): 338–40.

Sangster, Joan. 'Creating Social and Moral Citizens: Defining and Treating Delinquent Boys and Girls in Canada, 1920–1965.' In Robert Adamoski, Dorothy Chunn, and Robert Menzies, eds., *Contesting Canadian Citizenship: Historical Readings*, 337–58. Peterborough, ON: Broadview, 2002.

– 'Criminalizing the Colonized: Ontario Native Women Confront the Criminal Justice System, 1920–1960.' *Canadian Historical Review* 80(1) (1999): 32–60.

– 'Doing Two Jobs: The Wage Earning Mother, 1945–1970.' In Joy Parr, ed., *A Diversity of Women, Ontario, 1945–1980*, 98–134. Toronto: University of Toronto Press, 1995.

– 'Incarcerating Bad Girls: The Regulation of Female Sexuality through the Female Refuges Act in Ontario, Canada, 1920–1945.' *Journal of the History of Sexuality* 7(2) (1996): 239–75.

Schmitz, Cathryne. 'Reframing the Dialogue on Female-Headed Single-Parent Families.' *Affilia* 10(4) (Winter 1995): 426–41.

Schnell, R.L. 'Female Separatism and Institution-Building: Continuities and

Discontinuities in Canadian Child Welfare, 1913–1935.' *International Review of History and Political Science* 25(2) (May 1988): 14–46.

Schultz, Patricia. 'Day Care in Canada, 1850–1962.' In Kathleen Gallagher Ross, ed., *Good Day Care*. Toronto: Women's Press, 1978.

Scott, Joan Wallach. 'Response to Linda Gordon.' *Signs* 15(4) (Summer 1990): 853–8.

– 'Review of *Heroes of their Own Lives*.' *Signs* 15(4) (Summer 1990): 849–52.

Sethna, Christabelle. 'The Cold War and the Sexual Chill: Freezing Girls out of Sexual Education.' *Canadian Woman Studies/les cahiers de la Femme* 17(4) (Spring 1998): 57–61.

Smandych, Russell. 'Colonial Welfare Law and Practices: Coping Without and English Poor Law in Upper Canada, 1792–1837.' In Louis Knafla and Susan Binnie, eds., *Law, Society and the State: Essays in Modern Legal History*, 214–46. Toronto: University of Toronto Press, 1995.

Snell, James. 'The White Life for Two: The Defence of Marriage and Sexual Morality in Canada, 1880–1914.' *histoire sociale/Social History* 16(31) (1983): 111–28.

Solinger, Rickie. 'Race and Value: Black and White Illegitimate Babies in the U.S.A., 1945–1965.' *Gender and History* 4 (1992): 343–63.

Spelman, Elizabeth. 'Theories of Race and Gender: The Erasure of Black Women.' *Quest: A Feminist Quarterly* 4 (1982): 36–62.

Strange, Carolyn. 'Patriarchy Modified: The Criminal Prosecution of Rape in York County, 1880–1930.' In Jim Phillips, Tina Loo, and Susan Lewthwaite, eds., *Essays in the History of Canadian Law: Crime and Criminal Justice*, 207–51. Toronto: The Osgoode Society, 1994.

Strong-Boag, Veronica. 'Wages for Housework: Mothers' Allowances and the Beginnings of Social Security in Canada.' *Journal of Canadian Studies* 14(1) (Spring 1979): 24–34.

Struthers, James. 'A Profession in Crisis: Charlotte Whitton and Canadian Social Work in the 1930s.' *Canadian Historical Review* 62(2) (1981): 169–85.

Takas, Marianne. 'Assisting Young Mothers with Paternity and Child Support Services.' *Children's Legal Rights Journal* 13(1) (Winter 1992): 2–13.

Trocme, N. 'Child Welfare Services.' In R. Barnhorst and L. Johnson, eds., *The State of the Child in Ontario*, 63–91. Toronto: Oxford University Press, 1991.

Valverde, Mariana. 'Building Anti-delinquent Communities: Morality, Gender, and Generation in the City.' In Joy Parr, ed., *A Diversity of Women*, 19–45. Toronto: University of Toronto Press, 1995.

– 'When the Mother of the Race Is Free.' In Franca Iacovetta and Mariana Valverde, eds., *Gender Conflicts: New Essays in Women's History*, 3–26. Toronto: University of Toronto Press, 1992.

Ward, Peter. 'Unwed Motherhood in Nineteenth-Century English Canada.' *Canadian Historical Association Historical Papers* (1981): 34–71.

Zainaldin, Jamil. 'The Emergence of a Modern American Family Law: Child Custody, Adoption and the Courts, 1796–1851.' *Northwestern University Law Review* 73(6) (1979): 1038–89.

Unpublished Theses

Bator, Paul A. 'Saving Lives on [the] Wholesale Plan: Public Health Reform in the City of Toronto, 1900–1930.' PhD diss., University of Toronto, 1979.

Biggs, Catherine Lesley. 'The Response to Maternal Mortality in Ontario, 1920–1940.' MSc thesis, University of Toronto, 1983.

McConnachie, Kathleen. 'Science and Ideology: The Mental Hygiene and Eugenics Movements in the Inter-war Years, 1919–1939.' PhD diss., University of Toronto, 1987.

McGinnis, Janice Dickin. 'From Health to Welfare: The Development of Federal Government Policy Regarding Standards for Public Health for Canadians, 1919–1945.' PhD diss., University of Alberta, 1980.

Pollock, Edmund. 'An Investigation into Certain Personality Characteristics of Unmarried Mothers.' PhD diss., New York University, 1957.

Ramsay, Dean. 'The Development of Child Legislation in Ontario.' MA thesis, Toronto School of Social Work, 1949.

Index

2007　Robert J. Sharpe and Patricia I. McMahon, *The Persons Case: The Origins and Legacy of the Fight for Legal Personhood*
Lori Chambers, *Misconceptions: Unmarried Motherhood and the Ontario Children of Unmarried Parents Act, 1921–1969*
Jonathan Swainger, ed., *The Alberta Supreme Court at 100: History and Authority*
Martin Friedland, *My Life in Crime and Other Academic Adventures*

2006　Donald Fyson, *Magistrates, Police, and People: Everyday Criminal Justice in Quebec and Lower Canada, 1764–1837*
Dale Brawn, *The Court of Queen's Bench of Manitoba, 1870–1950: A Biographical History*
R.C.B. Risk, *A History of Canadian Legal Thought: Collected Essays*, edited and introduced by G. Blaine Baker and Jim Phillips

2005　Philip Girard, *Bora Laskin: Bringing Law to Life*
Christopher English, ed., *Essays in the History of Canadian Law: Volume IX – Two Islands: Newfoundland and Prince Edward Island*
Fred Kaufman, *Searching for Justice: An Autobiography*

2004　Philip Girard, Jim Phillips, and Barry Cahill, eds., *The Supreme Court of Nova Scotia, 1754–2004: From Imperial Bastion to Provincial Oracle*
Frederick Vaughan, *Aggressive in Pursuit: The Life of Justice Emmett Hall*
John D. Honsberger, *Osgoode Hall: An Illustrated History*
Constance Backhouse and Nancy Backhouse, *The Heiress versus the Establishment: Mrs Campbell's Campaign for Legal Justice*

2003　Robert J. Sharpe and Kent Roach, *Brian Dickson: A Judge's Journey*
Jerry Bannister, *The Rule of the Admirals: Law, Custom, and Naval Government in Newfoundland, 1699–1832*
George Finlayson, *John J. Robinette, Peerless Mentor: An Appreciation*
Peter Oliver, *The Conventional Man: The Diaries of Ontario Chief Justice Robert A. Harrison, 1856–1878*

2002　John T. Saywell, *The Lawmakers: Judicial Power and the Shaping of Canadian Federalism*
Patrick Brode, *Courted and Abandoned: Seduction in Canadian Law*
David Murray, *Colonial Justice: Justice, Morality, and Crime in the Niagara District, 1791–1849*
F. Murray Greenwood and Barry Wright, eds., *Canadian State Trials, Volume Two: Rebellion and Invasion in the Canadas, 1837–1839*

2001　Ellen Anderson, *Judging Bertha Wilson: Law as Large as Life*
Judy Fudge and Eric Tucker, *Labour before the Law: The Regulation of Workers' Collective Action in Canada, 1900–1948*
Laurel Sefton MacDowell, *Renegade Lawyer: The Life of J.L. Cohen*

2000　Barry Cahill, *'The Thousandth Man': A Biography of James McGregor Stewart*
A.B. McKillop, *The Spinster and the Prophet: Florence Deeks, H.G. Wells, and the Mystery of the Purloined Past*

Beverley Boissery and F. Murray Greenwood, *Uncertain Justice: Canadian Women and Capital Punishment*

Bruce Ziff, *Unforeseen Legacies: Reuben Wells Leonard and the Leonard Foundation Trust*

1999   Constance Backhouse, *Colour-Coded: A Legal History of Racism in Canada, 1900–1950*

G. Blaine Baker and Jim Phillips, eds., *Essays in the History of Canadian Law: Volume VIII – In Honour of R.C.B. Risk*

Richard W. Pound, *Chief Justice W.R. Jackett: By the Law of the Land*

David Vanek, *Fulfilment: Memoirs of a Criminal Court Judge*

1998   Sidney Harring, *White Man's Law: Native People in Nineteenth-Century Canadian Jurisprudence*

Peter Oliver, *'Terror to Evil-Doers': Prisons and Punishments in Nineteenth-Century Ontario*

1997   James W. St.G. Walker, *'Race,' Rights and the Law in the Supreme Court of Canada: Historical Case Studies*

Lori Chambers, *Married Women and Property Law in Victorian Ontario*

Patrick Brode, *Casual Slaughters and Accidental Judgments: Canadian War Crimes and Prosecutions, 1944–1948*

Ian Bushnell, *The Federal Court of Canada: A History, 1875–1992*

1996   Carol Wilton, ed., *Essays in the History of Canadian Law: Volume VII – Inside the Law: Canadian Law Firms in Historical Perspective*

William Kaplan, *Bad Judgment: The Case of Mr Justice Leo A. Landreville*

Murray Greenwood and Barry Wright, eds., *Canadian State Trials: Volume I – Law, Politics, and Security Measures, 1608–1837*

1995   David Williams, *Just Lawyers: Seven Portraits*

Hamar Foster and John McLaren, eds., *Essays in the History of Canadian Law: Volume VI – British Columbia and the Yukon*

W.H. Morrow, ed., *Northern Justice: The Memoirs of Mr Justice William G. Morrow*

Beverley Boissery, *A Deep Sense of Wrong: The Treason, Trials, and Transportation to New South Wales of Lower Canadian Rebels after the 1838 Rebellion*

1994   Patrick Boyer, *A Passion for Justice: The Legacy of James Chalmers McRuer*

Charles Pullen, *The Life and Times of Arthur Maloney: The Last of the Tribunes*

Jim Phillips, Tina Loo, and Susan Lewthwaite, eds., *Essays in the History of Canadian Law: Volume V – Crime and Criminal Justice*

Brian Young, *The Politics of Codification: The Lower Canadian Civil Code of 1866*

1993   Greg Marquis, *Policing Canada's Century: A History of the Canadian Association of Chiefs of Police*

Murray Greenwood, *Legacies of Fear: Law and Politics in Quebec in the Era of the French Revolution*

1992   Brendan O'Brien, *Speedy Justice: The Tragic Last Voyage of His Majesty's Vessel Speedy*

Robert Fraser, ed., *Provincial Justice: Upper Canadian Legal Portraits from the Dictionary of Canadian Biography*

1991 Constance Backhouse, *Petticoats and Prejudice: Women and Law in Nineteenth-Century Canada*

1990 Philip Girard and Jim Phillips, eds., *Essays in the History of Canadian Law: Volume III – Nova Scotia*
Carol Wilton, ed., *Essays in the History of Canadian Law: Volume IV – Beyond the Law: Lawyers and Business in Canada 1830–1930*

1989 Desmond Brown, *The Genesis of the Canadian Criminal Code of 1892*
Patrick Brode, *The Odyssey of John Anderson*

1988 Robert J. Sharpe, *The Last Day, the Last Hour: The Currie Libel Trial*
John D. Arnup, *Middleton: The Beloved Judge*

1987 C. Ian Kyer and Jerome Bickenbach, *The Fiercest Debate: Cecil A. Wright, the Benchers, and Legal Education in Ontario, 1923-1957*

1986 Paul Romney, *Mr Attorney: The Attorney General for Ontario in Court, Cabinet, and Legislature, 1791–1899*
Martin Friedland, *The Case of Valentine Shortis: A True Story of Crime and Politics in Canada*

1985 James Snell and Frederick Vaughan, *The Supreme Court of Canada: History of the Institution*

1984 Patrick Brode, *Sir John Beverley Robinson: Bone and Sinew of the Compact*
David Williams, *Duff: A Life in the Law*

1983 David H. Flaherty, ed., *Essays in the History of Canadian Law: Volume II*

1982 Marion MacRae and Anthony Adamson, *Cornerstones of Order: Courthouses and Town Halls of Ontario, 1784–1914*

1981 David H. Flaherty, ed., *Essays in the History of Canadian Law: Volume I*